典藏版

—— 英汉对照 ——

英国经典散文选
A Selection of English Classic Essays

[英] 乔纳森·斯威夫特 等 著   刘炳善 译

外语教学与研究出版社
FOREIGN LANGUAGE TEACHING AND RESEARCH PRESS
北京 BEIJING

图书在版编目(CIP)数据

英国经典散文选：典藏版／（英）乔纳森·斯威夫特（Jonathan Swift）等著；刘炳善译. -- 北京：外语教学与研究出版社，2024.1
ISBN 978-7-5213-5028-9

Ⅰ.①英… Ⅱ.①乔…②刘… Ⅲ.①英语-汉语-对照读物②散文集-英国-近现代 Ⅳ.①H319.4：I

中国国家版本馆 CIP 数据核字（2023）第 256359 号

出 版 人　王　芳
项目策划　易　璐
责任编辑　张路路
责任校对　段会香
装帧设计　范晔文　彩奇风
出版发行　外语教学与研究出版社
社　　址　北京市西三环北路 19 号（100089）
网　　址　https://www.fltrp.com
印　　刷　三河市紫恒印装有限公司
开　　本　889×1194　1/32
印　　张　8.5
版　　次　2024 年 1 月第 1 版 2024 年 1 月第 1 次印刷
书　　号　ISBN 978-7-5213-5028-9
定　　价　48.00 元

如有图书采购需求，图书内容或印刷装订等问题，侵权、盗版书籍等线索，请拨打以下电话或关注官方服务号：
客服电话：400 898 7008
官方服务号：微信搜索并关注公众号"外研社官方服务号"
外研社购书网址：https://fltrp.tmall.com

物料号：350280001

英国随笔简论

这本小书，以随笔为主，选录了从18世纪到20世纪的十位英国作家的部分散文作品。现在需要把英国随笔的发展概貌以及其他有关问题作一说明。

一

随笔（essay，过去曾用译名"小品文"），是散文（prose）的一种。从文学史的角度来看，散文的发展常常是在诗歌之后，而随笔在各类散文中更要晚出。近代西欧的随笔是在文艺复兴运动中诞生的，代表作就是法国蒙田的《随笔》（*Essais*，1580—1595）一书。英国随笔的发展略晚于法国，事实上，是以蒙田《随笔》的最初英译本（*John Florio's Translation of Montaigne's Essays*，1603）为其滥觞。因此，随笔在英国开初可以说是外来品，可是一旦移植到了英国，那块土地似乎特别适于这一株花木的生长，在三四百年间不断发展壮大，成为非常富于英国民族特色的一种散文形式。最初的硕果是培根的五十八篇《随笔》（Francis Bacon: *Essays*，1597—1625）。但培根的随笔是哲理性的，和蒙田随笔中富于个人风趣的亲切笔调不同。蒙田的随笔传统到了17世纪在英国才有较大的发展。伯顿的《忧郁的剖析》(Robert Burton: *The Anatomy of Melancholy*, 1621)和布朗的《一个医生的宗教观》(Thomas Browne: *Religio Medici*, 1643)虽是两部长篇散文著作,但它们那杂学旁搜的内容、兼容并包的观点,随作者兴之所至而漫谈的笔调却为随笔的发展开辟了先河。无怪乎后来的不少随笔作家都以这两部17世纪的"奇书"为其"枕中之秘",就好像我国的《世说新语》对后代笔记小品的影响一样。在17世纪还出现了两本模仿蒙田的作品,那就是考利的《随笔集》(Abraham Cowley: *Essays in Verse and Prose*, 1668)和坦普尔的《杂谈集》(William Temple: *Miscellanea*, 1680—1701)。但英国随笔的真正大发展却是在18世纪。当时文人办期刊蔚然成风。譬如说,大家熟知的笛福,在他六十岁写《鲁滨逊漂流记》之前,早就是办刊物的老手,而且是英国头一份期刊《评论报》(*Review*, 1704—1713)的主笔。此外,斯威夫特办过《检察者》(*The Examiner*, 1710—1711),斯梯尔和艾迪生办过《闲话报》(*The Tatler*, 1709—1711)和《旁观者》(*The Spectator*, 1711—1712; 1714),约翰逊博士办过《漫游者》(*The Rambler*, 1750—1752),后来哥尔德斯密斯也办过短期的小刊物《蜜蜂》(*The Bee*, 1759)。由于刊物的需要,随笔这一形式得到广泛的应用,作家用它来立论、抒情、写人、叙事,把随笔开拓成为一种贯穿着作者活泼个性的非常灵活、非常吸引读者的文学体裁。评论者往往把18世纪以后的这种英国随笔叫作familiar essays(漫笔、小品文、随笔)。

到了19世纪,随笔散文成为英国浪漫主义文学运动的一个分支,出现了一批著名的随笔作家,如兰姆、黑兹利特、德·昆西、利·亨特等。英国随笔到19世纪发展到了一个顶峰，题材扩展到日常生活各个方面，作者的个性色彩也更为浓厚，名篇佳作甚多。承上述诸名家的余绪，史蒂文森在19世纪末再次振兴随笔创作，是个承上启下的重要作者。

在史蒂文森之后，随笔在20世纪初期又繁荣了相当一段时间，出现一批作家，如切斯特顿（G. K. Chesterton）、贝洛克（H. Belloc）、比尔博姆（Max Beerbohm）、梅内尔（Alice Meynell）、卢卡斯（E. V. Lucas）、林德（R. Lynd）、米尔恩（A. A. Milne）等等。直到30年代以来，据说由于期刊减少，报纸版面紧张，具有亲切漫谈优点的随笔已被具有更大吸引力的广播和电视节目所取代，因而随笔这种文学体裁颇有衰落之势。（参见Ifor Evans: *A Short History of English Literature*, p.346）

虽然如此，随笔这一具有三四百年历史传统的英国文学样式，是不会一下子销声匿迹的，作者仍然时有出现，譬如说，小说家奥尔德斯·赫胥黎和吴尔夫就写过不少随笔作品。英国随笔的前途究竟如何，还需要看今后的事实如何发展才能断定。

二

比起莎士比亚的戏剧、弥尔顿的长诗、菲尔丁和狄更斯的小说这些鸿篇巨制，英国随笔不过是小品文字。然而，"虽小道，亦有可观者焉"。从历史角度来说，英国随笔的发展乃是自从欧洲文艺复兴以来人道主义觉醒、思想启蒙运动等等意识形态变化的结果；从社会条件来说，它是时代思潮激荡、报刊发达、读者需要的结果；从文学本身来说，它又是一个国家散文艺术发展到一定成熟水平之后的自然产物——譬如说，私人书信、日记、笔记、游记、政论、随感录、自传、传记、回忆录、文艺评论、各种"杂著"。这些散文作品的大量产生，就势必为随笔这种"杂文"形式的出现提供土壤和养料,提供素材和语言艺术的基础。在整个文学艺术的大花园里,随笔虽然不过只是一朵小花,但滋养着这一朵小花生长的却是一个国家民族的全部思想文化艺术成果;正因为如此,随笔才能具有那种非其他鸿篇巨制所能取代的独特的艺术魅力。而且,如果按照时代的顺序,把英国的随笔作品从18世纪到20世纪看下来,也可以窥察不同时代的英国社会风尚,可以看出英国文学的大致发展轨迹。这是因为:一个时代的生活状况和文学思潮既然要反映在诗歌、小说、戏剧之中,在随笔散文当中也自然要有所反映的。

然则,随笔究竟是怎样的一种文学形式呢?由于随笔的形式非常灵活、变化多端,要想给它下一个确切、固定、圆满的定义是很困难的。但是,我们可以试着给它笼统地画一个圈圈:首先,在文学的总范围内,我们先把诗歌、小说、戏剧放在一边。然后,在散文这个大范围内,再把纯理性的议论文(规规矩矩、方方正正的科学论文、文论、批评论著等)、纯叙事文(正儿八经的历史、传记、自传、大部头的回忆录等)以及纯抒情文(像屠格涅夫、泰戈尔或纪伯伦那样的散文诗等)当作三个极端,让它们"三足鼎立"。于是,我们再来看看在这个"三角地带"中间的那些五花八门的散文小品,那么,不管是偏于发发议论而夹杂着抒发作者个人之情的,或者是偏于个人抒情而又发发议论的,或者是偏于叙事而又夹杂着一点议论和抒情的,还有那些文采动人、富有个人风趣的短评(又不管是社会评论、文学评论、艺术评论)——这些议论、叙事、抒情浑然杂糅,并且富于个性色彩,运用漫谈方式、轻松笔调所写出的种种散文小品,统统都可以叫作"随笔"——也就是上边说过的familiar essays。随笔，可以说是一种笔谈——不过，一切写作都可以算是"笔谈"；但是，随笔是作者拿笔跟读者谈心、聊天。这种笔谈是推心置腹、直抒胸臆、真情毕露、个性鲜明的——没有个性特色，即不成其为随笔。随笔，又可以说是一种"小题大做"的文章。打个比方，就好像丢给小猫一个线团，让它抓住一个线头，它不把线团完全抖开绝不拉倒。让随笔作者抓住任何一个小题目，他开始从这个题目做起文章来；但是，"一不做，二不休"，他写着写着，不由得就把跟这个题目有关的一切见闻、体会、读书心得都谈了出来——不仅如此，有时候，甚至借此机会（只要能拉扯上）对于宇宙、人生、历史、文艺等等问题发表一番"高见"。表面看来，这种写法倒很"自由"，其实，事情又不这样简单。因为，作为一种文学艺术，随笔写作同样受着创作规律的制约，作者对于内容自然也要进行选择和剪裁。而且，用笔向读者谈心，发议论要娓娓动听，写人物要须眉如见，叙事件要引人入胜，抒私情要亲切感人，而作者自己的个性特色又要通过恰当的语言艺术鲜明地透露出来，可不是一件容易的事。——在这一方面，英国作家似乎是特别擅长的。总括一句，随笔可以说是一种题材广泛、形式自由、语言活泼的人生社会杂谈、人物风习散记和文学艺术漫评——贯穿其中的灵魂是作者的鲜明个性。

三

本书选录了18、19和20世纪的一些英国随笔名篇。所以这样选录，乃是因为除了培根那些偏重哲理的短论以外，18世纪以后的英国随笔才发展圆熟，留下大批脍炙人口的作品，足资欣赏、观摩、比较。下面试以艾迪生、兰姆和吴尔夫三位作家为例，说明英国随笔在18、19和20世纪的不同特色。

我们知道，在英国，17世纪是一个动荡剧烈的社会政治斗争的时代：新兴的资产阶级为了取得政权、封建势力为了维持自己的统治进行着生死斗争，差不多整个世纪都在君主专制与反君主专制、革命与复辟的反复较量中过去了；直到1688年的"光荣革命"，大资产阶级与土地贵族达成妥协，英国的国家制度在君主立宪的基础上稳定下来。这时候，成为统治者的资产阶级需要进行自我教育，使自己的成员在思想情操、文化教养、道德伦理、风俗习惯等等方面文明起来，适应自己作为国家新主人的地位。在这种时代需要的推动之下，英国的随笔散文在18世纪曾经起过非常活跃的作用：它被作家们广泛应用在报刊上，作为向上层市民进行思想启蒙的媒介；它被作家们用作表达自己各种思想见解的工具，在政治舞台上它还成为党派斗争的武器；而在个别具有强烈正义感的作家手里，它更成为替被压迫人民呼吁的喉舌。贯穿在这一切活动中的基本精神则是以理性为核心的启蒙主义，而在文学创作思想上又以祖述古希腊罗马（主要是罗马）文化的古典主义为准绳。

18世纪的英国随笔就在上述各种社会条件的推动下获得了空前的发展。18世纪的著名随笔作家艾迪生是一个温文尔雅的"君子人"，一帆风顺的政治活动家——辉格党的红人，牛津大学高才生出身的学者，优雅的文体家——这一切使他成为英国资产阶级启蒙作家的一个非常合适的人选。他和斯梯尔一起，用随笔散文这种轻松活泼的文学形式，把符合资产阶级需要的思想道德伦理原则向中上层的读者——那些咖啡馆和俱乐部里的常客们进行灌输推广，有利于巩固资本主义社会的上层建筑，当时受到极大欢迎。他的文章在整个18世纪被奉为英文散文的楷模。约翰逊博士说:"有志于学得那种亲切而不粗俗、优雅而不浮华的英语文体的人,都必须日日夜夜地攻读艾迪生著作。"可谓推崇备至。艾迪生文章的确写得炉火纯青、亲切有味,自是一代散文名手。但是,19世纪的历史家麦考利(Thomas Babington Macaulay)将艾迪生跟伏尔泰和斯威夫特相比,把艾迪生抬得高于后二人之上,却未免褒贬失当,缺乏一个历史家应有的公允了。作为一个启蒙者,艾迪生的思想高度远远不能和伏尔泰相比;作为一个触及当代时事的作家,艾迪生也没有斯威夫特那样深刻的洞察力、强烈的正义感、巨大的道义勇气以及对于人民的炽热同情。

艾迪生和斯威夫特——这是两个截然不同的作家。艾迪生是一位给英国绅士洗温水澡的作家,在他笔下也有些温和的讽刺和嘲弄,那等于让上流读者洗了澡再搔搔痒;所以英国绅士对他的文章能够舒舒服服读下去,即使受到一些嘲笑也不以为忤。但是,斯威夫特就不同了,他那刻骨的揭露、热辣辣的讽刺像烈火一样烧灼,那是绅士们受不了的。所以,二百多年来,评论家们对于艾迪生都是一路赞美,对于斯威夫特却往往是肯定其文笔、否定其内容,说他是什么"厌世者""憎恨人类的人"等等——近年来,对他的评语倒是渐渐好转了。站在今天时代的高度,对于斯威夫特和艾迪生这两位散文作家的历史地位和社会作用应该看得更清楚了。斯威夫特是像我国鲁迅那样的作家,他那如椽之笔能唤醒一代读者的强烈爱憎,他的文章能掀起一股巨大的精神力量,沉重打击邪恶的势力,热情扶持正义的势力——在向不合理的社会制度或者罪恶的势力斗争时,正需要这样的作家和作品,因为对于罪恶势力给它洗温水澡是无济于事的。但是,当新兴阶级业已取得领导权,需要一边扫除旧的垃圾、改革社会弊端，一边向本阶级的基本群众进行自我教育，并建设新的精神文化的时候，则从艾迪生的随笔作品中可以看出历史上的资产阶级曾经用什么样的内容、什么样的形式和什么样的语言来对自己的群众进行启蒙教育——这对于我们也不无可供参考借鉴之处。

兰姆是英国最有代表性的随笔作家。他的《伊利亚随笔》是19世纪初期英国浪漫主义文学运动的产物：从思想上摆脱理性主义的约束，任直感，师造化；从文学上摆脱古典主义的框框，虽然有时也引几句拉丁诗文，但心目中真正感到亲切的文学典范并不是远古的维吉尔、奥维德，而是从莎士比亚到华兹华斯这些英国本土的诗人。在这些基本特征上，兰姆和其他的浪漫主义诗人作家并无二致。不同之处仅仅在于：华兹华斯的诗歌以农村为自己的讴歌对象，而兰姆的随笔则以城市为自己的描写对象。喧闹繁华的伦敦几乎是他全部灵感的源泉。他从城市生活的种种平凡琐碎的小事中寻找富有诗意的东西，正如华兹华斯从乡间的山川湖泊和田野平民那里汲取自己诗歌的灵感。兰姆扩大了随笔作家的视野，把写作题材深入到以往随笔作家很少注意的日常生活的范围中去，赋予这些平凡小事以一种浪漫的异彩；但是，兰姆作品的浪漫主义情调披上了一层古色古香的外衣——他往往借用往昔诗人作家的一些古词古语。他在学问上是个爱读"奇书"的杂家，师承17世纪的两个"怪老头子"，即杂文作家伯顿和布朗；不过，在他肩头并没有压着思想启蒙或其他社会性的任务，所以他尽可自己说自己的话，他的作品里也就没有18世纪随笔作家那种劝善说教的气味。

在18世纪发展壮大了的英国随笔，到了兰姆手里，加进了新内容，换上了新写法，抒情、记事、议论互相穿插，文风或则秾丽或则简古，用语或则文言或则白话，跌宕多姿，妙趣横生。这时，随笔变成了一种具有高度艺术性的散文，说它是近于诗的散文，并不算过分。然而，若了解一下兰姆的生平，则知道：为了能够写出像《伊利亚随笔》这样的文章，作者本人是付出了沉重的代价的。一个有很高才能的作家，在雇佣劳动的社会条件下，不得不把自己的大半生为饭碗而卖掉，在枯燥的账房生活中度过了三十六年；自己本来在少年时代精神上就受过失恋的创伤，家庭又遭惨祸，遂毅然挑起了沉重的家务负担；心爱的文学事业只能在十小时的白日工作以外去进行……《伊利亚随笔》便是在这样万方多难的情况下写出来的。"风格即人"。他的生活遭遇，他的"杂学"，他的性格，决定了在他的随笔中所使用的不可能是那种爽朗明快、通俗易懂的风格——他的风格像是突破了重重的障碍、从大石下弯弯曲曲地萌发、艰艰难难地成长，而终于灿烂开放的异花奇葩。像安徒生一样，他把个人的不幸升华为美妙的文学作品。他的文章寓谐于庄，他常常板着面孔说笑话——但这是一种"含泪的微笑"。兰姆的含泪的微笑跟果戈理、契诃夫的有所不同：果戈理、契诃夫的含泪微笑成为俄国式的刻骨讽刺，最终融入变革社会的总精神动力之中去了；而兰姆的含泪微笑只能化为英国式的含蓄的幽默，让能够解得此中意味的读者去慢慢咀嚼这带点苦涩的芳香。作为一个幽默的散文家，兰姆在英国是独一无二的，他的作品给读者留下言之不尽的艺术享受。

若把培根的随笔和兰姆的随笔加以比较，更可看出英国随笔的发展变化：培根的随笔是一个参透了人生、世界的哲学家的文章，他那犀利的目光、斩截的判断、格言般精辟的语言令人叹为观止。他的文章闪着理性的白光，但缺少一点人情的温暖。作者自己不动声色、不苟言笑，跟读者不说什么"闲话"，读者对这样的作家只觉得敬佩而不感到亲切。兰姆可就完全不同了。他的随笔是个性毕露、披肝沥胆的；他拉住读者，无论识与不识，畅谈自己的私房话——"竹筒倒豆子"，不吐不快。所以，培根的随笔是浓缩型的，兰姆的随笔则是开放型的。随笔到了兰姆手里，写法完全放开了——这对于作者无论抒情、叙事、议论都非常方便。直到20世纪，还有一批英国作家模仿他的笔调写作随笔散文。

如果兰姆可以算作19世纪最有代表性的英国随笔作家的话，那么，我个人认为，吴尔夫可以算是20世纪最有代表性的英国随笔作家。吴尔夫的主要成就在小说方面——她是"意识流"文学的开创者之一。同时，她也是一个重要的散文家，善于用轻快活泼的笔调写出她对于自己所喜爱的作家和作品的印象。她在这方面的文章主要收在题为《普通读者》的两本文学评论集当中（*The Common Reader*, 1925; *The Second Common Reader*, 1932）。这些评论是一个具有高度文化修养、丰富创作经验的女作家，在她的创作事业之余，不摆学者架子，不拿作家身份，用随笔的形式向读者谈文学、谈历史、谈生活的文章。写到作者那些心爱的作家的生平逸事，她往往采用形象化的手法，使得读者好似看到一组组印象派的人物素描连续画。这是一种形式新颖的文学评论，是英国随笔一种新的发展，从独创性上胜过20世纪初期的有些随笔作者。因为20世纪初的那一批以兰姆、黑兹利特、利·亨特为师的英国随笔作者只是19世纪随笔传统的追随者；但是，吴尔夫的文章，既继承了19世纪英国随笔的传统，又采用了自己特有的"印象主义"的笔法，以女作家的细腻蕴藉巧妙地糅合了英国民族所固有的幽默风趣，文章写得行云流水、舒卷自如、清新活泼、别具一格。因此，如果选举具有20世纪特色的英国随笔名手，我愿意高高兴兴地投吴尔夫一票。

四

与随笔密切相关的还有两个问题，即文体与幽默。"言之不文，行之不远。"文章既是要做，总要讲究使用语言的艺术，这就牵扯到了文体问题。英国散文中自古以来就存在着两种写法：一种是以来源于古盎格鲁-撒克逊语的英语基本词汇和句式所写成的文章，特点是通俗易懂、质朴无华；另一种是受拉丁文影响并使用大量外来词汇所写出的文章，辞藻繁复、句式灵活而有时失之于芜杂。17世纪后期，英国文学受法国文学影响，重视文体之学，这对于提高文学语言的艺术性有很大好处。18世纪散文作家继承这种传统，写文章以准确、洗练、明晰、畅达为宗，像笛福、艾迪生、斯威夫特和哥尔德斯密斯都是如此。他们的文章语言平易、纯净、生动、流畅，为广大读者喜爱，在文体学上被称为"朴素的文体"（the plain style）。但在古典主义崇尚拉丁文学的风气影响之下，也出现了另一种高华典雅的文体，讲究用词古奥华丽、声调铿锵、句型对仗，这在文体学上叫作"高雅的文体"（the elegant style）。这两种文体在历史上或平行或交错地发展下来了，而且各有自己的代表作家和作品。

英国随笔，由它那信笔漫谈的根本特点所决定，自然是以朴素、平易、明晰、流畅的文体为主流。但朴素与高雅两种文体既然都流传下来，随笔作者兴趣爱好各异，他们所使用的语言手段自然也不是整齐划一的。兰姆虽然爱用冷僻的古字，就是在提倡平易文体的黑兹利特的文章中华丽的字句也不少见。但是，无论如何，平易的文体在随笔作品中总是占着主流罢了。随笔的艺术魅力在很大程度上还决定于每位作家自己独特的语言艺术风格——这是作者的个性通过恰当的语言艺术而体现出来的结果。但这一问题比一般的文体问题更为复杂，国外学者对不同作家的语言风格正在进行专门研究，浅学如我为见闻所限，只好在此存而不论。

随笔的另一个重要因素是幽默。幽默是一种性格特点和语言风趣，要给它下一个定义简直是不可能的，但在读英国随笔的时候又时时感到它的存在。有一位作者这样写道："心地善良的人们，在深知人性的真相之后，还能对它保持热爱，这才能领略幽默的意味。他们看清了人类的言行矛盾之处和种种弱点，但因为他们热爱自己的同类，便把这些傻事化为欢笑的源泉，化为理解和同情的根由。"（H. S. Canby: *Selections from R. L. Stevenson*, 1911）一位日本作家说，幽默是"寂寞的内心的安全瓣"，"多泪的内心的安全瓣"，"深味着人生的尊贵，不失却深的人类爱的心情，而笑着的，是幽默罢。"又说："泪和笑只隔一张纸。恐怕只有尝过了泪的深味的人，这才懂得人生的笑的心情。"（鹤见祐辅：《说幽默》——见鲁迅译《思想·山水·人物》）我们所熟悉的几位著名幽默作家，例如兰姆、马克·吐温和契诃夫，都是深知生活中的悲苦而又让读者发笑的作者。恩格斯也谈过幽默作家。他在《英国工人阶级状况》中提到英国诗人托马斯·胡德时，曾说他是"所有现代幽默作家中最有才能的一个，像所有的幽默作家一样，他有很敏锐的心灵，但没有一点精神力量"。恩格斯的这一论述，把幽默作家的长处和短处两个方面都谈到了。那么，要问：幽默这个东西到底有什么用呢？答曰：对这个问题要具体分析，分别论之。一方面，在需要正正经经去办的事情上，幽默恐怕是用不上的。譬如说，社会问题不可能靠着一点儿幽默或一阵感伤来解决。幽默作家开不出治疗社会溃疡的药方。不能靠幽默作家来解决邦国大事。但是，具体到一个人的情绪或精神状态这种小事情，幽默倒是有用的。它好像是一种精神上的润滑剂。润滑剂的作用，大家都知道。譬如说，高车、大马都有了，道路、方向也确定了，车轮子也是结结实实的；那么，车子朝着既定的方向前进就是。但是，走到中途，人需要休息一下，车子也需要停下来，在轮轴上抹点儿油润滑一下。固然，不润滑一下，车子仍然能走下去；但是，只靠着干燥的轮子摩擦着向前走，时间久了，轮子也许会转动不灵的。这也就是在严肃、紧张以外，还需要团结、活泼的道理。这也就是人在紧张工作之余，需要喝一杯茶、看一页"闲书"、稍事休息的道理。因此，对于学英文的人来说，在正襟危坐攻读莎士比亚、弥尔顿之余，不妨费上半个钟头看一篇亲切有味的随笔小品，也许会感觉到学习英文的一种意外的乐趣。正如"皓首穷经"的学者，在苦读经史之余，未尝不可偶尔看一下《陶庵梦忆》之类的笔记小品。

五

在我国，介绍翻译英国的随笔散文，历史也算不短了。一个多世纪以来，英国的随笔名篇不断出现在我国的英文课本里。五四运动中，新文学的斗士曾经抓住随笔这个文学形式作为武器向封建顽固派开战。《新青年》上钱玄同和刘半农那有名的"答王敬轩的双簧信"，很容易让我们联想到艾迪生和斯梯尔在《旁观者》上的那些俏皮的答读者问。当时和以后用随笔散文形式写出许多作品的还有一大批作家。五四时期对于英国随笔的借鉴和运用是成功的，所留下的大量泼辣生动的散文作品既是历史的里程碑，也是世代读者感到亲切有味的好文章。但是，到了国难当头的30年代，也有作家不顾时代人民的需要，生搬硬套西洋幽默，正当外寇入侵、国家处在存亡关键，却硬要引诱读者去"寄沉痛于悠闲"，因而受到多数有正义感的作者的反对，这也是一个历史教训。

鲁迅在《小品文的危机》一文中写道："到五四运动的时候，……散文小品的成功，几乎在小说戏曲和诗歌之上。这之中，自然含着挣扎和战斗，但因为常常取法于英国的随笔（essay），所以也带一点幽默和雍容；写法也有漂亮和缜密的，这是为了对于旧文学的示威，在表示旧文学之自以为特长者，白话文学也并非做不到。以后的路，本来明明是更分明的挣扎和战斗，因为这原是萌芽于'文学革命'以至'思想革命'的。但现在的趋势，却在特别提倡那和旧文章相合之点，雍容，漂亮，缜密，就是要它成为'小摆设'，供雅人的摩挲，并且想青年摩挲了这'小摆设'，由粗暴而变为风雅了。"实际上，从"五四"到20世纪30年代，由鲁迅所开创并奠定了坚实基础的杂文业已发展成熟。这是植根于中国土壤、深受中国读者喜爱的一种新的散文形式，也可以说是中国式的"随笔"。鲁迅之后，我国作家结合新时代的要求，对于杂文艺术又有许多创造性的发展——仅举一例，从抗日战争期间在桂林出版的随笔月刊《野草》就可看到我们的随笔作家在思想性与艺术性的结合上曾取得多么丰富多彩的成果。可见，在学习借鉴外国随笔散文时，正如在其他方面一样，也要遵循"拿来主义"的原则，从时代环境、人民需要出发，不可生搬硬套，要走自己的路子。

今天，我们的精神生活日益丰富，我们在散文创作方面的文路也会日益广阔，在坚持我们自己正确方向的前提下，借鉴一下英国的随笔散文，对于丰富我们自己的散文艺术应该说是有一定好处的。鲁迅还有一段名言："只要并不是靠这来解决国政，布置战争，在朋友之间，说几句幽默，彼此莞尔而笑，我看是无关大体的。就是革命专家，有时也要负手散步；理学先生总不免有儿女，在证明着他并非日日夜夜，道貌永远的俨然。小品文大约在将来也还可以存在于文坛，只是以'闲适'为主，却稍嫌不够。"让我们就在这个意义上、这个范围内来介绍这么一组英国的随笔作品吧。

刘炳善

目 录
Contents

2	**Joseph Addison & Richard Steele**	
	约瑟夫·艾迪生与理查德·斯梯尔	
6	On the Cries of London	伦敦的叫卖声
16	The Spectator Club	旁观者俱乐部
32	**Jonathan Swift** 乔纳森·斯威夫特	
36	A Meditation upon a Broomstick	关于一把扫帚的沉思
40	A Modest Proposal	育婴刍议
64	**Oliver Goldsmith** 奥利弗·哥尔德斯密斯	
66	The Man in Black	黑衣人
76	**Charles Lamb** 查尔斯·兰姆	
80	Dream-Children	梦幻中的小孩子
92	Detached Thoughts on Books and Reading	读书漫谈

114	**William Hazlitt** 威廉·黑兹利特
118	On Familiar Style 论平易的文体
140	**Thomas De Quincey** 托马斯·德·昆西
142	The Literature of Knowledge and the Literature of Power 知识的文学与力量的文学
160	**Charlotte Brontë** 夏洛特·勃朗特
162	Biographical Notice of Ellis and Acton Bell 埃利斯·贝尔与阿克顿·贝尔生平纪略
180	**Robert Louis Stevenson** 罗伯特·路易斯·史蒂文森
182	An Apology for Idlers 为闲人一辩
210	**Virginia Woolf** 弗吉尼亚·吴尔夫
212	Mary Wollstonecraft 玛丽·沃斯通克拉夫特
232	Dorothy Wordsworth 多萝西·华兹华斯

约瑟夫·艾迪生与理查德·斯梯尔

1672—1719　　　1672—1729

约瑟夫·艾迪生(Joseph Addison，1672—1719)与理查德·斯梯尔(Richard Steele，1672—1729)是继培根之后，在18世纪初出现的有代表性的英国随笔作家。他们两人从小就是好朋友，生于同年，一同上中学，一同在牛津大学读书，后来在政治活动中又同属辉格党，特别因为他们两人的文学成就密切联系在一起，所以在文学史上常把他们两人并称。

但是，这两位老朋友的脾气和经历是很不一样的：艾迪生性格沉稳、含蓄、温文尔雅而工于心计，一辈子一帆风顺。他在大学时代学习优异，用拉丁文写的诗得到好评。毕业后先做研究生，后来又到欧洲大陆见习外交。1704年，在西班牙王位继承战争中，英国在布莱尼姆(Blenheim)一役战胜法国，艾迪生写了颂诗《战役》，受到英国政府重视。从此，他宦途得意，连任要职：当过议会议员、爱尔兰总督助理、英国副国务大臣，最后升任国务大臣。他的经济状况自然也是优裕的。

斯梯尔却是一个热情、活跃、爱玩爱动的爱尔兰人，大学未毕业就离校当了骑兵，升到上尉。从军期间，他酗酒赌博，还与人决斗；经济上常常陷入困难，借到钱又去挥霍。据说，有一次他写信向艾迪生哀词告借，艾迪生借给他一百英镑。第二天，艾迪生去看他，却见他在家大摆酒宴，高朋满座。艾迪生气不过，叫法庭执行吏逼他还债。看来，斯梯尔的脾气像是绅士阶级当中的一个"浪子"。不过，他和他的老朋友艾迪生有一个重要的共同点，即文学的才能和事业心。他在军队里不断写诗、写喜剧。1707年，他被辉格党政府任命为官报主编。这

Joseph Addison

一官报，每周两期，刊载任免事项和国内外消息，这对他从事新闻事业是一种初步锻炼。

1709年，斯梯尔创办了《闲话报》。这个刊物每周三期，内容分为社交娱乐、诗歌、学术、新闻、随感录五项，把时事、闲谈、随笔文章巧妙地糅合在一起，富有文学趣味，面向伦敦的中、上层市民。斯梯尔说明："本报的目的在于揭穿生活中的骗术，扯下狡诈、虚荣和矫情的伪装，在我们的衣着、谈话和行为中提倡一种质朴无华的作风。"为了吸引读者，斯梯尔使用了"艾萨克·比克斯塔夫"这个笔名。这本来是斯威夫特在揭露伦敦一个骗人的星相家时所使用过的假名；斯梯尔接过来继续使用，大做文章。这时，艾迪生在爱尔兰做官，也为《闲话报》写文章。《闲话报》是英国第一家文学性期刊，出版后大受欢迎，成为当时俱乐部和咖啡馆里不可缺少的读物。

1710年，英国托利党上台，辉格党失势，艾迪生丢了官，斯梯尔的官报主编也被免掉。而且，《闲话报》后来也办不下去了，因为大家一旦知道实际主编是斯梯尔，再装作比克斯塔夫的口气写文章就没有意思了。所以，1711年，两个老朋友合办了另一种刊物《旁观者报》。《旁观者报》每天一期，每期一篇文章，从1711年3月1日创刊，到1712年12月6日停刊，出了五百多期。艾迪生和斯梯尔各写了二百多篇文章，其他作者写了一小部分。1714年6月，艾迪生又单独复刊，每周三期，出了半年。

艾迪生和斯梯尔对于英国文学的主要贡献就是在1709—

3

Richard Steele

1712四年间所办的这两种刊物。

《旁观者报》比《闲话报》办得更为精彩。刊物号称是由一位"旁观者先生"和他的俱乐部主办的。第一期（艾迪生执笔）登出旁观者的自我介绍：他学识渊博、阅历丰富，各行各业无不通晓，但从不插手任何实际事务，对于党派斗争更不介入，而且生性缄默，不在自己俱乐部里决不开口——这是"书生论事"的最佳人选。第二期（斯梯尔执笔）介绍"旁观者俱乐部"的六位成员，其中包括一个爱好戏剧的见习律师、一个牧师、一个军人、一个城市交际场老手，另有一个老乡绅罗杰·德·考福来爵士——代表旧贵族，还有一个伦敦富商——代表新兴的资产者。在第十期，介绍刊物的编辑宗旨。从这三篇文章，可以清清楚楚看出《旁观者报》所代表的社会力量。用我国"五四"时代的语言来说，它不是为"引车卖浆者流"所编的刊物，它的读者对象乃资产者和富裕市民。

《旁观者报》的编写方法非常别致。它那五六百篇文章中，有很大篇幅是描写旁观者俱乐部这六七个成员的日常活动，从伦敦各界写到乡绅田庄，形成了一组以考福来爵士为中心的人物特写、散记，反映出当时英国上层社会各种代表人物的生活、思想、风貌。这是英国小说发展的一种萌芽形式。另外，《旁观者报》还常常采用"来函照登"加上编者按语，或者"答读者问"的形式来发表议论。实际上，这些"来函"往往是作者自己杜撰，那些"读者问"也类似我国古代议论文中的"或曰"，便于使作者通过"答问"的形式把自己的社会、哲学、道德、美学观点广泛应用于社会生活的各个领域。因此,《旁观者报》在文学上的贡献有两个方面:一方面,它居于18世纪英国文学期刊之首,应用随笔散文写人、叙事、抒情、议论,大大发展了随笔这种文学形式;另一方面,它又是英国小说的先驱。

这里所介绍的两篇文章中,《旁观者俱乐部》的大意已如上述。《伦敦的叫卖声》,题材新鲜。无论中外古今,种种市声都引人入胜。陆游诗:"小楼一夜听春雨,深巷明朝卖杏花。"——那叫卖声自然是很美的。北京盛夏卖酸梅汤,重庆冬夜卖炒米糖开水,也各有不同的情趣。至于文章中那位怪客的设想,似怪而并不怪,不过是在两百多年前就提出了城市中的噪声问题,而噪声与污染直到今天仍是正在研究解决之中的环境保护课题。不过,作者对待劳动人民有时流露出的那种居高临下的绅士气味,叫人觉得不大舒服。譬如说,当萝卜上市时,农民急于求售的心情,他就不能理解,说什么萝卜不会放凉,何必那样急如星火?其实,道理很简单:萝卜虽然不会放凉,青菜究以趁新鲜早早卖出、吃掉为宜。

在《闲话报》和《旁观者报》所留下的大量随笔作品中,评论者谓艾迪生的文章写得优雅、洗练、幽默,斯梯尔则写得生动活泼,而功力似不如艾迪生那样炉火纯青。因此,一般认为艾迪生的散文艺术优于斯梯尔,但斯梯尔开创局面之功亦不可没。

On the Cries of London

Joseph Addison

There is nothing which more astonishes a foreigner, and frights a country squire, than the Cries of London. My good friend Sir Roger often declares that he cannot get them out of his head or go to sleep for them, the first week that he is in town. On the contrary, Will Honeycomb calls them the *Ramage de la Ville*, and prefers them to the sound of larks and nightingales, with all the music of fields and woods. I have lately received a letter from some very odd fellow upon this subject, which I shall leave with my reader, without saying anything further of it:

Sir,

I am a man out of all business, and would willingly turn my head to anything for an honest livelihood. I have invented several projects for raising many millions of money without burdening the subject, but I cannot get the parliament to listen to me, who look upon me, forsooth, as a crack , and a projector; so that despairing to enrich either myself or my country by this public-spiritedness, I would make some proposals to you relating to a design which I have very much at heart, and which may

伦敦的叫卖声

约瑟夫·艾迪生

初来乍到的外国人或者外地乡绅，最感到吃惊甚至会被惊吓到的莫过于伦敦的叫卖声了。我那位好朋友罗杰爵士常说，他刚到京城第一周里，脑子里装的全是这些声音，挥之不去，简直连觉都睡不成。相反，威尔·亨尼康却把这些声音称为"鸟喧华枝"，说是这比什么云雀、夜莺，连同田野、树林里的天籁加在一起还要好听呢。最近，我接到一位怪客来信，谈到这个问题。这封信，我不加任何按语，发表出来，请读者自己去看。

先生：

我是一个没有职业的人，只要能让我正正派派活下去，什么事情我都愿意去做。我制定了种种方案，实行起来可以叫人轻轻松松发财数百万之巨，可惜议院不肯听听我的意见。——他们不是以为我疯了，就是把我当作骗子。现在，我这一心造福大众、既能利己又能富国的事业既已落空，愿就个人潜心探讨的另一计划，向贵报略陈鄙见。此项计划，若蒙贵报向伦敦及

procure me a handsome subsistence, if you will be pleased to recommend it to the cities of London and Westminster.

The post I would aim at, is to be comptroller-general of the London Cries, which are at present under no manner of rules or discipline. I think I am pretty well qualified for this place, as being a man of very strong lungs, of great insight into all the branches of our British trades and manufactures, and of a competent skill in music.

The Cries of London may be divided into vocal and instrumental. As for the latter, they are at present under a very great disorder. A fireman of London has the privilege of disturbing a whole street for an hour together, with a twanking of a brass kettle or frying-pan. The watchman's thump at midnight startles us in our beds as much as the breaking in of a thief. The sowgelder's horn has indeed something musical in it, but this is seldom heard within the liberties[1]. I would therefore propose, that no instrument of this nature should be made use of, which I have not tuned and licensed, after having carefully examined in what manner it may affect the ears of her majesty's liege subjects.

Vocal cries are of a much larger extent, and indeed so full of incongruities and barbarisms, that we appear a distracted city to foreigners, who do not comprehend the meaning of such enormous outcries. Milk is generally sold in a note above E-la, and in sounds so exceedingly shrill, that it often sets our teeth on edge. The chimney-sweeper is confined to no certain pitch; he sometimes utters himself in

---

1 the liberties: the limits within which certain immunities are enjoyed, or jurisdiction is exercised. 暂译为"市区"。

威斯敏斯特[2]二市当局惠予推荐,本人说不定还可以找到一个体面的职业。

鉴于叫卖之声目前处于一种无章可循的状态,我想来谋求伦敦市声总监一职。这个职位,我自认为还是满能胜任的,因为我本人嗓门很高,对于我们英国工商各业又了如指掌,而且还精通音乐。

伦敦的市声可以分为声乐、器乐两大类。后一类现在特别杂乱无章。在伦敦,救火员是有特权的人物,他可以敲打着一只铜壶,或者一口煎锅,接连一个钟头不停,把整整一条街的人全都惊动起来。更夫半夜敲梆,把我们从梦中惊醒,好像屋子里突然闯进了一个贼。阉猪匠的号角声倒还有点悦耳,可惜在市区里难得听见。因此,我想建议:此类发声器具必先经过仔细检验,测定它对于女王陛下[3]忠实臣民的耳鼓究竟产生何种影响,然后由敝人将其音量加以调整,逐一批准,否则,不得擅自使用。

口头的叫卖声包括的范围则要广泛得多,而且又是那样聒聒噪噪,野调无腔。外地人听不懂这许多嚎叫到底是什么意思,说不定以为我们全城的人都发了疯。卖牛奶的人所采用的音调一般都在E调la以上,声音又特别尖细,听起来碜得我牙痒痒的。扫烟囱的人音调不受什么固定限制,有时候用最深沉的低音,有时候又用最

---

2 威斯敏斯特是伦敦市的一个区,当时是一个独立的城市。
3 当时(本文成于1711年)英国安妮女王在位。

the deepest bass, and sometimes in the sharpest treble; sometimes in the highest, and sometimes in the lowest, note of the gamut. The same observation might be made on the retailers of small-coal, not to mention broken glasses, or brick-dust. In these, therefore, and the like cases, it should be my care to sweeten and mellow the voices of these itinerant tradesmen, before they make their appearance in our streets, as also to accommodate their cries to their respective wares; and to take care in particular, that those may not make the most noise who have the least to sell, which is very observable in the vendors of card-matches, to whom I cannot but apply that old proverb of "Much cry, but little wool."

Some of these last-mentioned musicians are so very loud in the sale of these trifling manufactures, that an honest splenetic gentleman of my acquaintance bargained with one of them never to come into the street where he lived. But what was the effect of this contract? Why, the whole tribe of card-match-makers which frequent that quarter passed by his door the very next day, in hopes of being bought off after the same manner.

It is another great imperfection in our London Cries, that there is no just time nor measure observed in them. Our news should indeed be published in a very quick time because it is a commodity that will not keep cold. It should not, however, be cried with the same precipitation as fire. Yet this is generally the case. A bloody battle alarms the town from one end to another in an instant. Every motion of the French is published in so great a hurry, that one would think the enemy were at our gates. This likewise I would take upon me to regulate in such a manner, that

尖锐的高音来吐露自己的心意，在全音阶中从最高音到最低音都可以。同样的评语也适用于那些卖煤末的，更适用于卖碎玻璃和砖渣的小贩。对于这些以及其他类似的行当，我职责所在，理应加以调整，先要使得这些流动商贩的叫卖声柔和、悦耳，方才准许他们在街头出现；还要使得他们的叫卖声适应各自的货物，特别要防止的是卖的东西最少、喊的声音最凶的人——这在卖纸片火柴[1]的小贩那里是最明显不过了。对于他们，我只好照搬一句老话："声音很大，货色可怜。"

上面说的那些卖纸片火柴的音乐家们，为了兜售他们那些微不足道的商品，有时候吆喝的声音实在太大了。我认识的一位患有脾脏病的老好先生只好掏腰包请他们当中的某一位再也不要到他住的那条街上来了。可是，这笔交易结果怎样？第二天，那一带所有的纸片火柴贩子一个接一个到他门口叫卖，指望那位先生以同样方式拿钱出来把他们打发走。

我们伦敦的叫卖声还有一个大毛病，就是吆喝起来不顾时间，也不讲分寸。譬如说，新闻自应以快速公布为是，因为这种商品是经不起久放的。但是，卖报的时候也不必那样风是风火是火，跟闹了火灾似的。然而，这却是通常现象。一眨眼工夫，一场血战的消息就从伦敦这一头吆喝到那一头，弄得全城轰动。法国人有一点点动向[2]，总是急匆匆登出来，让人觉得好像已经兵临城下似的。此种弊端，本人自当负责予以适当纠正。在

---

[1] 早期的火柴以硬纸片蘸硫黄制成，用以燃火、点蜡烛等。
[2] 在18世纪初，英法两国之间为争夺殖民地以及西班牙王位继承问题，发生过一系列战争。

there should be some distinction made between the spreading of a victory, a march, or an encampment, a Dutch, a Portugal, or a Spanish mail. Nor must I omit under this head those excessive alarms with which several boisterous rustics infest our streets in turnip season; and which are more inexcusable, because they are wares which are in no danger of cooling upon their hands.

There are others who affect a very slow time, and are in my opinion much more tunable than the former. The cooper in particular swells his last note in a hollow voice, that is not without its harmony; nor can I forbear being inspired with a most agreeable melancholy, when I hear that sad and solemn air with which the public are very often asked if they have any chairs to mend? Your own memory may suggest to you many other lamentable ditties of the same nature, in which the music is wonderfully languishing and melodious.

I am always pleased with that particular time of the year which is proper for the picking of dill and cucumbers; but alas! this cry, like the song of the nightingale, is not heard above two months. It would therefore be worth while to consider whether the same air might not in some cases be adapted to other words.

It might likewise deserve our most serious considerations, how far, in a well-regulated city, those humourists are to be tolerated, who, not contented with the traditional cries of their forefathers, have invented particular songs and tunes of their own: such as was, not many years since, the pastry-man, commonly known by the name of the Colly-Molly-Puff; and such as is at this day the vendor of powder and wash-balls, who, if I am rightly informed, goes under the name of Powder-Wat.

卖报声中，对于胜利消息、行军消息、野营消息，以及荷兰、葡萄牙和西班牙各国邮件中所传来的消息，务必有所区别。在这一方面，我还必须指出：每当萝卜上市，总有许多乡下人大吵大嚷，沿街叫卖，满城为之骚然，实属不可原谅；因为萝卜这种商品即使在卖方手里放一放，并没有放凉的危险。

另外有些商贩爱拉长腔，在我看来，这比前面说的那些叫卖声要更有韵味。特别是箍桶匠爱用闷声，送出他那最后的尾音，不失为具有和谐动人之处。修理匠常用他那悲怆、庄严的语调向居民们发问："有修理椅子的没有？"我每当听见，总禁不住感到有一种忧郁情调沁入心脾。——这时，你的记忆会联想出许许多多类似的哀歌，它们那曲调都是缠绵无力、哀婉动人的。

每年，到了该摘黄瓜、收荨萝的季节，那叫卖声让我听了格外高兴。可惜，这种叫卖像夜莺的歌唱似的，让人听不上两个月就停了。因此，倒是值得考虑一下，是不是在其他场合把这个调调儿再配上别的什么词儿。

还有些人——譬如说，不几年以前大家叫作"松软-可口-蓬蓬酥"的卖点心小贩，以及现在（如果我没有弄错的话）通称为"香粉沃特"[1]的脂粉货郎，不以他们祖祖辈辈留传下来的叫卖为满足，还特别编出自己的歌曲来，以吟唱代替叫卖。在一个管理完善的城市里，对于这些市廛奇人究竟应该宽容到何等程度，也值得我们认真考虑。

---

1 指贩卖妇女化妆品的小贩的绰号。"沃特"为"瓦尔特"的简称。

I must not here omit one particular absurdity which runs through this whole vociferous generation, and which renders their cries very often not only incommodious, but altogether useless to the public. I mean that idle accomplishment which they all of them aim at, of crying so as not to be understood. Whether or no they have learned this from several of our affected singers, I will not take upon me to say; but most certain it is, that people know the wares they deal in rather by their tunes than by their words; insomuch that I have sometimes seen a country boy run out to buy apples of a bellows-mender, and gingerbread from a grinder of knives and scissors. Nay, so strangely infatuated are some very eminent artists of this particular grace in a cry, that none but their acquaintance are able to guess at their profession; for who else can know, that "work if I had it" should be the signification of a corn-cutter?

Forasmuch, therefore, as persons of this rank are seldom men of genius or capacity I think it would be very proper that some men of good sense and sound judgement should preside over these public cries, who should permit none to lift up their voices in our streets that have not tunable throats, and are not only able to overcome the noise of the crowd, and the rattling of coaches, but also to vend their respective merchandises in apt phrases, and in the most distinct and agreeable sounds. I do therefore humbly recommend myself as a person rightly qualified for this post; and if I meet with fitting encouragement, shall communicate some other projects which I have by me, that may no less conduce to the emolument of the public.

I am, Sir, &c.
Ralph Crotchet.

在这些高声叫卖之徒当中还普遍流行一种荒唐行径，对此我不能放过不提，因为那使得他们的叫嚷不仅嘈杂不堪，而且也于公众无益。我指的是他们在叫卖时拼命不让人听懂的那种无补实际的本领。在这方面，他们究竟是不是在向我们那些装腔作势的歌唱家学习，我且不去说它。但是，有一点可以肯定：市民判断他们卖的什么货色，并不是根据他们叫喊的词儿，而是听他们叫喊的调调儿。有时候，我看见一个从乡下来的孩子跑出来，向风箱修理匠买苹果，向磨剪刀师傅买姜面包，这就可见一斑。有些高级花腔叫卖家对于这门艺术钻研到了如此入迷的地步，结果，除了他们自己的熟人，谁也猜不出他们干的到底是哪一行。譬如说，谁能想到，修脚工喊的词儿竟是："给活儿就干哪！"

准此，既然在这个阶层里天才能人甚少，一切公共叫卖之声应该统归明理善断之士主管，嗓音不美者不得在街头大喊大叫，叫卖声不仅要压倒人声喧哗、车声轧轧，而且要使用恰当词句将各自贩卖的货色加以说明，发音也要清晰、悦耳。我谦卑地把自己推荐出来，担此重任。倘蒙奖掖，本人还有其他方案，也将一一献出，以惠公益。

余不一一。

狂想客谨白

The Spectator Club

Richard Steele

The first of our society is a gentleman of Worcestershire, of ancient descent, a baronet, his name Sir Roger de Coverley. His great-grandfather was inventor of that famous country-dance which is called after him. All who know that shire are very well acquainted with the parts and merits of Sir Roger. He is a gentleman that is very singular in his behaviour, but his singularities proceed from his good sense, and are contradictions to the manners of the world only as he thinks the world is in the wrong. However, this humour creates him no enemies, for he does nothing with sourness of obstinacy; and his being unconfined to modes and forms makes him but the readier and more capable to please and oblige all who know him. When he is in town, he lives in Soho Square. It is said he keeps himself a bachelor by reason he was crossed in love by a perverse, beautiful widow of the next county to him. Before this disappointment, Sir Roger was what you call a fine gentleman, had often supped with

---

1 英国西部的一个郡名。

旁观者俱乐部

理查德·斯梯尔

在我们俱乐部里，头一个要介绍的是伍斯特郡[1]的一位绅士。他出身望族，封号从男爵，名叫罗杰·德·考福来爵士。他的曾祖父是一种著名土风舞的发明者——这组对舞就是拿他的名字做名称的。凡是熟悉那一带地方的人都十分了解罗杰爵士的才干和建树。这位绅士立身行事的态度跟别人大不相同。不过，他之所以与众不同只是因为他那真知灼见跟世俗格格不入，而在他看来错在世俗方面。尽管如此，他这种脾气并没有给他招惹出怨敌来，因为他做事并不尖酸刻薄，也不刚愎自用。所以，他那不拘繁文缛节的性格倒让熟人觉得痛快，对他感到高兴。他每次进京，都住在苏豪广场[2]，过着独身生活——据说这是因为他曾经追求过邻郡的一个长相漂亮、脾气乖张的寡妇，结果失败的缘故。在这次挫折之前，罗杰爵士却是一个所谓风流倜傥

---

2 伦敦的一个繁华区。

my Lord Rochester and Sir George Etherege, fought a duel upon his first coming to town, and kicked Bully Dawson in a public coffeehouse for calling him "youngster". But being ill used by the above-mentioned widow, he was very serious for a year and a half; and though, his temper being naturally jovial, he at last got over it, he grew careless of himself, and never dressed afterward. He continues to wear a coat and doublet of the same cut that were in fashion at the time of his repulse, which, in his merry humours, he tells us, has been in and out twelve times since he first wore it. 'Tis said Sir Roger grew humble in his desires after he had forgot this cruel beauty, insomuch that it is reported he has frequently offended in point of chastity with beggars and gypsies; but this is looked upon by his friends rather as matter of raillery than truth. He is now in his fifty-sixth year, cheerful, gay, and hearty; keeps a good house both in town and country; a great lover of mankind; but there is such a mirthful cast in his behaviour that he is rather beloved than esteemed. His tenants grow rich, his servants look satisfied, all the young women profess love to him, and the young men are glad of his company; when he comes into a house he calls the servants by their names, and talks all the way upstairs to a visit. I must not omit that Sir Roger is a justice of the quorum; that he fills the chair at a quarter session with great abilities; and, three months ago, gained universal applause by explaining a passage in the Game Act.

---

1 罗切斯特爵爷（John Wilmot, Earl of Rochester，1647—1680）是英王查理二世的宠臣，宫廷浪子，能诗。

之士,常常跟罗切斯特爵爷[1]、乔治·埃瑟里奇爵士[2]共进晚餐。他第一次到京城来,就跟人决斗过,还在一个热闹的咖啡馆里把青皮陶三一脚踢翻,因为那个家伙竟敢叫他"小子"!然而,在受到上面说的那个寡妇的折磨之后,有一年半的时间他的脸上失去了笑影。尽管他天性爱说爱笑,后来也恢复了常态,但是从此他就不修边幅、邋遢起来,身上一直穿着他恋爱失败时风行的那种外套和紧身上衣。他心情高兴的时候,还对我们说:这种衣服,自打他穿在身上,时兴了又不时兴,已经变了十二回了。据说,罗杰爵士把那个冷心肠的美人一抛到脑后,私生活上有些饥不择食,道路传闻,甚至说他和乞丐、吉卜赛人搞在一道,殊于令名有伤。但据他的知交们看来,这多半出于嘲弄,并非事实。他今年五十六岁,乐乐呵呵,无忧无虑,热情豪爽,不管在京城、外乡都广交朋友,慷慨好客。只是他一高兴起来就不顾身份,因此别人对他也就亲近多于尊敬。他的佃客家家富裕,他的仆人个个满意,年轻妇女纷纷向他表示爱慕,青年男子高高兴兴和他来往。他每到别人家里做客,脚刚一进门,就喊着仆人的名字,边走边谈,说说笑笑上楼。我还得补充一句:罗杰爵士是郡里一位特邀治安法官,每季开庭,他坐在席上问事,表现出干练才能。三个月前,他对于田猎法令[3]的一项条款进行阐述,赢得法庭上一致喝彩。

---

2 乔治·埃瑟里奇爵士(Sir George Etherege,约1635—约1692)是查理二世的另一宠臣,英国王政复辟时期的戏剧家。
3 鸟兽保护法令。

The gentleman next in esteem and authority among us is another bachelor, who is a member of the Inner Temple; a man of great probity, wit, and understanding; but he has chosen his place of residence rather to obey the direction of an old humoursome father, than in pursuit of his own inclinations. He was placed there to study the laws of the land, and is the most learned of any of the house in those of the stage. Aristotle and Longinus are much better understood by him than Littleton or Coke. The father sends up, every post, questions relating to marriage articles, leases, and tenures, in the neighborhood; all which questions he agrees with an attorney to answer and take care of in the lump. He is studying the passions themselves, when he should be inquiring into the debates among men which arise from them. He knows the argument of each of the orations of Demosthenes and Tully, but not one case in the reports of our own courts. No one ever took him for a fool, but none, except his intimate friends, know he has a great deal of wit. This turn makes him at once both disinterested and agreeable; as few of his thoughts are drawn from business, they are most of them fit for conversation. His taste of books is a little too just for the age he lives in; he has read all, but approves of very few. His familiarity with the customs, manners, actions, and writings of the ancients makes him a very delicate observer of what occurs to him in the present world. He

---

1 朗吉努斯（Longinus，约213—273），希腊哲学家，著有文论《论崇高》。
2 利特尔顿（Sir Thomas de Littleton，1422—1481），英国法学家。
3 科克（Sir Edward Coke，1552—1634），英国法学家。

在我们当中次有威望的是法律公会的一位见习员，也是一个单身汉。他是个性格正直的人，很有聪明才智，不过他选择了这么一个栖身之地，与其说是出自个人爱好，不如说是为了服从脾气古怪的老父亲的命令。他被送到那里去，本来是让他研究土地法，但他却成了一位剧坛内行，在这方面和他同学的人谁也比不上他。他对于亚里士多德和朗吉努斯[1]比对于利特尔顿[2]和柯克[3]要熟悉得多。每趟邮车进城，都送来他父亲转给他的左邻右舍有关婚姻条款、租赁契约、田地租佃的问题——这些问题，他统统交给一个律师包干答复、处理，自己概不过问。他本应探讨由于人类七情六欲而产生出来的种种争执，但他却对这七情六欲本身尽自钻研不休。狄摩西尼[4]和西塞罗[5]的每篇演说词的内容他无不通晓，但是我国法庭记录的案情他却毫无所知。当然，别人还不至于把他当成傻瓜，但是，除了他那些知心好友，谁也不知道他原来是一个具有大才大智的人。他不为名利所牵，性情自然随和，种种想头多与正事无关，倒很适于娓娓清谈。他于书无所不读而赞许者甚少，对于我们这个时代来说，他那欣赏趣味未免有点儿曲高和寡。正因为他熟知古代的风俗、习惯、行为、著作，观察起当今社会上发生的事情来也就能明察秋毫。他是

---

4 狄摩西尼（Demosthenes，前384—前322），希腊演说家。
5 西塞罗（Marcus Tullius Cicero，即Tully，前106—前43），罗马演说家、哲学家。

is an excellent critic, and the time of the play is his hour of business; exactly at five he passes through New Inn, crosses through Russell Court, and takes a turn at Will's till the play begins; he has his shoes rubbed and his periwig powdered at the barber's as you go into the Rose. It is for the good of the audience when he is at a play, for the actors have an ambition to please him.

The person of next consideration is Sir Andrew Freeport, a merchant of great eminence in the city of London, a person of indefatigable industry, strong reason, and great experience. His notions of trade are noble and generous, and (as every rich man has usually some sly way of jesting, which would make no great figure were he not a rich man) he calls the sea the British Common. He is acquainted with commerce in all its parts, and will tell you that it is a stupid and barbarous way to extend dominion by arms; for true power is to be got by arts and industry. He will often argue, that if this part of our trade were well cultivated, we should gain from one nation; and if another, from another. I have heard him prove that diligence makes more lasting acquisitions than valour, and that sloth has ruined more nations than the sword. He abounds in several frugal maxims, among which the greatest favourite is, "A penny saved is a penny got." A general trader of good sense is pleasanter company than a general scholar; and Sir Andrew having a natural unaffected eloquence, the perspicuity of his discourse gives the same pleasure that wit would in another man. He

---

1 伦敦法律公会所在地之一。

位高明的评论家,以看戏为正业:五点整,他走过新会馆[1],穿过拉塞尔小巷[2];然后,在开戏之前,他到威尔咖啡店稍事停留;乘别人去玫瑰酒店[3]的工夫,让人给他把鞋子刷刷,到理发店给假发上上粉。戏院里有他在座,对观众有好处,因为演员为了讨他的好,特别卖力气。

下一个要说的重要人物是伦敦市有名的富商安德鲁·弗里波特爵士——这是一位具有坚强理智、丰富经验,而又孜孜不倦的事业家。他对于贸易颇有一些恢宏大度的看法,而且,有钱人都爱说句俏皮话(他们若不是富翁,别人恐怕也就看不出那俏皮话到底有何出色之处),他把海洋叫作英国的公共领地。有关商业的种种事务他都精通,常常说:武力不过是主权扩张的一种愚蠢而野蛮的方式,真正的权力是靠着工业、技术而赢得的。他常发议论说:只要我国在某一方面的贸易充分发展起来,就会从甲国那里赚钱;在另一方面发展,又会从乙国获利。他亲口对我说:作战勇敢,不如勤奋获利最长远;又说:懒惰足以亡国,其害甚于刀剑。他肚子里装了许许多多关于节俭的格言,最爱说的一句是:"一便士不花,等于一便士挣下。"跟一个普通的聪明商人打交道,比跟一个普通学者打交道要愉快得多。别人说话机智俏皮,叫人高兴;安德鲁爵士说话直来直去,发表什么意见明明白白,同样叫人觉得愉快。他的家私是

---

2 伦敦一条小街,仅可步行而不能通马车。
3 祝来巷戏院附近的一家酒馆。

has made his fortunes himself, and says that England may be richer than other kingdoms by as plain methods as he himself is richer than other men; though at the same time I can say this of him, that there is not a point in the compass but blows home a ship in which he is an owner.

Next to Sir Andrew in the clubroom sits Captain Sentry, a gentleman of great courage, good understanding, but invincible modesty. He is one of those that deserve very well, but are very awkward at putting their talents within the observation of such as should take notice of them. He was some years a captain, and behaved himself with great gallantry in several engagements and at several sieges; but having a small estate of his own, and being next heir to Sir Roger, he has quitted a way of life in which no man can rise suitably to his merit who is not something of a courtier as well as a soldier. I have heard him often lament that in a profession where merit is placed in so conspicuous a view, impudence should get the better of modesty. When he has talked to this purpose, I never heard him make a sour expression, but frankly confess that he left the world, because he was not fit for it. A strict honesty and an even, regular behaviour are in themselves obstacles to him that must press through crowds, who endeavour at the same end with himself—the favour of a commander. He will, however, in this way of talk, excuse generals for not disposing according to men's desert, or inquiring into it, "for", says he, "that great man, who has a mind to help me, has as many to break through to come at me as I have to come at him"; therefore he will conclude that the man who would make a figure, especially in a military way, must get over all false modesty, and assist his patron against the importunity of other

靠自己挣来的。他说：英国只要采用他自己那一套简简单单的致富办法，便可以比其他国家富裕。关于安德鲁爵士，我不妨再说一句：不管罗盘针指着哪一个方向，都会有属于他的船只给英国运来财富。

在俱乐部里，安德鲁爵士之下就是森特里上尉了。这是一位勇敢过人、洞察世事而又无比谦逊的绅士。有这样一些人，按他们的才能来说，本来是极该受到赏识的，可惜他们偏不善于在应该赏识他们的人面前显露自己，而森特里上尉便是这么一个人。他担任上尉军职数年之久，也曾在多次作战、围城中表现得英勇善战；只是因为他在家薄有田产，又是罗杰爵士的近亲继承人，所以就离开了军界；其实，换了别人，若非文武全才，要想挣得他那样大的战功，是根本办不到的。我常听得他叹气说：在军人这一行里，战功摆在那里，本来大家明明都看得见，然而，无耻幸进之徒仍然要比谦谦君子吃得开。不过，他在说这一派话的时候，从来不作尖酸刻薄之语，只是爽快承认自己生性与时不合，理当避世索居。大家都在争先恐后巴结官长，不把头皮挤破休想博得一顾，他一个人却尽在那里古板正直、循规蹈矩做人，前途自然障碍重重。不过，他尽管这样议论，对于将帅们不能论功行赏、又不去查问清楚，倒能给予谅解："因为，"他说，"大人物即使有心提携，却要突破一层又一层阻塞才能见得着我这么一个人，我要想见他也是一样困难。"所以，他下结论说：一个人要想出人头地，尤其在军人这一行里，一定得把假谦虚统统扔到一边，该为自己辩护，就毫不含糊把话说明，帮助自己

pretenders by a proper assurance in his own vindication. He says it is a civil cowardice to be backward in asserting what you ought to expect, as it is a military fear to be slow in attacking when it is your duty. With this candour does the gentleman speak of himself and others. The same frankness runs through all his conversation. The military part of his life has furnished him with many adventures, in the relation of which he is very agreeable to the company; for he is never overbearing, though accustomed to command men in the utmost degree below him; nor ever too obsequious, from an habit of obeying men highly above him.

But that our society may not appear a set of humourists unacquainted with the gallantries and pleasures of the age, we have among us the gallant Will Honeycomb, a gentleman who, according to his years, should be in the decline of his life, but having ever been very careful of his person, and always had a very easy fortune, time has made but very little impression either by wrinkles on his forehead or traces in his brain. His person is well turned and of a good height. He is very ready at that sort of discourse with which men usually entertain women. He has all his life dressed very well, and remembers habits as others do men. He can smile when one speaks to him, and laughs easily. He knows the history of every mode, and can inform you from which of the French king's wenches our wives and daughters had this manner of curling their hair, that way of placing their hoods; whose frailty was covered by such a sort of petticoat, and whose vanity to show her foot made that part of the dress so short in such a year. In a word, all his conversation and knowledge has been in the female world. As other men of his age

的恩人摆脱那些冒功请赏的家伙的歪缠。他说：应该理直气壮、当仁不让的时候，却文文气气，畏畏缩缩，正同需要冲锋陷阵、义无反顾的时候，却临阵不前、坐误战机一样，都是胆小懦弱的行为。这位先生不论谈到别人、谈到自己，都是这么一副爽快口吻。他的谈吐都是这么坦率。在他以往的军事生涯当中有不少惊险遭遇，他对我们谈起这些来，大家都很爱听，因而喜欢他这个人；因为，尽管他指挥过级别最低的下等兵打仗，他却从不盛气凌人；尽管他服从高级长官的命令成为习惯，他也从不谄媚奉承。

为了不让别人把我们这些人看成是一批对于当代声色之乐、风流韵事一窍不通的冬烘怪物，我们团体里吸收了一位时髦绅士威尔·亨尼康。这位先生按岁数说也该算垂垂老矣，但他身体保养得好，家道也还富裕，所以年岁对他影响甚微，额头上皱纹不多，脑子也还清楚。他长得高高大大，一表人才。凡是男人们为了讨女人欢心而常说的那一套甜言蜜语，他嘴巴上说得极熟。他一辈子衣冠楚楚，对于种种时装记得最清，正如别人专记熟人名字一样。别人讲话，他总微笑听着，动不动发出笑声。每一种时兴装束的来龙去脉，他都清清楚楚。他能告诉你：咱们的太太小姐们把头发这么样卷起来、把头巾那么样摆弄，都是从法国国王的哪一位情妇那里学来的。他还能说出：在何年何月，某位轻佻的女士为了遮羞设计了一种什么样的内裙，另一位女士为了显示自己的纤足，又裁制出什么样的一种短裙。一言以蔽之，他口之所言、生平所学都不离闺阃之事。别人

will take notice to you what such a minister said upon such and such an occasion, he will tell you when the Duke of Monmouth danced at court, such a woman was then smitten, another was taken with him at the head of his troop in the Park. In all these important relations, he has ever about the same time received a kind glance or a blow of a fan from some celebrated beauty, mother of the present Lord Such-a-one. If you speak of a young commoner that said a lively thing in the House, he starts up: "He has good blood in his veins; Tom Mirabell begot him. The rogue cheated me in that affair; that young fellow's mother used me more like a dog than any woman I ever made advances to." This way of talking of his very much enlivens the conversation among us of a more sedate turn; and I find there is not one of the company, but myself, who rarely speak at all, but speaks of him as of that sort of man who is usually called a well-bred, fine gentleman. To conclude his character, where women are not concerned, he is an honest worthy man.

I cannot tell whether I am to account him whom I am next to speak of as one of our company, for he visits us but seldom; but when he does, it adds to every man else a new enjoyment of himself. He is a clergyman, a very philosophic man, of general learning, great sanctity of life, and the most exact good breeding. He has the misfortune to be of a very weak constitution, and consequently cannot accept of such cares and business as preferments in his function would oblige him to; he is therefore among divines what a chamber-counsellor is among lawyers. The probity of his mind and the integrity of his life create him followers, as being eloquent or loud advances others. He seldom introduces the subject he speaks upon; but we are so far gone in years that he observes,

到了他这把年纪，来找你谈话，说的都是某某大臣在某某场合发表了什么高见。而他一开口，说的却是某年蒙茅斯公爵[1]在宫中跳舞，某女士为之芳心揉碎；他率领随从在海德公园露面，某女士为之一见钟情，等等。他一边谈着诸如此类的要闻，在座的某位著名美人儿，即现今某贵族阁下的妈妈，往往要向他投一个温柔的飞眼，或者拿扇子头敲他一下。如果你提到某位年轻下议员在议院发表了什么精彩演说，他就会惊叫起来："那可是个好种，汤姆·米拉博下的崽子嘛！那个坏蛋把我骗得好苦。哼，小家伙的妈妈也厉害，把我折腾得连个狗都不如——我追过的女人谁也不敢那样！"我们这些人都是古板脾气，聊天时，他说话的这种调调儿给大家增添不少活泼气氛。大家在一起，我很少开口，但是别人众口一词说他可称为风流雅士。关于他的为人，一句话说完：在和女人无关的事情上，他是一个正人君子。

我最后要谈到的这个人究竟算不算我们俱乐部的一员，我说不准，因为他不常在我们这里露面；不过，他每来一次，都让我们对他更加喜爱。这是一位牧师，一位学识渊博、心地圣洁、品行方正的哲学家。不幸他体质虚弱，不能操心劳神、亲自过问本职事务，这也就影响了他的升迁。因此，他在神职人员当中的地位，犹如律师业中的法律顾问一样。别人靠着夸夸其谈扬名于世，他只有纯正思想、敦厚言行，却也仍然有人追随。他要讲的正题，不必由他自己多作引导；因为我们大家

---

1 蒙茅斯公爵（James Scott，Duke of Monmouth，1649—1685）是英王查理二世的私生子。

when he is among us, an earnestness to have him fall on some divine topic which he always treats with much authority, as one who has no interest in this world, as one who is hastening to the object of all his wishes and conceives hope from his decays and infirmities. These are my ordinary companions.

年事已高,他一来就看出我们盼望他谈谈宗教方面的问题——在这方面,他谈论起来总是引经据典、头头是道。因为,他自己对尘世并无牵挂,急于归依那一心向往的未来目标,因此倒把疾病衰残看作是永生希望之所寄。以上各位便是我日常过从的友伴。

乔纳森·斯威夫特

1667—1745

《格列佛游记》的作者乔纳森·斯威夫特(Jonathan Swift, 1667—1745)生在爱尔兰一个英国移民家庭。自幼父死母去，他靠叔父资助，在都柏林三一学院读书。毕业后，他给一门远亲、退休外交官威廉·坦普尔做私人秘书，实际上过的是寄人篱下的生活。他希望通过坦普尔找一个好工作，但做了十年秘书，这个目的终未达到。不过他在坦普尔家里写了两部使他在文坛初露头角的作品:《木桶的故事》(关于基督教中天主教、英国国教和清教三派的讽喻故事)和《书籍之战》(关于古代作品和近代作品优劣比较的寓言)。

此后，他担任了英国国教会的职务，在爱尔兰做牧师，有时也到伦敦。1707年，他在伦敦结识了艾迪生、斯梯尔、蒲柏等著名作家，参加文学活动。他在政治上本来属于辉格党，后来转到托利党立场，担任其党刊《考察者》的主笔，成为托利党的舆论台柱。这时斯威夫特声誉日隆，托利党又是执政党，以他的威望本应得到高官；但由于他生性孤傲，鄙视权贵，加之他在《木桶的故事》中所流露的宗教观点为正统的绅士们所疑惧，所以就连托利党的掌权者对于把这么一个能够左右社会舆论而性格又不同流俗的大才子放在英国的重要位置上，也不那么放心。因此，在1713年，斯威夫特被派回爱尔兰，在都柏林圣帕特里克教堂担任副主教，直到他在1745年去世。

回爱尔兰任职后，斯威夫特对于多难的爱尔兰人民产生了强烈的同情，并且投入了保卫他们权利的正义斗争。

爱尔兰与英伦三岛一水之隔，从12世纪开始成为英国的第一

Jonathan Swift

个殖民地。在那一时期，英国殖民者任意圈占土地，使爱尔兰农民流离失所，变成乞丐；英国工厂主在爱尔兰办炼铁所，并且砍伐森林烧炭做燃料，把大片森林烧光；英国政府任意禁止爱尔兰产品出口，断绝爱尔兰工农业产品的国外销路；此外，爱尔兰人大部分信仰天主教，还受到宗教歧视。很多爱尔兰人在国内无法生存，大量逃亡海外，远到西印度群岛，为种植园主做奴隶。

斯威夫特眼见故乡人民所遭受的深重苦难，奋起如椽之笔，写出一系列关于爱尔兰的文章。这些文章，统称为"爱尔兰政论"(the Irish Pamphlets)，与他的杰作《格列佛游记》一起被当作斯威夫特的重要代表作品。而在这些政论中最常为人称引的则是《布商信札》("The Drapier's Letters")和此处所介绍的《育婴刍议》[又译作《一个小小的建议》("A Modest Proposal")]。

《布商信札》共四篇，写于1724年。当时一个名叫威廉·伍德的英国商人向国王的情妇行贿，取得权力，铸造成色不足的半便士铜币(Wood's Halfpenny)，准备在爱尔兰流通，牟取四万英镑的暴利。斯威夫特假托一个爱尔兰布商的名义，发表了四篇书信体的政论，揭穿英国的骗局。他指出：如果使用这种钱币，就意味着爱尔兰人民的进一步贫困；而且，英国国王根本无权强迫爱尔兰接受这种贬值钱币。书信向英国在爱尔兰的统治权提出挑战，呼吁爱尔兰人民掌握自己国家的命运。《布商信札》一出，不胫而走，在爱尔兰全国点燃起反英的怒火。英国总督悬赏寻找这几封信的匿名作者。在都柏林，尽管人人知道作者是谁，却没有一个人说出斯威夫特的名字。英国政府

Jonathan Swift

不得不撤销已经发给伍德的特许状。

为了爱尔兰的民族利益,斯威夫特劳心焦思,写了许多文章,提过许多建议,英国统治者自然不会采纳。在爱尔兰的英国绅士贵妇也豪奢如故,人民依然陷在水深火热之中,乞丐成群,哀鸿遍野,大批人逃亡国外求生。义愤之火促使斯威夫特写出他震撼人心的政论名作《育婴刍议》(1729)。在这篇文章中,作者假托为一个向英国统治者献策的谋士,采用一副悲天悯人、同情爱尔兰人民的口吻,提出自己解决爱尔兰问题的"理论"和"建议",最后拿出来的"使爱尔兰穷人子女不但不拖累其父母国家且能为社会造福"的方案,原来竟是建议把爱尔兰穷人的小孩子,除"留种"者外,一律卖给英国地主贵妇做餐桌上的食物!全文用反语冷嘲的手法,把这么一种血淋淋的计划说得理由十足,轻轻松松,好像一件十分平常的事情一样。然而,把文章读完以后,英国殖民者及其帮凶的吃人面目也就昭然若揭了!

以往国外有的评论者谈到这篇文章,往往说作者过于刻毒,甚至说斯威夫特是"憎恨人类的人"。这未免是皮相之见。近来的评论才比较客观公允了。例如,《诺顿英国文学选集》的编者在此文的题解中说它"表达出斯威夫特对于受压迫、愚昧无知、人口众多、忍饥挨饿、信仰天主教的爱尔兰人民的同情,以及对于住在国外的、贪得无厌的英国地主的愤怒——他们在英国议院、大臣和国王的默许下把这个国家的全部膏血都榨干了"。确实,冷酷刻毒的并不是斯威夫特,而是英国殖民主义者和地主贵族。斯威夫特在《育婴刍议》中所写的穷人婴儿被当作食料，也和鲁迅在《狂人日记》中所写的人吃人一样，都是作者在对于某种社会罪恶进行长期深刻观察之后，用形象加以概括，向恶势力发出的一种"诛心之论"。

斯威夫特的文章特点，除了他这种强大的讽刺力量，还有另外一个重要方面，那就是他的幽默风趣。此处所选的另一短文《关于一把扫帚的沉思》即是一例。斯威夫特三十二岁时，为爱尔兰法官伯克莱伯爵做家庭牧师。他除了要主持这位贵族家里的宗教仪式之外，还得为伯爵夫人念书。而这位夫人喜欢的又是枯燥乏味的宗教伦理著作。有一阵，伯爵夫人叫斯威夫特给她念化学家兼神学家波义耳（Robert Boyle，1627—1691）的《关于各种问题的随想》（*Occasional Reflections upon Several Subjects*，1665），又名《沉思录》（*Meditations*）。看此书名，其沉闷可知。斯威夫特对这个差使实在讨厌透了，就想出一个办法来摆脱。一天，他模拟这位神学家道貌岸然的教训口吻，写了一篇《关于一把扫帚的沉思》，暗暗夹在那本大著里。第二天，伯爵夫人叫他念书，他就把自己的作品翻出来，板着面孔朗诵。伯爵夫人一听题目吃了一惊，但又莫测高深，听完以后，还赞不绝口，连说：波义耳真是奇才，能从一件完全微不足道的东西身上想出这么一大篇人生哲理。斯威夫特心中好笑，表面上不动声色，离开了。以后，又来了客人，伯爵夫人又把这一篇《沉思录》夸奖一番，别人也吃一惊。最后，大家把书翻开一看，发现了斯威夫特的手稿，这才知道他开了一个大玩笑。

A Meditation upon a Broomstick

This single stick, which you now behold ingloriously lying in that neglected corner, I once knew in a flourishing state in a forest. It was full of sap, full of leaves, and full of boughs; but now in vain does the busy art of man pretend to vie with nature, by tying that withered bundle of twigs to its sapless trunk; it is now at best but the reverse of what it was, a tree turned upside-down, the branches on the earth, and the root in the air; it is now handled by every dirty wench, condemned to do her drudgery, and, by a capricious kind of fate, destined to make other things clean, and be nasty itself; at length, worn to the stumps in the service of the maids, it is either thrown out of doors or condemned to the last use—of kindling a fire. When I beheld this I sighed, and said within myself, "Surely mortal man is a broomstick!" Nature sent him into the world strong and lusty, in a thriving condition, wearing his own hair on his head, the proper branches of this reasoning vegetable, till the axe of intemperance has lopped off his green boughs, and left him a withered trunk; he then flies to art, and puts on a periwig, valuing

关于一把扫帚的沉思

——拟可敬的波义耳阁下《沉思录》体

君不见,眼前这根孤零零、灰溜溜、羞怯怯歪在壁角里的扫帚,往年在森林里它也曾有过汁液旺盛、枝叶繁茂、欣欣向荣的日子。然而,如今呵,它生机早已枯萎,人类偏偏多事,拿一把枯枝绑在它那赤条条的躯干之上,妄想以人工与造化相颉颃,而又终归徒然。它现在的模样恰好跟过去翻了一个个儿:枝条委之于地,根梢朝向天空,成为一株上下颠倒的树,掌握在某个做苦工的贱丫头手里,受着命运任意拨弄,注定了要把别的东西清扫干净,而自己只落得一身腌臜晦气。而在为女仆效劳、磨损得四肢不全之后,到头来或被随手抛出门外,或则最后再派它一个用场——当作引火之物一烧了之。有鉴于此,敝人不禁喟然自叹:"人生在世,岂不和这把扫帚一模一样吗?"造化将人送到世上来的时候,他身强力壮,精神奋发,头上毛发蓬松,恰似一棵有理性的树木枝叶扶疏一般。不料,贪欲失度犹如一柄巨斧,将其青枝绿叶戕伐殆尽,空留下光秃秃枯干一条。

himself upon an unnatural bundle of hairs, all covered with powder, that never grew on his head; but now should this our broomstick pretend to enter the scene, proud of those birchen spoils it never bore, and all covered with dust, through the sweepings of the finest lady's chamber, we should be apt to ridicule and despise its vanity. Partial judges that we are of our own excellencies, and other men's defaults!

But a broomstick, perhaps you will say, is an emblem of a tree standing on its head; and pray what is a man but a topsy-turvy creature, his animal faculties perpetually mounted on his rational, his head where his heels should be, grovelling on the earth? And yet, with all his faults, he sets up to be a universal reformer and corrector of abuses, a remover of grievances, rakes into every slut's corner of nature, bringing hidden corruptions to the light and raises a mighty dust where there was none before, sharing deeply all the while in the very same pollutions he pretends to sweep away. His last days are spent in slavery to women, and generally the least deserving; till, worn to the stumps, like his brother besom, he is either kicked out of doors, or made use of to kindle flames for others to warm themselves by.

此时，他只好乞灵于人工，戴上头套，借助于虽则撒满香粉、却非自家头皮长出的一副假发来撑一撑门面。然而，我们眼前这把扫帚，倘若仗恃这些并非自身所生、实系夺自他人的桦树枝条，曾在某位勋贵佳丽的闺房中扫出一堆又一堆垃圾，弄得尘土满身，因而洋洋得意，妄图在人前冒充角色。对于它这种妄自尊大，我们该会怎样嘲笑和鄙夷！然则，在判断自己的长处和别人的短处时，我们又是多么偏执的法官呵！

　　阁下也许会说：一把扫帚所代表的不过是区区一棵头朝下的树木而已。但是，请问：如果一个人的动物本能总是凌驾在他的理性本能之上，如果他总是摧眉折腰，把脑袋放在脚后跟才该放的地方，那么，他不是一种上下颠倒的动物又是什么？然而，尽管他自身毛病百出，他还要做出改革社会、匡正时弊、消除不平的样子，世间一切腌臜角落都要去亲自探查一番，把隐藏着的败德秽行扫到光天化日之下，结果本来清清净净的地方，也被他搅得甚嚣尘上。虽然他自以为是在澄清乾坤，其实他自己早在不知不觉之中深受尘垢污染了。到了晚年，他又为那些往往不值一提的妇人做牛做马，以此卒岁，直到手脚残废；然后，就像那些长把扫帚一样，不是被一脚踢出门外，就是被用来点火，好让他人取暖。

39

A Modest Proposal

For Preventing the Children of Poor People in Ireland from Being a Burden to Their Parents or Country, and for Making Them Beneficial to the Public

It is a melancholy object to those who walk through this great town or travel in the country, when they see the streets, the roads, and cabin doors, crowded with beggars of the female sex, followed by three, four, or six children, all in rags and importuning every passenger for an alms. These mothers, instead of being able to work for their honest livelihood, are forced to employ all their time in strolling to beg sustenance for their helpless infants, who, as they grow up, either turn thieves for want of work, or leave their dear native country to fight for the Pretender in Spain, or sell themselves to the Barbadoes.

I think it is agreed by all parties that this prodigious number of children in the arms, or on the backs, or at the heels of their mothers, and frequently of their fathers, is in the present deplorable state of the kingdom a very great additional grievance; and therefore whoever could

---

1 《育婴刍议》这个题目采自周作人的早年译本，见于1927年出版的"苦雨斋小书"之一《冥土旅行》。我之所以采用这个中文题目，是因为它颇能传达出这篇文章一方面使用当时侵略弱小国家的英国统治者及其帮凶们惯用的"悲天悯人"、一本正经的正人君子口吻，另一方面深刻讽刺、揭露他们血腥、凶恶的本质。
2 指爱尔兰首都都柏林。

育婴刍议[1]

——关于如何使爱尔兰穷人子女
不但不拖累其父母国家
且能为社会造福的一个小小的建议

凡从这个大城市[2]走过或在乡间旅行的人，常常看见街头、路边、小屋门口挤满了女乞丐，后边跟着三四个、五六个小孩子，全都衣衫褴褛，哀求过路人施舍，这真是一种凄惨的景象。这些做母亲的人，不能去做工以谋求正当的生计，只得天天四处漂流，为她那些哀哀无告的婴儿讨一口饭吃；而这些婴儿长大以后，不是因为无工可做而去做贼，便是离乡背井去为躲在西班牙的冒牌国王[3]当兵打仗，再不然就自愿卖身远到巴巴多斯岛[4]去。

我想，各方人士定会一致同意，这些母亲们（时常也是父亲们）怀里抱着、身上背着、脚后跟着的多得惊人的小孩子，在我国[5]当前的可悲状况下实在是一个很

---

3 指在1688年英国"光荣革命"后，荷兰的奥仑治亲王威廉及其子孙已经成为英国国王之后，仍企图复辟斯图亚特王朝的詹姆斯二世之子詹姆斯·爱德华·斯图亚特（James Edward Stuart）及其子孙——他们先后在法国和西班牙支持下多次起事，均告失败。
4 西印度群岛中的一个岛屿，英国殖民地。当时在国内无以为生的爱尔兰人多逃往西印度群岛为种植园主去做苦工。
5 指爱尔兰。

find out a fair, cheap, and easy method of making these children sound, useful members of the commonwealth would deserve so well of the public as to have his statue set up for a preserver of the nation.

But my intention is very far from being confined to provide only for the children of professed beggars; it is of a much greater extent, and shall take in the whole number of infants at a certain age who are born of parents in effect as little able to support them as those who demand our charity in the streets.

As to my own part, having turned my thoughts for many years upon this important subject, and maturely weighed the several schemes of other projectors, I have always found them grossly mistaken in their computation. It is true, a child just dropped from its dam may be supported by her milk for a solar year with little other nourishment; at most not above the value of two shillings, which the mother may certainly get, or the value in scraps, by her lawful occupation of begging, and it is exactly at one year old that I propose to provide for them in such a manner as, instead of being a charge upon their parents or the parish, or wanting food and raiment for the rest of their lives, they shall on the contrary contribute to the feeding, and partly to the clothing, of many thousands.

There is likewise another great advantage in my scheme, that it will prevent those voluntary abortions, and that horrid practice of women murdering their bastard children, alas, too frequent among us, sacrificing the poor innocent babes, I doubt, more to avoid the expense

---

1 指当时以关心国计民生为名，向统治者献策献计，以捞取个人私利的人。

大的额外灾难。因此，若有人能够想出一个周到、省钱、简单可行的办法，使得这些小孩子也能成为国家中健壮有用的分子，大家理当对他奖赏，甚至应该把他当作民族救星，为他建立雕像。

但是，我这种意图并非专为那些职业乞丐设想。其范围要广泛得多，在某种年龄以内的全体婴儿都要包括在内，因为他们的父母养活他们不起，一如那些在街头告怜的人。

说到我自己，对于这样一个重要问题，敝人业已动了多年脑筋，而且连其他献策人[1]的种种方案也都加以细细掂量。不过，我发现他们在计算方面都有严重失误之处。确切地说，一个刚刚落地的婴儿，只要靠着母奶，没有别的什么养料也可以活上整整一个年头，其用度至多不超过两先令，即使再加上一点别的琐屑花费，也统统可以靠着母亲的合法乞讨[2]来取得。我所要提出解决的却是那些满了一周岁的小儿。只要按照我这种办法，他们不但不会成为父母和教区的累赘，而且自己一辈子也不再缺吃少穿，相反，还能给数千人提供食品甚至一部分衣着。

同时，我这个方案还有另外一种莫大的好处，它可以阻止自愿堕胎以及有些妇女弄死自己私生婴儿的骇人行为——可惜，这在我们同胞当中发生的次数太多了。我想，她们拿那些可怜无辜的小生命做牺牲，与其说是为

---

2 根据英国传统法律，一部分因老弱而失去劳动力的人求乞，属于"合法乞讨"，青壮年乞丐则受到严刑峻法的禁止。

than the shame, which would move tears and pity in the most savage and inhuman breast.

The number of souls in this kingdom being usually reckoned one million and a half, of these I calculate there may be about two hundred thousand couple whose wives are breeders; from which number I subtract thirty thousand couples who are able to maintain their own children, although I apprehend there cannot be so many under the present distresses of the kingdom; but this being granted, there will remain an hundred and seventy thousand breeders. I again subtract fifty thousand for those women who miscarry, or whose children die by accident or disease within the year. There only remain an hundred and twenty thousand children of poor parents annually born. The question therefore is, how this number shall be reared and provided for, which, as I have already said, under the present situation of affairs, is utterly impossible by all the methods hitherto proposed. For we can neither employ them in handicraft or agriculture; we neither build houses (I mean in the country) nor cultivate land. They can very seldom pick up a livelihood by stealing till they arrive at six years old, except where they are of towardly parts; although I confess they learn the rudiments much earlier, during which time they can however be looked upon only as probationers, as I have been informed by a principal gentleman in the county of Cavan, who protested to me that he never knew above one or two instances under the age of six, even in a part of the kingdom so renowned for the quickest proficiency in that art.

I am assured by our merchants that a boy or a girl before twelve years old is no saleable commodity; and even when they come to this

了遮羞，不如说是为了省钱。这样的事，即使让那些最无人性的野蛮人听了，也不免要流下怜悯的泪水！

爱尔兰的人口一般计算为一百五十万。我估计，其中大约有二十万对能够生养；从这个数字当中，我除去有抚养子女能力者三万对——虽然，现今国家灾难深重，恐怕未必能有这么多；即便如此，仍然还有十七万对生殖者。我再除去五万，包括那些小产的或者在一周岁之内因事故、疾病而死亡的婴儿。这么一来，穷人的年产子女就只剩下十二万了。问题在于拿什么来供养这么多小孩子——这个，我已经说过，在目前的局面下，无论什么办法也都不能解决。因为，我们既不能使唤这些小孩子做手艺、种田，也不能（我说的是乡下）叫他们去盖房、开荒。他们不到六岁，也很难依靠盗窃为生，除非某些地方小孩子特别早熟。虽然，我也承认，在这方面的基本知识他们很早就已无师自通，不过他们那时候顶多只能算是练习生罢了。卡文郡一位要人对我说过，即使在那么一个以精通此道名闻全国的地方，他所知道的案例中，六岁以下的也仅有那么一两起。

商人们告诉我说，十二岁以下的男孩、女孩根本不可能上市；即使到了十二岁，行市也超不过三镑，最多

age they will not yield above three pounds, or three pounds and half a crown at most on the Exchange; which cannot turn to account either to the parents or the kingdom, the charge of nutriment and rags having been at least four times that value.

I shall now therefore humbly propose my own thoughts, which I hope will not be liable to the least objection.

I have been assured by a very knowing American of my acquaintance in London, that a young healthy child well nursed is at a year old a most delicious, nourishing, and wholesome food, whether stewed, roasted, baked, or boiled; and I make no doubt that it will equally serve in a fricassee or a ragout.

I do therefore humbly offer it to public consideration that of the hundred and twenty thousand children, already computed, twenty thousand may be reserved for breed, whereof only one fourth part to be males, which is more than we allow to sheep, black cattle, or swine; and my reason is that these children are seldom the fruits of marriage, a circumstance not much regarded by our savages, therefore one male will be sufficient to serve four females. That the remaining hundred thousand may at a year old be offered in sale to the persons of quality and fortune through the kingdom, always advising the mother to let them suck plentifully in the last month, so as to render them plump and fat for a good table. A child will make two dishes at an entertainment for friends; and when the family dines alone, the fore or hind quarter will make a reasonable dish, and seasoned with a little pepper or salt will be very good boiled on the fourth day, especially in winter.

I have reckoned upon a medium that a child just born will weigh

三镑零半克朗[1]。这对于父母或国家都无利可图,因为光拿他们的嚼谷和破衣烂衫这么两项来说,价钱就起码四倍于此数。

准此,我谨略陈愚见,希望不至引起任何异议。

我在伦敦认识的一位深明内情的美国人对我说,一个喂养得壮壮实实的一岁小儿,无论炖、烤、烘、煮,都是一种非常可口、营养、卫生的食物。而且,我也毫不怀疑,如果把它做成炸丸子或炒肉丝[2],大概也同样不差。

所以,我谨将鄙见提出,以供大家斟酌:从刚才算出的十二万口小儿当中,可以抽出两万留种,其中雄性仅占四分之一;这比起我们所留养的雄绵羊、黑牛或猪仔来,已经要算多了。我这样主张,乃因为这些小儿多半不是正式婚姻所生(我国的乡野愚民对于这一点是不大在乎的),因此,一雄四雌也就足够了。其余十万小儿养到周岁便可拿出来卖给全国的富贵人家,但要切记交代母亲在那最后一个月里给小儿喂足了奶,把他们弄得肥肥胖胖,才好上得席面。遇到招待亲友,一个小儿可做两道佳肴。如果家里平素吃饭,一条前腿或者后腿就尽够做一盘合适的菜;若能加上一点椒盐,放到第四天煮了吃,则更有风味,尤其是在冬天。

我计算过,初生小儿平均体重十二磅[3],只要喂养得

---

[1] 克朗是英国货币名,值五先令。
[2] 对fricassee和ragout这两种菜名,各家说法不一。此处暂斟酌译为"炸丸子"和"炒肉丝",以与上文的"炖、烤、烘、煮"稍示区别。
[3] 英制质量单位,1磅约等于453.6克。

twelve pounds, and in a solar year if tolerably nursed increaseth to twenty-eight pounds.

I grant this food will be somewhat dear and therefore very proper for landlords, who, as they have already devoured most of the parents, seem to have the best title to the children.

Infant's flesh will be in season throughout the year, but more plentiful in March, and a little before and after. For we are told by a grave author, an eminent French physician, that fish being a prolific diet, there are more children born in Roman Catholic countries about nine months after Lent than at any other season; therefore, reckoning a year after Lent, the markets will be more glutted than usual, because the number of popish infants is at least three to one in this kingdom; and therefore it will have one other collateral advantage, by lessening the number of Papists among us.

I have already computed the charge of nursing a beggar's child (in which list I reckon all cottagers, labourers, and four fifths of the farmers) to be about two shillings per annum, rags included; and I believe no gentleman would repine to give ten shillings for the carcass of a good fat child, which, as I have said, will make four dishes of excellent nutritive meat, when he hath only some particular friend or his own family to dine with him. Thus the squire will learn to be a good landlord, and grow popular among the tenants; the mother will have eight shillings net profit, and be fit for work till she produces another child.

Those who are more thrifty (as I must confess the times require) may flay the carcass; the skin of which artificially dressed will make admirable gloves for ladies, and summer boots for fine gentlemen.

法，经过一年就能长到二十八磅。

我承认，这种食物略嫌昂贵，因此对于地主们特别合适：因为他们既然已经把许多父母吃掉，看来也最有资格来吃他们的子女。

婴儿的肉全年均可上市，3月前后尤其是旺季。一位严肃的作家[1]又是法国的名医说过：鱼是促进生育的食品，所以在四旬斋[2]九个月以后，天主教国家的产子率要比其他任何时期都高；因此，从四旬斋往后推算一年，市场上一定货源充足；而且，由于我国天主教徒的婴儿至少三倍于其他教派[3]，这件事还兼有另一种好处，那就是可以减少我们人口中天主教徒的数目。

我业已算过，养育一个乞丐小孩（我把佃农、工人和五分之四的农夫都划进这一类），包括他们身上的破衣，一年大约花费两个先令。我相信，无论哪位绅士都不惜拿出十个先令买下一具肥壮小儿的尸体；因为，我已说过，如果他要招待稀客，或同家人共餐，这可以做成四盘滋养丰富的菜。这样一来，乡绅就懂得怎样做一个好东家，受到佃户们爱戴；而小孩的母亲净赚八先令的纯利之后，还可照常干活，直到她生产下一个小孩。

那些还想再节省一点的人（我承认，这是时势使然），可以把尸首剥了皮；皮子经过精工处理，能为贵妇人做成漂亮的手套，或给文雅绅士们做成夏天穿的凉鞋。

---

1 这是反话。作者此处指法国著名的讽刺、滑稽作家，《巨人传》的作者拉伯雷（François Rabelais，1494—1553）。
2 指复活节前四十日间。在此期间，天主教徒不能吃肉，只能吃鱼，而多吃鱼有助于繁殖。
3 爱尔兰人大部分信仰天主教，故云。

As to our city of Dublin, shambles may be appointed for this purpose in the most convenient parts of it, and butchers we may be assured will not be wanting; although I rather recommend buying the children alive, and dressing them hot from the knife as we do roasting pigs.

A very worthy person, a true lover of his country, and whose virtues I highly esteem, was lately pleased in discoursing on this matter to offer a refinement upon my scheme. He said that many gentlemen of this kingdom, having of late destroyed their deer, he conceived that the want of venison might be well supplied by the bodies of young lads and maidens, not exceeding fourteen years of age nor under twelve, so great a number of both sexes in every county being now ready to starve for want of work and service; and these to be disposed of by their parents, if alive, or otherwise by their nearest relations. But with due deference to so excellent a friend and so deserving a patriot, I cannot be altogether in his sentiments; for as to the males, my American acquaintance assured me from frequent experience that their flesh was generally tough and lean, like that of our schoolboys, by continual exercise, and their taste disagreeable; and to fatten them would not answer the charge. Then as to the females, it would, I think with humble submission, be a loss to the public, because they soon would become breeders themselves: and besides, it is not improbable that some scrupulous people might be apt to censure such a practice (although indeed very unjustly) as a little bordering upon cruelty; which, I confess, hath always been with me the strongest objection against any project, how well soever intended.

But in order to justify my friend, he confessed that this expedient was put into his head by the famous Psalmanazar, a native of the island Formosa,

我们都柏林市，可在适当地点设立专用的屠宰场，我相信，屠夫是不会缺少的；不过，我建议还是买活小孩现宰现做，就像烤小猪那样。

一位品德高尚、为我仰慕的名士，真正的爱国者，最近动了雅兴，也谈起这个问题，打算把我的方案加以修订。他说，近来我国许多绅士滥杀鹿群，引起鹿肉缺乏；他认为，这可用十四岁以下、十二岁以上的少年男女的肉来加以补充，因为我国各地大批男男女女正由于无活可干、无事可做而在那里挨饿。可以趁这些人一息尚存，由他们父母加以处理，或由他们近亲代劳。然而，尽管我对这位高贵的朋友、功勋卓著的爱国人士十分敬仰，对于他的高见却未便苟同；因为我那位美国朋友曾经说过，根据他自己的多次试验，少男们由于活动频繁，像我们的小学生那样，肉质一般硬而且瘦，味道不好，把他们养肥了再卖又怕亏本。说到少女呢，鄙见以为吃掉恐于社会有损，因为稍待时日她们自己就能繁殖了。而且，某些谨小慎微之徒说不定还要谴责（虽然很不公平），说这种行为几近残忍。实在话，对于任何方案，如果手段残忍，我也向来强烈反对，不管那动机是多么良好。

不过，我还是要为我那位朋友辩护一句，因为他倒是说过，他之所以想出这么一种权宜之计，是受了那个出了名的"台湾岛土著"普萨尔马纳扎[1]的启发。约当

---

[1] 普萨尔马纳扎（George Psalmanazar, 1679—1763），文学骗子，法国人，冒充中国台湾居民，捏造事实写了一本关于台湾的书。作者在此转述的就是其中任意杜撰的内容。Formosa是16至17世纪殖民主义者对中国台湾的称呼。

who came from thence to London above twenty years ago, and in conversation told my friend that in his country when any young person happened to be put to death, the executioner sold the carcass to persons of quality as a prime dainty; and that in his time the body of a plump girl of fifteen, who was crucified for an attempt to poison the emperor, was sold to his Imperial Majesty's prime minister of state, and other great mandarins of the court, in joints from the gibbet, at four hundred crowns. Neither indeed can I deny that if the same use were made of several plump young girls in this town, who without one single groat to their fortunes cannot stir abroad without a chair, and appear at the playhouse and assemblies in foreign fineries which they never will pay for, the kingdom would not be the worse.

Some persons of a desponding spirit are in great concern about that vast number of poor people who are aged, diseased, or maimed, and I have been desired to employ my thoughts what course may be taken to ease the nation of so grievous an encumbrance. But I am not in the least pain upon that matter, because it is very well known that they are every day dying and rotting by cold and famine, and filth and vermin, as fast as can be reasonably expected. And as to the younger labourers, they are now in almost as hopeful a condition. They cannot get work, and consequently pine away for want of nourishment to a degree that if at any time they are accidentally hired to common labour, they have not strength to perform it; and thus the country and themselves are happily delivered from the evils to come.

I have too long digressed, and therefore shall return to my subject. I think the advantages by the proposal which I have made are obvious

二十年前，那个人从他本土来到伦敦，在交谈中对我那朋友说，在他本国，如有青年人被处死刑，刽子手就把犯人尸体当作一种珍馐美味卖给王公贵人；还说，当时有一个十五岁少女因为图谋毒死皇帝而被处磔刑，她那肥胖的身体挂在刑架上，肉给一片一片割下来，卖给万岁爷的宰相和其他宫廷大员，一共卖了四百克朗。我直话直说，我们都城里有不少胖姑娘，自己一个钱也没有，可是一出门就得坐轿子，穿着并非自己挣钱买来的进口华丽衣裳，在剧院和交际场进进出出；要是把她们也照那样利用一下子，对于国家大概不会有什么损失。

有些意气消沉的人非常担心那许多穷苦的老弱病残者，要求我动动脑筋想个什么办法来减轻国家的这一项沉重负担。但我丝毫不必为这件事操心，因为，众所周知，他们这些人由于寒冷、饥荒、污秽、害虫，天天都在死亡、烂掉，正像我们所料想的那样快。至于那些青年劳工，他们的当前处境也差不多同样大有希望。他们找不到工作，由于缺乏营养而日渐憔悴，即使偶尔被人雇去做工，也没有力气干活；因此，国家和他们本人也就非常圆满地摆脱了未来的灾难。

话扯得远了，我现在回到正题。我认为，我所提出

53

and many, as well as of the highest importance.

For first, as I have already observed, it would greatly lessen the number of Papists, with whom we are yearly overrun, being the principal breeders of the nation as well as our most dangerous enemies; and who stay at home on purpose to deliver the kingdom to the Pretender, hoping to take their advantage by the absence of so many good Protestants, who have chosen rather to leave their country than stay at home and pay tithes against their conscience to an Episcopal curate.

Secondly, the poorer tenants will have something valuable of their own, which by law may be made liable to distress, and help to pay their landlord's rent, their corn and cattle being already seized and money a thing unknown.

Thirdly, whereas the maintenance of an hundred thousand children, from two years old and upwards, cannot be computed at less than ten shillings a piece per annum, the nation's stock will be thereby increased fifty thousand pounds per annum, besides the profit of a new dish introduced to the tables of all gentlemen of fortune in the kingdom who have any refinement in taste. And the money will circulate among ourselves, the goods being entirely of our own growth and manufacture.

Fourthly, the constant breeders, besides the gain of eight shillings sterling per annum by the sale of their children, will be rid of the charge of maintaining them after the first year.

Fifthly, this food would likewise bring great custom to taverns, where the vintners will certainly be so prudent as to procure the best receipts for dressing it to perfection, and consequently have their houses frequented by all the fine gentlemen, who justly value themselves upon

的这个建议好处很明显,很多,而且事关重大。

第一,我已经说过,这个方案能大大减少天主教徒的人数。他们在我国到处蔓延,成为本民族的主要生殖者,也是我们最危险的敌人。他们趁许多善良新教徒出走之机,自己留在国内,图谋把国家送给那个冒牌国王[1];那些新教徒则不愿待在本国,违背良心向副牧师交纳什一税,只好出国他走。

第二,那些穷苦佃户也因此有了一点属于自己的值钱东西,依法还可以没收,以抵押应该交给地主的一部分田租,因为他们的谷物和耕牛早被夺走了,更不知道钱是什么样子。

第三,十万个两岁以上小儿的养育费,每人每年非十先令不办,因此,国库每年就可增加五万镑的收入;这还不算摆到全国有口福的富家绅士餐桌上的那一道新鲜菜肴。而赚来的钱仍可在我们自己当中流通,因为这种货物完全是本国自产自造。

第四,常年的生育者[2],在卖掉子女之后,除了每年八先令的收益,小儿一周岁后的一切养育费也一并免掉了。

第五,这种食品还能给酒馆招来大批顾客。酒馆主人一定会细心访求烹制妙方,以吸引那些讲究美食的风雅绅士川流不息地到酒馆里来;而手艺高明的厨师既懂

---

1 指"僭位者"詹姆斯·爱德华·斯图亚特。
2 指只会生育的动物,即爱尔兰的妇女、母亲。

their knowledge in good eating; and a skillful cook, who understands how to oblige his guests, will contrive to make it as expensive as they please.

Sixthly, this would be a great inducement to marriage, which all wise nations have either encouraged by rewards or enforced by laws and penalties. It would increase the care and tenderness of mothers toward their children, when they were sure of a settlement for life to the poor babes, provided in some sort by the public, to their annual profit instead of expense. We should see an honest emulation among the married women, which of them could bring the fattest child to the market. Men would become as fond of their wives during the time of their pregnancy as they are now of their mares in foal, their cows in calf, or sows when they are ready to farrow; nor offer to beat or kick them (as is too frequent a practice) for fear of a miscarriage.

Many other advantages might be enumerated. For instance, the addition of some thousand carcasses in our exportation of barreled beef, the propagation of swine's flesh, and improvement in the art of making good bacon, so much wanted among us by the great destruction of pigs, too frequent at our tables, which are no way comparable in taste or magnificence to a well-grown, fat, yearling child, which roasted whole will make a considerable figure at a lord mayor's feast or any other public entertainment. But this and many others I omit, being studious of brevity.

Supposing that one thousand families in this city would be constant customers for infants' flesh, besides others who might have it at merry meetings, particularly weddings and christenings, I compute that Dublin would take off annually about twenty thousand carcasses, and the rest of the kingdom (where probably they will be sold somewhat

得如何投客人之所好，自然要想尽法子把这道菜做得愈贵重愈好。

第六，这将大大推动人们结婚。本来，对于这件事，凡是贤明的政府不是用奖赏来鼓励，就是拿法律和刑罚来强迫的。做母亲的对她们的子女也会因此特别加以关心和爱护，因为她们知道社会上对于这些可怜的小宝宝已经作好了某种安排，她们自己每年无须花钱，还有赚头。这样，我们就会看到，在已婚妇女之间将会出现一种正当的竞赛活动，看哪一个能为市场提供最肥的小儿。男人们在妻子怀孕期间也会对她们格外爱惜，正如他们现在爱惜那怀驹的母马、怀犊的母牛或者就要下仔的母猪，而不对她们拳打脚踢(这本来是家常便饭)，因为怕她们小产。

此外，还有很多好处可以列举出来。譬如说，能为我国出口桶装牛肉增加几千头牛，有利于猪肉推销，以及提高咸肉的加工技术，等等。咸肉本为我们餐桌上必不可少之物，近来却因生猪大量死亡而变得奇缺；但要论起风味和豪华来，它断断比不上养得肥壮的小儿，整只烤了摆在市长的酒席上或者其他公共宴会上，那才真显出十足的派头。然而，凡此种种，为了行文简洁，我都略过不提了。

假定在这个城里有一千户人家是小儿肉的常年主顾，再加上为了庆祝婚礼和命名日而欢宴时的零买，计算起来都柏林一地每年可销去将近两万具尸体，剩下

cheaper) the remaining eighty thousand.

I can think of no one objection that will possibly be raised against this proposal, unless it should be urged that the number of people will be thereby much lessened in the kingdom. This I freely own, and it was indeed one principal design in offering it to the world. I desire the reader will observe, that I calculate my remedy for this one individual kingdom of Ireland and for no other that ever was, is, or I think ever can be upon earth. Therefore let no man talk to me of other expedients: of taxing our absentees at five shillings a pound: of using neither clothes nor household furniture except what is of our own growth and manufacture: of utterly rejecting the materials and instruments that promote foreign luxury: of curing the expensiveness of pride, vanity, idleness, and gaming in our women: of introducing a vein of parsimony, prudence, and temperance: of learning to love our country, in the want of which we differ even from Laplanders and the inhabitants of Topinamboo: of quitting our animosities and factions, nor acting any longer like the Jews, who were murdering one another at the very moment their city was taken: of being a little cautious not to sell our country and conscience for nothing: of teaching landlords to have at least one degree of mercy toward their tenants: lastly, of putting a spirit of honesty, industry, and skill into our shopkeepers, who, if a resolution could now be taken to buy only our native goods, would immediately unite to cheat and exact upon us in the price, the measure, and the goodness, nor could ever yet be brought to make one fair proposal of just dealing, though often and earnestly invited to it.

八万具(售价或许要略予降低)则可运销到全国各地。

对于我这个建议,我想别人不至于提出什么反对意见,除非有人要说全国人口定会因此大为减少。这一点我坦白承认,而且它也正是我把这一方案公之于众的主要目的所在。我还要请读者明鉴,这套济世方略是专为爱尔兰这个国家而制订,并不适用于过去、现在以至将来世界上其他任何国家。所以,别人就不必再向我提别的什么办法,例如,对于国外居住者[1]的收入每镑课以五先令的税金;对于非本国产制的衣物、家具一律不用;抵制一切容易助长外国奢靡之风的材料和器件;对于妇女的傲慢、虚荣、懒惰、赌博加以纠正,以杜绝浪费;提倡一种俭约、谨慎、节制之风;学习热爱祖国——在这方面,我们甚至还比不上拉普兰人和托品南布的土著;停止敌对、派别活动,不要像犹太人那样,国破家亡关头还在自相残杀;[2]要稍稍留神,不要把祖国和自己的良心白白出卖给人;教育地主们对于佃户至少发那么一点善心;最后,要在我国商人们当中灌输一种诚实、勤勉、干练的精神——现在只要刚一做出购买国货的决定,他们就立刻串通一气,在价格、分量、货色方面对大家进行欺骗和勒索,无论怎样经常对他们加以劝说,他们总不肯公平交易,信诚无欺。[3]

---

[1] 指在爱尔兰之外的英国或欧洲居住,但以在爱尔兰收租为其财富来源的英国地主们。
[2] 公元前70年,罗马帝国军队包围耶路撒冷,城破之前,城内的犹太人各派之间还在自相残杀。
[3] 在此段最后一个长句中所列举的是作者的正面主张,与全文中作为讽刺的反话而提出的"建议"不同。

Therefore I repeat, let no man talk to me of these and the like expedients, till he hath at least some glimpse of hope that there will ever be some hearty and sincere attempt to put them in practice.

But as to myself, having been wearied out for many years with offering vain, idle, visionary thoughts, and at length utterly despairing of success, I fortunately fell upon this proposal, which, as it is wholly new, so it hath something solid and real, of no expense and little trouble, full in our own power, and whereby we can incur no danger in disobliging England. For this kind of commodity will not bear exportation, the flesh being of too tender a consistence to admit a long continuance in salt, although perhaps I could name a country which would be glad to eat up our whole nation without it.

After all, I am not so violently bent upon my own opinion as to reject any offer proposed by wise men, which shall be found equally innocent, cheap, easy, and effectual. But before something of that kind shall be advanced in contradiction to my scheme, and offering a better, I desire the author or authors will be pleased maturely to consider two points. First, as things now stand, how they will be able to find food and raiment for an hundred thousand useless mouths and backs. And secondly, there being a round million of creatures in human figure throughout this kingdom, whose sole subsistence put into a common stock would leave them in debt two millions of pounds sterling, adding those who are beggars by profession to the bulk of farmers, cottagers, and labourers, with their wives and children who are beggars in effect; I desire those politicians who dislike my overture, and may perhaps be so bold to attempt an answer, that they will first ask the parents of these

因此，我在此重申，别人不必向我再提以上这些以及其他类似的办法，除非他们能看到一线希望的光芒，真有什么热心人要把它们付诸实践。

至于我自己，多年以来虽然提过不少空洞、迂阔，不切实际的意见，但是毫无成功之望，早已心灰意冷，幸亏最后才想出这么一个方案。它不落陈套，切实可行，既不花钱，又不费事，可以完全由我们自己做主，也不会得罪英国。因为，这一类商品无法输出，小儿肉质太嫩，禁不起在盐里久放；虽然，我能指出一个国家[1]，它不要盐也可以高高兴兴吃掉我们的整个民族。

说到底，我并不刚愎自用，对于时贤高见一概排斥，只要有人能提出同样纯正、省钱、简便易行、效果显著的建议。但是，在没有人能够针对鄙人方案提出那种建议，并且拿出更好的方案之前，我恳求其他献策人对于以下两点惠予过细考虑。第一，目前就有十万个无用的小儿，张嘴要吃，光背要穿，怎样去为他们找到衣食？第二，现在全国各地的职业乞丐，连同那些实际上也等同乞丐的多数农夫、村民、工人和他们的妻子儿女，加起来整整一百万之多；这一百万徒具人类模样的动物[2]，仅仅为了维持生存就得陷入两百万英镑的债务。我恳求那些反对我的建议并且胆敢提出反驳的政治家们，请他们先去问一问那些人的父母，看看他们是否

---

1 即英国。
2 指爱尔兰的穷苦人民。

mortals whether they would not at this day think it a great happiness to have been sold for food at a year old in the manner I prescribe, and thereby have avoided such a perpetual scene of misfortunes as they have since gone through by the oppression of landlords, the impossibility of paying rent without money or trade, the want of common sustenance, with neither house nor clothes to cover them from the inclemencies of the weather, and the most inevitable prospect of entailing the like or greater miseries upon their breed forever.

I profess, in the sincerity of my heart, that I have not the least personal interest in endeavouring to promote this necessary work, having no other motive than the public good of my country, by advancing our trade, providing for infants, relieving the poor, and giving some pleasure to the rich. I have no children by which I can propose to get a single penny; the youngest being nine years old, and my wife past childbearing.

觉得如果自己早在一周岁时,就照我说的办法被卖作食料,倒真是一种莫大的幸福,可以免除他们一生所经历过的那种漫长的苦难,包括:受地主压迫,无钱无业,交不起租子,生活上又缺社会补助,既无房屋又无衣裳可以遮风蔽雨,以及他们子孙后代将要不可避免永远陷入类似或更为悲惨的境地。

我恳切声明,本人倡导此项急需事业,除为促进贸易、抚育幼儿、救苦济贫、娱乐富户而竭尽微力,且为国家造福之外,别无他图;我个人是一丝好处也得不到的。我的子女中最小的一个已经九岁,所以不能拿出去赚钱;我的老伴呢,生育期也早过去了。[1]

---

[1] 作者一生未婚,也无子女,他的这句话模拟"献策人"的口吻。

奥利弗·哥尔德斯密斯

1728—1774

奥利弗·哥尔德斯密斯(Oliver Goldsmith, 1728—1774)是18世纪中叶的著名英国作家。他生于爱尔兰一个穷牧师的家庭。他性格纯朴而不善理家，是一个善良可爱、耽于幻想而极不实际的人。他以工读生资格上了都柏林大学。有时候穷得没办法，他就为街头艺人写写歌谣，挣很可怜的一点钱；到晚上跑出学校，偷偷去听人家演唱自己的作品，暗自高兴一番。大学毕业，想当牧师、律师、教员、演员，一一失败；又到爱丁堡学医，中途离开英国，跑到欧洲大陆流浪。他会唱爱尔兰民歌、吹笛子、讲故事。在各国，靠着这种本领讨饭吃，当了一两年"快活的乞丐"。回到英国，他自称在意大利（一说在法国）得了医学博士，别人对此持怀疑态度，不敢让他看病。

他当过校对员、学堂传达、药剂师助手，后来成为书店老板的雇佣文人，过着"从手到口"的苦日子。几年后，他为文学界所承认，加入了著名的"约翰逊俱乐部"。

哥尔德斯密斯著作很多。他的代表作有小说《威克菲尔德的牧师》、长诗《荒村》、喜剧《屈身求爱》以及随笔《世界公民》等。文学史上常常把他列入感伤主义流派，也就是说，从人道主义的思想出发，歌颂纯朴的人性和感情，向往古老的田园之乐。

哥尔德斯密斯成名之后，经济情况好转。但他不会过日子，又爱周济穷人，所以总是有钱就乱花，无钱就借债。到他四十六岁死的时候，还欠着两千英镑的外债。

哥尔德斯密斯的散文以语言平易畅达、笔调幽默而著称。

Oliver Goldsmith

这从他的《世界公民》一书中可以看出。在这部随笔集中，作者假托住在伦敦的一个名叫李安济（Lien Chi Altangi）的中国哲学家，给他在北京礼部任职的朋友付和（Fum Hoam）写信，[1]叙述他在英国的种种见闻，议论英国人的风俗习惯、社会制度，还穿插一些性格特殊的人物素描，叙述、描写、议论三者熔为一炉，把作者对于英国社会的看法用轻松、幽默的笔调巧妙地传达出来。这部书现在已被公认为哥尔德斯密斯的一部重要代表作，英国的随笔名著。这里所介绍的《黑衣人》是《世界公民》中的第二十六封信。这是一篇人物特写，写一个表面上性情乖僻，故作自私悭吝，其实却是一片赤子之心，急他人之难的"怪人"。据说，哥尔德斯密斯本人做事就往往颠三倒四，亲戚为之绝望，朋友也只好说"可怜的哥尔德斯密斯"。《约翰逊传》的作者博斯韦尔则把他写成一个傻瓜。不过，在他死的时候，哀悼的除了他那几个文学好友，还有他平日周济过的那些穷朋友。当然，点点滴滴的救济解决不了社会根本问题，但对这种好心人也未可厚非。高尔基说过："我们大家都饥渴于对人的爱，而人饿着的时候，即使是烤得坏的面包，吃起来也是香的。"（《安东·契诃夫》）

---

[1] "李安济"这一译名根据范存忠教授《中国的思想文物与哥尔斯密斯的〈世界公民〉》一文。"付和"一名则由笔者根据范文考证试译。

The Man in Black

Though fond of many acquaintances, I desire an intimacy only with a few. The Man in Black, whom I have often mentioned, is one whose friendship I could wish to acquire, because he possesses my esteem. His manners, it is true, are tinctured with some strange inconsistencies; and he may be justly termed a humorist in a nation of humorists. Though he is generous even to profusion, he affects to be thought a prodigy of parsimony and prudence; though his conversation be replete with the most sordid and selfish maxims, his heart is dilated with the most unbounded love. I have known him profess himself a man-hater, while his cheek was glowing with compassion; and, while his looks were softened into pity, I have heard him use the languages of the most unbounded ill-nature. Some affect humanity and tenderness, others boast of having such dispositions from Nature; but he is the only man I ever knew who seemed ashamed of his natural benevolence. He takes as much pains to hide his feelings, as any hypocrite would to conceal his indifference; but on every unguarded moment the mask drops off, and reveals him to the most superficial observer.

黑衣人

我虽然广爱交游,却只愿跟少数知己亲密来往。我常常提起的那位黑衣人,就是因为我敬重他的为人,这才愿意同他做朋友的。自然,他做起事情来顾前不顾后,有些古怪,在一个专出滑稽人物的民族当中算得一个地地道道的滑稽人物。他的脾气本来是慷慨大方到了挥金如土的地步,却爱在人前装出一副特别吝啬小气的样子;他心里对人们充满着无限的热爱,满嘴里说的却是卑鄙自私的口头禅。我曾经见他嘴里一边说自己多么厌恶人类,脸上却因为同情别人而涨得通红;而当他的面容现出一派温柔悲悯的表情的时候,嘴里说的却是一个性情恶毒的人才能说出的话。有的人假装仁慈厚道,还有的人吹嘘自己生来就有这种脾气;在我认识的人当中,只有他一个人生怕暴露自己天生的仁爱心肠。伪君子掩饰自己的冷漠无情不遗余力,他却竭力掩饰自己的真情实意;不过,不定什么时候他一不小心,假面具掉下来,再粗心大意的人也能看出他的本来面目。

In one of our late excursions into the country, happening to discourse upon the provision that was made for the poor in England, he seemed amazed how any of his countrymen could be so foolishly weak as to relieve occasional objects of charity, when the laws had made such ample provision for their support. "In every parish-house," says he, "the poor are supplied with food, clothes, fire, and a bed to lie on; they want no more, I desire no more myself; yet still they seem discontented. I'm surprised at the inactivity of our magistrates in not taking up such vagrants, who are only a weight upon the industrious; I'm surprised that the people are found to relieve them, when they must be at the same time sensible that it, in some measure, encourages idleness, extravagance, and imposture. Were I to advise any man for whom I had the least regard, I would caution him by all means not to be imposed upon by their false pretences; let me assure you, sir, they are imposters, every one of them; and rather merit a prison than relief."

He was proceeding in this strain earnestly, to dissuade me from an imprudence of which I am seldom guilty, when an old man, who still had about him the remnants of tattered finery, implored our compassion. He assured us that he was no common beggar, but forced into the shameful profession to support a dying wife and five hungry children. Being prepossessed against such falsehoods, his story had not the least influence upon me; but it was quite otherwise with the Man in Black; I could see it visibly operate upon his countenance, and effectually interrupt his harangue. I could easily perceive that his heart burned to relieve the five starving children but he seemed ashamed to discover his weakness to me. While he thus hesitated between

我们最近到乡下旅行,偶然谈起英国的贫民救济问题,他表示惊讶,觉得在他的同胞当中有人真是心软得可笑,既然法律已经对于救济穷人做出那样周密的规定,他们见了乞丐还要给予施舍。"在每一个教区的救济院里,"他说,"那些穷人们有吃,有穿,有火烤,有床睡。他们还想要什么?就是我自己,也不贪图别的什么了。然而,他们还是不满足。我真奇怪,地方官怎么那样无能,为什么不把这些无业游民统统抓起来——他们简直是压在勤快人身上的包袱!可是,竟然还有人去救济他们;实际上,他们应该知道,他们这样做,在某种程度上是鼓励懒惰、放纵和欺骗。要是让我对于自己稍稍关心的人给一点忠告的话,我就要千方百计地提醒他:千万不要被那些人的虚假借口所蒙蔽。我向你保证,先生,他们是骗子,一个个都是骗子,应该进监狱,而不该得到救济。"

他尽在那里如此这般说下去,还一本正经地劝我无论如何不要去犯那种我很少犯过的轻率错误。这时候,一个身上还穿着破破烂烂的华丽服装的老头子走过来,恳求我们怜悯。他向我们郑重地说,他并不是普普通通的叫花子,只因家里有一个垂危的妻子,五个挨饿的儿女需要抚养,被逼无奈,这才干上这种丢脸的行当。对于诸如此类的谎言,我心中早有戒备,所以他这一套我丝毫不去理睬。但是黑衣人可就大不一样了。我看得清清楚楚,他的脸色顿时变了,他那长篇大论停了下来。看得出,他心急火燎地想要解救那五个嗷嗷待哺的小孩,但是又不好意思在我面前暴露出他那软心肠,因

compassion and pride, I pretended to look another way and he seized this opportunity of giving the poor petitioner a piece of silver, bidding him at the same time, in order that I should hear, go work for his bread, and not tease passengers with such impertinent falsehoods for the future.

As he had fancied himself quite unperceived, he continued, as we proceeded, to rail against beggars with as much animosity as before; he threw in some episodes on his own amazing prudence and economy, with his profound skill in discovering impostors; he explained the manner in which he would deal with beggars, were he a magistrate, hinted at enlarging some of the prisons for their reception, and told two stories of ladies that were robbed by beggarmen. He was beginning a third to the same purpose, when a sailor with a wooden leg once more crossed our walks, desiring our pity, and blessing our limbs. I was for going on without taking any notice, but my friend, looking wistfully upon the poor petitioner, bade me stop, and he would show me with how much ease he could at any time detect an impostor.

He now, therefore, assumed a look of importance, and in an angry tone began to examine the sailor, demanding in what engagement he was thus disabled and rendered unfit for service. The sailor replied in a tone as angrily as he, that he had been an officer on board a private ship of war, and that he had lost his leg abroad, in defence of those who did nothing at home. At this reply, all my friend's importance vanished in a moment; he had not a single question more to ask; he now only studied what method he should take to relieve him unobserved. He

此就在怜悯心和自尊心之间犹豫不决、左右为难。这时候，我装作往另外一边看，他抓住这个机会往那个可怜的求乞者手里塞了一块银币；同时，为了说给我听，吩咐他快去自食其力，以后再也不要拿这些岂有此理的谎言老缠着过路人不放。

他以为我什么也没有看见，所以，我们一边往前走，他一边仍然跟先前一样怒气冲冲地骂那些乞丐，还补充一些小插曲，以表明他自己是多么谨慎、多么节约，在识破骗子方面又是多么老练。他还说如果他做了官，他要怎么样对付那些叫花子，暗示要扩充监狱，把他们都关进去；此外，还说了两个关于妇女遭乞丐抢劫的小故事。他正要说第三个意思差不多的故事时，一个安着一条木腿的水兵走过来，挡住我们的去路，向我们的好腿表示祝福，求我们怜悯。我想走过去不理他，可是我的朋友眼巴巴盯住那可怜的求乞者，叫我停下来，好看一看他怎样轻而易举地随时揭穿这一类的骗子。

这时候，他做出一脸傲慢的神气，带着不高兴的口吻盘查那个水兵，追问他到底是在哪一次战斗中受伤致残，不能服役的。那个水兵也用同样不客气的口吻回答，说他原来是一条私家战船[1]上的军官，只因为保卫那些躺在国内什么事情也不干的人，这才在海外作战中失去了一条腿。听到这句答话，我那朋友的傲慢劲儿一下子消失得无影无踪，他什么也不问了，现在他唯一要考虑的只是用什么办法来周济眼前这个人而又不致露出

---

[1] 指在战时受本国政府之命攻击敌船的民船。

had, however, no easy part to act, as he was obliged to preserve the appearance of ill-nature before me, and yet relieve himself by relieving the sailor. Casting, therefore, a furious look upon some bundles of chips which the fellow carried in a string at his back, my friend demanded how he sold his matches; but not waiting for a reply, desired in a surly tone to have a shilling's worth. The sailor seemed at first surprised at his demand, but soon recollecting himself, and presenting his whole bundle—"Here, master", says he, "take all my cargo, and a blessing into the bargain".

It is impossible to describe with what an air of triumph my friend marched off with his new purchase; he assured me that he was firmly of opinion that these fellows must have stolen their goods who could thus afford to sell them for half value. He informed me of several different uses to which those chips might be applied; he expatiated largely upon the savings that would result from lighting candles with a match instead of thrusting them into the fire. He averred, that he would as soon have parted with a tooth as his money to those vagabonds, unless for some valuable consideration. I cannot tell how long this panegyric upon frugality and matches might have continued, had not his attention been called off by another object more distressful than either of the former. A woman in rags with one child in her arms, and another on her back, was attempting to sing ballads, but with such a mournful voice that it was difficult to determine whether she was singing or crying. A wretch who in the deepest distress still aimed at good-humour, was an object my friend was by no means capable of withstanding; his vivacity and

任何痕迹。然而，要做到这一点可不那么容易，因为他还得在我面前撑起一副恶声恶气的架势，又要救济那个水兵，这才能救他自己脱出苦恼。于是，他狠狠瞪了一眼，瞥见他身后背了用绳子捆着的几捆火柴。我的朋友问他火柴怎么卖，不等他开口，就粗声粗气地说要买一先令的火柴[1]。那个水兵一开始对他这句话感到奇怪，可是很快就明白过来，把他那一捆火柴全捧出来，一边说："请吧，先生，把我的存货都拿去吧——此外，再饶上我的祝福。"

我这位朋友带着新买的东西扬长而去，他那得意扬扬的神气是无法形容的。他对我说他坚决相信这些东西一定是那些家伙偷来的，所以才肯以半价卖掉。他告诉我火柴的许多用处，还说用火柴点燃蜡烛比起拿着蜡烛直接去引火是一种大大的节省。他断言：要不是有便宜可捞，他宁可拔下自己的牙齿送给他们，也不愿把钱花在那些无赖身上。这时候，如果不是一种比前面那两个人更为凄惨的景象引起了他的注意，我不知道他对于节俭与火柴的赞美还要继续多久。因为，一个衣衫褴褛的妇女，怀里抱一个小孩，身上还背一个，正在那里勉强唱着小曲乞讨；她那声音悲悲咽咽，说不清她究竟是在歌唱，还是在哭泣。一个苦人，深陷在不幸之中而又强颜欢笑，看到此情此景，我的朋友再也受不住了。他那兴致勃勃的长篇大论戛然而止，

---

[1] 火柴价值很低，黑衣人拿出一先令来买，等于白送给那个水兵。水兵开始不解，想一想才明白对方是以买火柴为借口来周济自己。

his discourse were instantly interrupted; upon this occasion his very dissimulation had forsaken him. Even in my presence, he immediately applied his hands to his pockets, in order to relieve her; but guess his confusion, when he found he had already given away all his money he carried about him to former objects. The misery painted in the woman's visage was not half so strongly expressed as the agony in his. He continued to search for some time, but to no purpose, till, at length, recollecting himself, with a face of ineffable good-nature, as he had no money, he put into her hands his shilling's worth of matches.

他再也伪装不下去了。甚至当着我的面，他立刻就要给那个妇女一点儿周济。可是，你就想一下他那狼狈劲儿吧——他把手伸进口袋，发现身上的钱已经完全打发给以前那两个人了。那个妇女脸上的愁容还抵不上他那痛苦表情的一半。他掏了好一阵，还是一点钱也找不到。最后，他醒悟过来，脸上现出一种无可名状的和蔼神情，由于没钱，就把那价值一先令的火柴送到那个妇女的手里。

查尔斯·兰姆

1775—1834

查尔斯·兰姆（Charles Lamb，1775—1834）生于伦敦法学院一个律师的用人之家。他在一个为穷苦子弟办的"基督慈幼学校"念了七年书，十四岁就做事，先在伦敦的南海公司，后在东印度公司，直到1825年退休为止，当了整整三十六年职员。1796年，他家里发生了一桩惨剧：比他大十岁的姐姐玛丽突然神经错乱，拿刀子刺死了他们的母亲。此后，养活老父亲、照料疯姐姐的沉重家庭负担就落到他的肩上。玛丽的病时好时坏——病好的时候，姐弟在一起进行文学活动（因为玛丽也是一个文学才能很高的人）。玛丽发病前常有预感，每到此时，姐弟俩就手拉手哭着向疯人院走去。姐弟俩就这样相依为命地生活着。当时的人们都被这一情景所感动。为了不让玛丽流离失所，查尔斯牺牲了个人幸福，一生未婚。他这种无私的精神，常为评论家所称道。但长期的贫困和焦虑也影响了他的健康。查尔斯·兰姆死于1834年。他姐姐比他多活了十多年，于1847年去世。

兰姆一生大部分消磨在东印度公司的账房里，每天要工作八至十小时，只能在晚上读书、写作、会见文学界的朋友。他写过诗歌、散文传奇、喜剧和文学评论，但他最成功的作品是和玛丽合作的《莎士比亚戏剧故事集》以及他自己的代表作《伊利亚随笔》初集、续集（The Essays of Elia，1823；The Last Essays of Elia，1833）。他的信札也很有名。

兰姆发表他的随笔时用的笔名"伊利亚"，取自和他同事的一位老职员的名字。他的两集随笔共六十多篇，其内容或写

Charles Lamb

他青少年时代的回忆，或写他的亲属、朋友、熟人，或写他当小职员的生涯，或写他忙里偷闲之中的小小快乐和种种遐想，或评论他读过的书、看过的戏，或写伦敦的市风，写醉鬼，写单身汉，并对各种社会现象发发议论：从内容来说，可谓庞杂。然而，在所有这些随笔之中都贯穿着作者自己善良、正直、乐观的个性，贯穿着他那别人无从模仿的幽默感。这就使得兰姆的随笔成为英国文学中所独有的、非常富于民族特色的散文名作。

这里介绍的两篇兰姆随笔中，《梦幻中的小孩子》选自《伊利亚随笔》初集，《读书漫谈》选自《伊利亚随笔》续集。

《梦幻中的小孩子》一文，正如副题所云，是"一段奇想"。兰姆少年时代，在他外祖母做管家的那个田庄上认识一位叫安妮·西蒙斯的姑娘，爱上了她。但这次恋爱失败了，安妮后来嫁给伦敦的一个当铺老板。兰姆为此一度精神失常，不久精神恢复。此后，他曾和一个女演员谈过婚姻之事，那个演员要求他离开患精神病的姐姐，他不答应，又吹了。从此他就独身过了一辈子。然而，正如安徒生一样，他是很爱小孩子的。《梦幻中的小孩子》描写他在哥哥约翰去世的刺激下，对于少年时代恋人的怀念，对于下一代的热爱以及对于外祖母和哥哥的回忆，交织一起，产生一种不寻常的感情的升华。文章本身是很美的，构思也很巧妙，然而作者当时内心的悲痛也是可以想见的。实在说，写这样的文章也太难为他了。

在《读书漫谈》一文中，兰姆从一个文学爱好者的角度漫

Charles Lamb

谈各类书籍以及种种不同条件下的读书之乐。他不喜欢硬性的、枯燥的书，但有时"玉石不分"，把吉本的《罗马帝国衰亡史》和亚当·斯密的《原富》这些科学名著也排除在"可读之书"范围以外了，这未免有点偏颇。不过，一个普通读者要想遍读群籍，事实上也难以办到，除了阅读与本职工作和业余事业直接有关的书籍以外，所余时间无几，也只好各自方便了。但兰姆关于书籍出版问题所发的议论，有些颇有道理：如少数学者、藏书家所需要的珍本书，读者范围有限，尽可出一部分豪华版、精装本。而为广大读者着想，则将已有定评的文学杰作，多出廉价普及版，实在是功德无量的好事。这个意见或可供我国文学出版工作参考。

兰姆的随笔写得亦庄亦谐，在谐谑之中又包藏着个人的辛酸。这是一种"含泪的微笑"。兰姆的文风跌宕多姿，或秾丽或简古，或文言或白话，写得意到笔随、不受拘束。

在我国，兰姆的《莎士比亚戏剧故事集》，最早有林纾以《吟边燕语》为名的文言译本；"五四"以后，又有以《莎氏乐府本事》为名的各种注释本、对照本和汉译本；新中国成立后又出了新的译本。他的随笔，自"五四"以来，也有人介绍。梁遇春不仅译过他的随笔（当时叫作"小品文"），还写过这一类华丽而活泼的抒发个人思想感情的散文。因此，郁达夫在《中国新文学大系·散文二集·导言》中称梁遇春为"中国的伊利亚"。

我国的现代文学中，鲁迅先生所开创并奠定坚实基础的杂文,从形式上说,是与随笔相当近似的(虽然在内容上各有千秋)。为了丰富我国的散文艺术,介绍一点兰姆的随笔,想来还不算多余吧!

Dream-Children

A Reverie

Children love to listen to stories about their elders, when *they* were children; to stretch their imagination to the conception of a traditionary great-uncle or grandame, whom they never saw. It was in this spirit that my little ones crept about me the other evening to hear about their great-grandmother Field, who lived in a great house in Norfolk (a hundred times bigger than that in which they and papa lived) which had been the scene—so at least it was generally believed in that part of the country—of the tragic incidents which they had lately become familiar with from the ballad of "The Children in the Wood". Certain it is that the whole story of the children and their cruel uncle was to be seen fairly carved out in wood upon the chimney-piece of the great hall, the whole story down to the Robin Redbreasts, till a foolish rich person pulled it down to set up a marble one of modern invention in its stead, with no

---

1 兰姆一生未婚，这篇文章里说他有两个孩子，是虚构的。
2 兰姆的外祖母叫玛丽·菲尔德，曾在英国赫特福德郡的布来克斯威尔一个叫作普鲁默的乡绅家里做总管五十余年。

梦幻中的小孩子

——一段奇想

小孩子爱听关于他们长辈的故事——他们做小孩子的时候怎么样;这样可以驰骋想象,对于他们从未见过、只听大人传说的某位叔爷爷、老奶奶进行一番揣想。正是出于这种心情,有一天晚上,我的一对小儿女[1]偎在我的脚边,听我讲他们外曾祖母菲尔德[2]的事:她住在诺福克郡的一所大宅院里(那可比他们和爸爸住的房子要大一百倍),那所宅子恰好又是(至少,在那一带乡间大家都这么相信)他们最近念的那首《林中小儿》[3]歌谣里的悲剧故事的发生地点。不管怎么说,那一对小兄妹,和他们那狠心的叔叔,还有那红胸脯的知更鸟[4],都雕刻在大厅壁炉面的木板上,原原本本,丝毫不差。可是,一个煞风景的阔人后来把那块雕花木板拆掉,换上一块时新样式的大理石壁炉面,什么故事也没

---

3 英国一首有名的歌谣,叙述一对小兄妹,他们的父亲死后,其叔为夺取财产,派两个凶手到森林中去杀害他们。其中一人不忍下手,杀死另一人,然后自杀。但小兄妹也在森林中冻饿而死。

4 上述歌谣叙述小兄妹死后,红胸的知更鸟衔树叶把他们覆盖起来。

story upon it. Here Alice put out one of her dear mother's looks, too tender to be called upbraiding. Then I went on to say, how religious and how good their great-grandmother Field was, how beloved and respected by everybody, though she was not indeed the mistress of this great house, but had only the charge of it (and yet in some respects she might be said to be the mistress of it too) committed to her by the owner, who preferred living in a newer and more fashionable mansion which he had purchased somewhere in the adjoining county; but still she lived in it in a manner as if it had been her own, and kept up the dignity of the great house in a sort while she lived, which afterwards came to decay, and was nearly pulled down, and all its old ornaments stripped and carried away to the owner's other house, where they were set up, and looked as awkward as if some one were to carry away the old tombs they had seen lately at the Abbey and stick them up in Lady C.'s tawdry gilt drawing-room. Here John smiled, as much as to say, "that would be foolish indeed." And then I told how, when she came to die, her funeral was attended by a concourse of all the poor, and some of the gentry too, of the neighbourhood for many miles round, to show their respect for her memory, because she had been such a good and religious woman; so good indeed that she knew all the Psaltery by heart, ay, and a great part of the Testament besides. Here little Alice spread her hands. Then I told what a tall, upright, graceful person their great-grandmother Field once was; and how in her youth she was esteemed the best dancer—here Alice's little right foot played an involuntary movement,

有了。听到这里,艾丽斯[1]脸上做出一副表情,酷像她那亲爱的妈妈,那么温柔动人,简直无法算是责备。于是,我接着说他们的外曾祖母菲尔德信教多么虔诚,为人多么能干,如何受到人人敬爱,虽然她并不是那所大宅子的主人,只是受人之托,代为看管(因此,在某种程度上,她又可以说是宅子的主人)。她的主人在邻郡购置了一所更讲究的新宅子,也就住在那里,而把老宅子交给了她。然而,她在那里居住时的派头倒好像那宅子属于她自己的,她活一天就要使它多多少少保持着一所大宅院的尊严。可是,那宅院后来还是破落了,几乎倒坍了。它那些古色古香的装饰部件统统被拆了下来,运到主人的新宅子里,重新安装起来,但是看起来很别扭,仿佛有人把他们最近参观过的那些古人墓葬从西敏大寺搬走,迁移到某位贵夫人金碧辉煌的客厅里。听到这里,约翰[2]微笑起来,好像在说:"真蠢!"我接着又说,外曾祖母死的时候,周围多少里的人成群结队参加她的葬礼。穷人们全来了,也有一些绅士,都向她的亡灵表示敬意,因为她是一个又能干、又虔诚的人——她是那么能干,把一整本《赞美诗》——嘿,还有大半本《新约》——都能背得下来。听到这里,小艾丽斯惊奇得摊开了小手。然后,我告诉他们,外曾祖母菲尔德长得个子高高,身材笔直,风度娴雅。在她年轻的时候,别人说她跳舞跳得最好——听到这里,艾丽斯小小的右脚

---

[1] 作者假想中的女儿。
[2] 作者假想中的儿子。

till upon my looking grave, it desisted—the best dancer, I was saying, in the county, till a cruel disease, called a cancer, came, and bowed her down with pain; but it could never bend her good spirits, or make them stoop, but they were still upright, because she was so good and religious. Then I told how she was used to sleep by herself in a lone chamber of the great lone house; and how she believed that an apparition of two infants was to be seen at midnight gliding up and down the great staircase near where she slept, but she said "those innocents would do her no harm"; and how frightened I used to be, though in those days I had my maid to sleep with me, because I was never half so good or religious as she—and yet I never saw the infants. Here John expanded all his eyebrows and tried to look courageous. Then I told how good she was to all her grandchildren, having us to the great house in the holydays, where I in particular used to spend many hours by myself, in gazing upon the old busts of the Twelve Caesars, that had been Emperors of Rome, till the old marble heads would seem to live again, or I to be turned into marble with them; how I never could be tired with roaming about that huge mansion, with its vast empty rooms, with their worn-out hangings, fluttering tapestry, and carved oaken panels, with the gilding almost rubbed out—sometimes in the spacious old-fashioned gardens, which I had almost to myself, unless when now and then a solitary gardening

---

1 据说，在普鲁默家庭里，17世纪曾有两个小孩子失踪。

不由自主地做出一种轻快的动作,我把面孔一板,它才停止——我刚才正说,在全郡她跳舞跳得最好;可是,有一种叫癌症的残酷疾病,使她痛苦得弯下了腰;然而,它压不倒她那愉快的心情,不能使她屈服,她在精神上还是挺然屹立,始终是那样能干,那样虔诚。然后,我又说,她总是独自一人睡在那所寂静的大院子里的一个寂静的房间里;她说,半夜里有人看见,在她房间附近有两个小孩子[1]的幽灵沿着一座大楼梯上上下下,滑来滑去;但是她说,"那两个天真的小东西是不会伤害她的"。不过,那一阵我可害怕,尽管晚上有女仆跟我睡在一起也不行,因为我连外祖母那样能干而虔诚的一半都没有——然而,我也从来没有看见过那两个小孩子。听到这里,约翰大大地舒展一下他的眉心,竭力做出勇敢的样子。于是,我又说她待我们这些外孙儿外孙女们多么好,到了节假日就叫我们到那个大宅子去住。尤其我在那里一待就是很久,一个人盯着那十二座恺撒[2]像,也就是说古时候十二个罗马皇帝的胸像出神。看着看着,那些古代的大理石头像仿佛变成了活人,我也仿佛跟他们一同变成了大理石像。我在那所很大很大的宅院里满世界地跑,从来不知什么是疲倦。那里有许许多多又大又空的房间和破破烂烂的帷帐,墙上的幔子还随风飘动,橡木雕花嵌板上的金粉却已剥落了——我常常到那座古老的大花园里去玩,那花园简直叫我一个人独占了,偶尔才碰上一个孤零零的老园丁——那园

---

2 古罗马皇帝的称号,此处指从奥古斯都到多米蒂安十二个罗马皇帝。他们的大理石胸像是当时富家房间里的一种摆设。

man would cross me—and how the nectarines and peaches hung upon the walls, without my ever offering to pluck them, because they were forbidden fruit, unless now and then, —and because I had more pleasure in strolling about among the old melancholy-looking yew-trees, or the firs, and picking up the red berries, and the fir-apples, which were good for nothing but to look at—or in lying about upon the fresh grass, with all the fine garden smells around me—or basking in the orangery, till I could almost fancy myself ripening too along with the oranges and the limes in that grateful warmth—or in watching the dace that darted to and fro in the fish-pond, at the bottom of the garden, with here and there a great sulky pike hanging midway down the water in silent state, as if it mocked at their impertinent friskings,—I had more pleasure in these busy-idle diversions than in all the sweet flavours of peaches, nectarines, oranges, and such like common baits of children. Here John slyly deposited back upon the plate a bunch of grapes, which, not unobserved by Alice, he had meditated dividing with her, and both seemed willing to relinquish them for the present as irrelevant. Then in somewhat a more heightened tone, I told how, though their great-grandmother Field loved all her grand-children, yet in an especial manner she might be said to love their uncle, John L—, because he was so handsome and spirited a youth, and a king to the rest of us; and, instead of moping about in solitary corners, like some of us. He would mount the most mettlesome horse he could get, when but an imp no bigger than themselves, and make it carry him half over the county in a

子里，油桃和桃子垂在墙头上，我根本不去碰它，因为那是禁果，除非偶然一回两回——因为，我更高兴在那些带着忧郁神情的老水松树或者枞树之间跑来跑去，从地上捡那么几颗红浆果、几只枞果，而那些枞果只能看、不能吃——有时候，我随便躺在嫩草地上，让自己完全沉浸在满园子的芳香之中——要不然，我就在橘子园里晒太阳，晒得暖洋洋的，一边想象自己也跟那些橘子、那些菩提树一同成熟起来——再不然，我就去到花园深处，看那些鲦鱼在鱼池里穿梭般游来游去，不定在哪里还会发现一条很大的梭子鱼冷冷落落地停在深水之间，一动也不动，好像对于那些小鱼们的轻狂样儿暗中表示鄙夷，——我喜欢的是诸如此类无事忙的消遣，而对于像桃子呀，油桃呀，橘子呀等等这些普通的小孩子们的诱饵，碰也不去碰它。听到这里，约翰把一串葡萄又悄悄放回到碟子里去。这串葡萄，艾丽斯刚才也看在眼里，约翰正盘算着如何跟她分吃，可是此时此刻又不大合适，于是两个人就决心把它放回去了。接着，我提高声音说，虽然他们的外曾祖母菲尔德对于外孙儿外孙女们全都喜欢，但是她特别疼爱的却是他们的约翰伯伯[1]，因为他是那么漂亮、那么活泼的一个小伙子，简直是我们一伙人当中的国王。他从来不会像我们当中有的人那样，一个人闷头闷脑待在什么角落里；即使在他还是像他们这么一点点大的小鬼的时候，不管多么烈性的马，他也敢抓住跳上去，叫它驮着他跑一个上午，走遍

---

[1] 指兰姆的哥哥约翰，死于1821年(此文写作之前)。

morning, and join the hunters when there were any out—and yet he loved the old great house and gardens too, but had too much spirit to be always pent up within their boundaries—and how their uncle grew up to man's estate as brave as he was handsome, to the admiration of everybody, but of their great-grandmother Field most especially; and how he used to carry me upon his back when I was a lame-footed boy—for he was a good bit older than me—many a mile when I could not walk for pain;—and how in after life he became lame-footed too, and I did not always (I fear) make allowances enough for him when he was impatient and in pain, nor remember sufficiently how considerate he had been to me when I was lame-footed; and how when he died, though he had not been dead an hour, it seemed as if he had died a great while ago, such a distance there is betwixt life and death; and how I bore his death as I thought pretty well at first, but afterwards it haunted and haunted me; and though I did not cry or take it to heart as some do, and as I think he would have done if I had died, yet I missed him all day long, and knew not till then how much I had loved him. I missed his kindness, and I missed his crossness and wished him to be alive again, to be quarrelling with him (for we quarrelled sometimes), rather than not have him again, and was as uneasy without him, as he, their poor uncle must have been when the doctor took off his limb. Here the children fell a crying, and asked if their little mourning which they had on was not for uncle John, and they looked up, and prayed me not to go on about their uncle, but to tell them some stories about their pretty dead mother. Then I told how for seven long years, in hope sometimes, sometimes in despair, yet persisting ever, I courted the fair Alice W—n;

半个郡,去赶上那些行围的猎手——自然,他也爱那所古老的大宅子和那些花园,不过他精力太旺盛了,哪肯把自己永远关在那高高的院墙里——后来,他们这位伯伯长大成人,一表人才,气宇轩昂,人人看了夸奖,尤其是他们的外曾祖母菲尔德。我小时候跛脚,他常常把我背在背上——因为他比我大好几岁——背着我走好多英里[1],因为我脚疼,走不得路。我又说,后来他脚也跛了,而我呢,碰上他痛苦、烦躁的时候,恐怕对他不够那么体谅;而过去自己脚跛,他对自己多么体贴的事,也不怎么记得了。可是,他一死,虽然刚刚死了还不到个把钟头,就叫人觉得他好像已经死了很久似的,因为生与死之间的悬殊太大了。他死了以后,刚开始我觉得也还受得了,但后来这件事一次又一次袭上心头;尽管我并不像别人那样又是哭,又是伤心(我想,如果死的是我,他一定会哭的),我仍然整天想他,这时候我才知道自己是多么爱他。我想念他对我友好,我也想念他对我发脾气,我盼望他能够再活着,哪怕还跟他吵架也行(因为我们过去吵过架),也不愿意再也见不着他,因为失去他而心神不安,就像他,他们可怜的伯伯,被大大截了肢以后那样。——听到这里,孩子们哭了,问我他们臂上一圈小小的黑纱是不是为了约翰伯伯而佩戴的;他们抬起头来,求我不要再讲伯伯的事了,给他们讲讲他们死去的可爱的妈妈吧。于是,我就说,在整整七年当中,有时候满怀希望,有时候灰心丧气,然而我没有

---

[1] 英制长度单位,1英里约等于1.6千米。

and, as much as children could understand, I explained to them what coyness, and difficulty, and denial meant in maidens—when suddenly, turning to Alice, the soul of the first Alice looked out at her eyes with such a reality of representment, that I became in doubt which of them stood there before me, or whose that bright hair was; and while I stood gazing, both the children gradually grew fainter to my view, receding, and still receding till nothing at last but two mournful features were seen in the uttermost distance, which, without speech, strangely impressed upon me the effects of speech; "We are not of Alice, nor of thee, nor are we children at all. The children of Alice call Bartrum father. We are nothing; less than nothing, and dreams. We are only what might have been, and must wait upon the tedious shores of Lethe millions of ages before we have existence, and a name"—and immediately awaking, I found myself quietly seated in my bachelor armchair where I had fallen asleep, with the faithful Bridget unchanged by my side—but John L. (or James Elia) was gone for ever.

---

1 即 Alice Winterton，兰姆为自己曾爱过的一位姑娘所起的假名——那个姑娘本名为安·西蒙斯，嫁给一个叫巴特鲁姆的当铺老板。(兰姆幻想自己与恋人结婚，并生下一双儿女。)

间断地追求着艾丽斯·温特顿[1]。我按照小孩子所能理解的程度,向他们说明什么叫作少女的羞羞答答、左右为难和婉言谢绝——说到这里,我一扭头,只见过去那个艾丽斯的眼神突然从小艾丽斯的眼睛中活生生再现出来,我简直说不清到底是哪一个艾丽斯坐在我的面前,也说不清那满头亮闪闪的金发到底是哪一个人的。我兀自凝眸细看,眼前的两个小孩子却渐渐模糊起来,向后愈退愈远,最后,在非常遥远之处只剩下两张悲伤的面容依稀可辨。他们默默无语,却好似向我说道:"我们不是艾丽斯的孩子,也不是你的孩子,我们压根儿就不是小孩子。艾丽斯的孩子们管巴特鲁姆[2]叫爸爸。我们只是虚无,比虚无还要空虚,不过是梦中的幻觉。我们仅仅是某种可能性,要在忘川[3]河畔浑浑茫茫等待千年万载,才能取得生命,具有名字。"——我立刻醒来,发现自己安安静静坐在单身汉的圈手椅里,刚才原来是酣然一梦,只有忠实的布里奇特[4]依然坐在我的身边——而约翰·兰(又名詹姆斯·伊利亚)却是永远地消逝了。

---

2 即作者恋人的真正丈夫。
3 希腊神话中的"阴阳河",死者饮其水,则尽忘生前之事。
4 兰姆在文中给姐姐Mary起的假名。

Detached Thoughts on Books and Reading

To mind the inside of a book is to entertain one's self with the forced product of another man's brain. Now I think a man of quality and breeding may be much amused with the natural sprouts of his own.

Lord Foppington in The Relapse

 An ingenious acquaintance of my own was so much struck with this bright sally of his Lordship, that he has left off reading altogether, to the great improvement of his originality. At the hazard of losing some credit on this head, I must confess that I dedicate no inconsiderable portion of my time to other people's thoughts. I dream away my life in others' speculations. I love to lose myself in other men's minds. When I am not walking, I am reading; I cannot sit and think. Books think for me.

 I have no repugnance. Shaftesbury is not too genteel for me, nor

---

1《旧病复发》，又名《美德遇险记》，英国王政复辟时期的戏剧家约翰·范布勒（John Vanbrugh，1664—1726）所写的喜剧，福平顿勋爵是剧中人物。

读书漫谈

把心思用在读书上，不过是想从别人绞尽脑汁、苦思冥想的结果中找点乐趣。其实，我想，一个有本领、有教养的人，灵机一动，自有奇思妙想联翩而来，这也就尽够他自己受用的了。

——《旧病复发》[1]福平顿勋爵的台词

我认识的一位生性伶俐的朋友，听了爵爷这段出色的俏皮话，在惊佩之余，完全放弃了读书；从此他遇事独出心裁，比往日大有长进。我呢，冒着在这方面丢面子的危险，却只好老实承认：我把相当大的一部分时间用来读书了。我的生活，可以说是在与别人思想的神交中度过的。我情愿让自己淹没在别人的思想之中。除了走路，我便读书，我不会坐在那里空想——自有书本替我去想。

在读书方面，我百无禁忌。高雅如沙夫茨伯里[2]，低

---

2 沙夫茨伯里(Anthony Ashley Cooper, the Third Earl of Shaftesbury, 1671—1713), 英国伦理学家，著有《关于道德的探索》。

Jonathan Wild too low. I can read anything which I call a *book*. There are things in that shape which I cannot allow for such.

In this catalogue of *books which are no books—biblia a-biblia—*I reckon Court Calendars, Directories, Pocket Books, Draught Boards bound and lettered on the back, Scientific Treatises, Almanacks, Statutes at Large; the works of Hume, Gibbon, Robertson, Beattie, Soame Jenyns, and, generally, all those volumes which "no gentleman's library should be without": the Histories of Flavius Josephus (that learned Jew), and Paley's *Moral Philosophy*. With these exceptions, I can read almost anything. I bless my stars for a taste so catholic, so unexcluding.

I confess that it moves my spleen to see these *things in books' clothing* perched upon shelves, like false saints, usurpers of true shrines, intruders into the sanctuary, thrusting out the legitimate occupants. To reach down a well-bound semblance of a volume, and hope it some kind-hearted play-book, then, opening what "seem its leaves", to come bolt upon a withering *Population Essay*. To expect a Steele, or a Farquhar, and find—Adam Smith. To view a well-arranged assortment

---

1 此书全名为《大伟人江奈生·魏尔德传》，亨利·菲尔丁（Henry Fielding，1707—1754）的小说，写一个强盗头子的一生并尖锐讽刺了当时的英国政府的大臣。
2 休谟（David Hume，1711—1776），苏格兰哲学家和历史家；吉本（Edward Gibbon，1737—1794），英国著名历史家，著有《罗马帝国衰亡史》；罗伯逊（William Robertson，1721—1793），苏格兰历史家；贝蒂（James Beattie，1735—1803），苏格兰诗人、伦理学教授；索姆·杰宁斯（1704—1787），英国神学家，著有《论罪恶的本性与起源》等。
3 弗莱维厄斯·约瑟夫斯（Flavius Josephus，约37—100），犹太学者，著有《犹太战争史》与《犹太古史考》。

俗如《魏尔德传》[1]，我都一视同仁。凡是我可以称之为"书"的，我都读。但有些东西，虽具有书的外表，我却不把它们当作书看。

在"非书之书"这一类别里，我列入了：《宫廷事例年表》《礼拜规则》，袖珍笔记本，订成书本模样而背面印字的棋盘，科学论文，日历，《法令大全》，休谟、吉本、罗伯逊、贝蒂、索姆·杰宁斯[2]等人的著作，以及属于所谓"绅士必备藏书"的那些大部头，例如弗莱维厄斯·约瑟夫斯[3]（那位有学问的犹太人）的历史著作和佩利[4]的《道德哲学》。把这些东西除外，我差不多什么书都可以读。我庆幸自己命交好运，得以具有如此广泛而无所不包的兴趣。

老实说，每当我看到那些"披着书籍外衣的东西"高踞在书架之上，我就禁不住怒火中烧，因为这些假圣人篡夺了神龛，侵占了圣堂，却把合法的主人赶得无处存身。从书架上拿下来装订考究、书本模样的一大本，心想这准是一本叫人开心的"大戏考"，可是掀开它那"仿佛书页似的玩意儿"一瞧，却是叫人扫兴的《人口论》[5]。想看看斯梯尔或是法夸尔[6]，找到的却是亚当·斯密。[7]有时候，

---

4 威廉·佩利（William Paley，1743—1805），英国神学家，著有《道德哲学与政治哲学》等。

5 全名为 *An Essay on the Principle of Population*，作者马尔萨斯（Thomas Robert Malthus，1766—1834）。

6 乔治·法夸尔（George Farquhar，1678—1707），英国王政复辟时期的喜剧家，爱尔兰人。

7 作者在上段和这里列举了一批他所不喜欢的书。他这样说，是从一个文学爱好者的个人兴趣出发的。但是亚当·斯密的《国富论》和吉本的《罗马帝国衰亡史》这样的书的学术价值是不能否定的。

95

of blockheaded Encyclopaedias (Anglicanas or Metropolitanas) set out in an array of Russia, or Morocco, when a tithe of that good leather would comfortably reclothe my shivering folios; would renovate Paracelsus himself, and enable old Raymund Lully to look like himself again in the world. I never see these impostors, but I long to strip them, to warm my ragged veterans in their spoils.

To be strong-backed and neat-bound is the desideratum of a volume. Magnificence comes after. This, when it can be afforded, is not to be lavished upon all kinds of books indiscriminately. I would not dress a set of Magazines, for instance, in full suit. The dishabille, or half-binding (with Russia backs ever) is *our* costume. A Shakespeare, or a Milton (unless the first editions), it were mere foppery to trick out in gay apparel. The possession of them confers no distinction. The exterior of them (the things themselves being so common), strange to say, raises no sweet emotions, no tickling sense of property in the owner. Thomson's *Seasons*, again, looks best (I maintain it) a little torn, and dog's-eared. How beautiful to a genuine lover of reading are the sullied leaves, and worn-out appearance, nay, the very odour (beyond Russia), if we would not forget kind feelings in fastidiousness, of an old "Circulating Library" *Tom Jones*, or *Vicar of Wakefield*! How they speak of the

---

1 帕拉塞尔苏斯(Philippus Aureolus Paracelsus, 1493—1541), 瑞士炼金术士、占星学家和医生。
2 雷蒙德·吕里(约1232—约1315), 西班牙哲学家、神秘主义者。(帕拉塞尔苏斯和吕里二人为欧洲中古时代的"奇人"。)

我看见那些呆头呆脑的百科全书(有的叫"大英",有的叫"京都"),分门别类,排列齐整,一律用俄罗斯皮或摩洛哥皮装订;然而,相比之下,我那一批对开本的老书却是临风瑟缩,衣不蔽体——我只要能有那些皮子的十分之一,就能把我那些书气气派派地打扮起来,让帕拉塞尔苏斯[1]焕然一新,让雷蒙德·吕里[2]能够在世人眼中恢复本来面目。每当我瞅见那些衣冠楚楚的欺世盗名之徒,我就恨不得把它们身上那些非分的装裹统统扒下来,穿到我那些衣衫褴褛的旧书身上,让它们也好避避寒气。

对于一本书来说,结结实实、齐齐整整地装订起来,是必不可少的事情,豪华与否倒在其次。而且,装订之类即使可以不计工本,也不必对各类书籍不加区别,统统加以精装。譬如说,我就不赞成对杂志合订本实行全精装——简装或半精装(用俄罗斯皮)也就足矣。而把一部莎士比亚或是一部弥尔顿(除非是第一版)打扮得花花绿绿,则是一种纨绔子弟习气。而且,收藏这样的书,也不能给人带来什么不同凡响之感。说来也怪,由于这些作品本身如此脍炙人口,它们的外表如何并不能使书主感到高兴,也不能让他的占有欲得到什么额外的满足。我以为,汤姆逊[3]的《四季》一书,样子以稍有破损、略带卷边儿为佳。对于一个真正爱读书的人来说,只要他没有因为爱洁成癖而把老交情抛在脑后,当他从"流通图书馆"借来一部旧的《汤姆·琼斯》或是《威克菲尔德牧师传》的时

---

3 汤姆逊(James Thomson,1700—1748),英国诗人,《四季》为其代表作。

thousand thumbs, that have turned over their pages with delight!—of the lone sempstress, whom they may have cheered (milliner, or hard-working mantua-maker) after her long day's needle-toil, running far into midnight, when she has snatched an hour, ill-spared from sleep, to steep her cares, as in some Lethean cup, in spelling out their enchanting contents! Who would have them a whit less soiled? What better condition could we desire to see them in?

In some respects the better a book is, the less it demands from binding. Fielding, Smollet, Sterne, and all that class of perpetually self-reproductive volumes—Great Nature's Stereotypes—we see them individually perish with less regret, because we know the copies of them to be "eterne". But where a book is at once both good and rare where the individual is almost the species and when *that* perishes,

> We know not where is that Promethean torch
> That can its light relumine—

such a book, for instance, as *The Life of the Duke of Newcastle*, by his Duchess—no casket is rich enough, no casing sufficiently durable, to honour and keep safe such a jewel.

---

1 斯摩莱特（Tobias George Smollett，1721—1771），英国小说家，著有《兰登传》。
2 斯特恩（Laurence Sterne，1713—1768），英国小说家，著有《感伤的旅行》和《项狄传》。

候,那污损的书页、残破的封皮以及书上(除了俄罗斯皮以外)的气味,该是多么富有吸引力呀!它们表明成百上千读者曾经带着喜悦的心情用拇指翻弄过这些书页,表明了这本书曾经给某个孤独的缝衣女工带来快乐。这位缝衣女工、女帽工或者辛辛苦苦工作的女装裁缝,在干了长长的一天针线活之后,到了深夜,为了把自己的一肚子哀愁暂时浸入忘川之水,好不容易挤出个把钟头的睡眠时间,一个字一个字拼读出这本书里的迷人的故事。在这种情况之下,谁还去苛求这些书页是否干干净净、一尘不染呢?难道我们还会希望这些书的外表更为完美无缺吗?

从某些方面说,愈是好书,对于装订的要求就愈低。像菲尔丁、斯摩莱特[1]、斯泰恩[2]以及这一类作家的书,似乎是版藏宇宙之内,不断重印,源源不绝。因此,对于它们个体的消灭也就毫不可惜,因为我们知道这些书的印本是绵绵不断的。然而,当某一本书既是善本,又是珍本,仅存的一本就代表某一类书,一旦这一孤本不存——

天上火种何处觅,
再使人间见光明?

例如,纽卡斯尔公爵夫人[3]写的《纽卡斯尔公爵传》就是这么一本书。为把这颗文学明珠加以妥善保存,使用再贵重的宝盒、再坚固的铁箱都不算过分。

---

[3] 纽卡斯尔公爵夫人,名玛格利特(Margaret Lucas Cavendish,1623—1673),英国女作家,写了一部她丈夫的传记。兰姆对她评价很高。

Not only rare volumes of this description, which seem hopeless ever to be reprinted; but old editions of writers, such as Sir Philip Sydney, Bishop Taylor, Milton in his prose-works, Fuller—of whom we *have* reprints, yet the books themselves, though they go about, and are talked of here and there, we know, have not endenizened themselves (nor possibly ever will) in the national heart, so as to become stock books—it is good to possess these in durable and costly covers. I do not care for a First Folio of Shakespeare. I rather prefer the common editions of Rowe and Tonson without notes, and with *plates*, which, being so execrably bad, serve as maps, or modest remembrancers, to the text; and without pretending to any supposable emulation with it, are so much better than the Shakespeare gallery *engravings*, which *did*. I have a community of feeling with my countrymen about his Plays, and I like those editions of him best, which have been oftenest tumbled about and handled.— On the contrary, I cannot read Beaumont and Fletcher but in Folio. The Octavo editions are painful to look at. I have no sympathy with them. If they were as much read as the current editions of the other poet, I should prefer them in that shape to the older one. I do not know a more heartless sight than the reprint of *The Anatomy of Melancholy*. What need was there of unearthing the bones of that fantastic old great man, to expose them in a winding-sheet of the newest fashion to modern

---

1 菲利普·锡德尼（Philip Sydney，1554—1586），英国文艺复兴时期的著名诗人，著有《阿尔卡迪亚》《爱星者与星》和《为诗辩护》。
2 泰勒（Jeremy Taylor，1613—1667），英国主教和散文家。
3 富勒（Thomas Fuller，1608—1661），英国牧师和散文家。兰姆很欣赏以上他与泰勒的文章。

不仅这一类的珍本书，眼见得重版再印渺渺无期，就是菲利普·锡德尼爵士[1]、泰勒主教[2]、作为散文家的弥尔顿以及富勒[3]这些作家，尽管他们著作的印本已经流行各地，成为街谈巷议之资，然而由于这些作品始终未能（也永远不会）成为全民族喜闻乐见之文、雅俗共赏之书，因此，对于这些书的旧版，最好还是用结实、贵重的封套好好保存起来。我并无意搜求第一版的莎士比亚对开本。我倒宁愿要罗和汤森[4]的通行本。这种版本没有注释，插画虽有但拙劣之极，仅足以起那么一点儿图解、说明原文的作用而已。然而，正因为如此，它们却远远胜过其他莎士比亚版本的豪华插图，原因是那些版画太不自量，竟然妄想与原文争个高下。在对于莎剧的感情上，我和我的同胞们心心相印，所以我最爱看的乃那种万人传阅、众手捧读的版本。对于博蒙特和弗莱彻[5]却恰恰相反——不是对开本，我就读不下去；八开本看着都觉得难受，因为我对它们缺乏感情。如果这两位作家像那位诗人那样受到万口传诵，我自然读读通行本也就心满意足，而不必仰仗旧版了。有人把《忧郁的剖析》[6]一书加以翻印，真不知是何居心。难道有必要把那位怪老头的尸首重新刨出来，裹上最时髦的寿衣，摆

---

4 罗（Nicholas Rowe，1674—1718），英国的莎剧编订者，他所编辑的莎士比亚全集由当时的出版商汤森（Jacob Tonson，1655—1736）出版。

5 博蒙特（Francis Beaumont，约1585—1616）、弗莱彻（John Fletcher，1579—1625），与莎士比亚同时的两个英国戏剧家，二人合写了一批剧本。

6 英国散文家罗伯特·伯顿（Robert Burton，1577—1640）的名著。作者原计划写一部分析治疗忧郁症的医学论著，结果写成了一部旁征博引、富有文学趣味的散文"杂著"。

censure? What hapless stationer could dream of Burton ever becoming popular?—The wretched Malone could not do worse, when he bribed the sexton of Stratford church to let him white-wash the painted effigy of old Shakespeare, which stood there, in rude but lively fashion depicted, to the very colour of the cheek, the eye, the eyebrow, hair, the very dress he used to wear—the only authentic testimony we had, however imperfect, of these curious parts and parcels of him. They covered him over with a coat of white paint. By—if I had been a justice of peace for Warwickshire, I would have clapt both commentator and sexton fast in the stocks, for a pair of meddling sacrilegious varlets.

I think I see them at their work—these sapient trouble-tombs.

Shall I be thought fantastical, if I confess, that the names of some of our poets sound sweeter, and have a finer relish to the ear—to mine, at least—than that of Milton or of Shakespeare? It may be, that the latter are more staled and rung upon in common discourse. The sweetest names, and which carry a perfume in the mention, are, Kit Marlowe, Drayton, Drummond of Hawthornden, and Cowley.

---

1 马隆（Edmund Malone，1741—1812），英国莎士比亚学者，编有一部莎士比亚全集。
2 即Stratford-on-Avon，莎士比亚的家乡埃文河畔斯特拉特福，在英格兰的沃里克郡（Warwickshire）。

出来示众，让现代人对他评头品足吗？莫非真有什么不识时务的书店老板想让伯顿变成家喻户晓的红人吗？马隆[1]干的蠢事也不能比这个再糟糕了——那个卑鄙小人买通了斯特拉特福教堂[2]的职员，得到许可把莎翁的彩绘雕像刷成一色粉白。然而，雕像的原貌尽管粗糙，却甚逼真，就连面颊、眼睛、须眉、生平服装的颜色也都一一描画出来。虽不能说十全十美，但毕竟是诗人身上的细部，而且我们也有了一个唯一可靠的见证。但是，这一切都被他们用一层白粉统统覆盖了。我发誓，如果我那时候恰好是沃里克郡的治安法官，我定要将那个注释家和那个教堂职员双双箍上木枷，把他们当作一对无事生非、亵渎圣物的歹徒加以治罪。

我眼前似乎看见他们正在现场作案——这两个自作聪明的盗墓罪犯。

我有个感觉，直说出来，不知是否会被人认为怪诞？我国有些诗人的名字，在我们（至少在我）耳朵里听起来要比弥尔顿或莎士比亚更为亲切有味，那原因大概是后面这两位的名字在日常谈话中翻来覆去说得太多，有点俗滥了。我觉得，最亲切的名字，提起来就口角生香的，乃马洛[3]、德雷顿[4]、霍桑登的德拉蒙德[5]和考利[6]。

---

3 马洛（Kit Marlowe 即 Christopher Marlowe，1564—1593），英国著名戏剧家，写有《浮士德博士的悲剧》等。
4 德雷顿（Michael Drayton，1563—1631），英国诗人。
5 德拉蒙德（William Drummond，1585—1649），英国诗人、作家。
6 考利（Abraham Cowley，1618—1667），英国诗人和散文家。

Much depends upon *when* and *where* you read a book. In the five or six impatient minutes, before the dinner is quite ready, who would think of taking up *The Fairy Queen* for a stop-gap, or a volume of Bishop Andrewes' sermons?

Milton almost requires a solemn service of music to be played before you enter upon him. But he brings his music, to which, who listens, had need bring docile thoughts, and purged ears.

Winter evenings—the world shut out—with less of ceremony the gentle Shakespeare enters. At such a season, *The Tempest,* or his own *The Winter's Tale*—

These two poets you cannot avoid reading aloud—to yourself, or (as it chances) to some single person listening. More than one—and it degenerates into an audience.

Books of quick interest, that hurry on for incidents, are for the eye to glide over only. It will not do to read them out. I could never listen to even the better kind of modern novels without extreme irksomeness.

A newspaper, read out, is intolerable. In some of the Bank offices it is the custom (to save so much individual time) for one of the clerks—who is the best scholar—to commence upon *The Times,* or *The Chronicle,* and recite its entire contents aloud *pro bono publico.* With every advantage of lungs and elocution, the effect is singularly vapid. In barbers' shops and public-houses a fellow will get up, and spell out a paragraph which he communicates as some discovery. Another follows with *his* selection. So

---

1 英国著名诗人埃德蒙·斯宾塞(Edmund Spenser，约1552—1599)的长诗。

这在很大程度上取决于读书的时间和地点。譬如说,开饭前还有五六分钟,为了打发时间,谁还能有耐心拿起一部《仙后》[1]或者安德鲁斯主教[2]的布道文来读呢?

开卷读弥尔顿的诗歌之前,最好能有人为你演奏一曲庄严的宗教乐章。不过,弥尔顿自会带来他自己的音乐。对此,你要摒除杂念,洗耳恭听。

严冬之夜,万籁俱寂,温文尔雅的莎士比亚不拘形迹地走进来了。在这种季节,自然要读《暴风雨》或者他自己讲的《冬天的故事》。

对这两位诗人的作品,当然忍不住要朗读——独自吟哦或者(凑巧的话)读给某一知己均可。听者超过两人——就成了开朗诵会了。

为了一时一事而赶写出来、只能使人维持短暂兴趣的书,很快浏览一下即可,不宜朗读。时新小说,即便是佳作,每听有人朗读,我总觉讨厌之极。

朗读报纸尤其要命。在某些银行的写字间里,有这么一种规矩:为了节省每个人的时间,常由某位职员(同事当中最有学问的人)给大家念《泰晤士报》或者《纪事报》,将报纸内容全部高声宣读出来,"以利公众"。然而,可着嗓子、抑扬顿挫地朗诵的结果,却是听者兴味索然。理发店或酒肆之中,每有一位先生站起身子,一字一句拼读一段新闻——此系重大发现,理应告知诸君。另外一位接踵而上,也念一番他的"选段"——整

---

[2] 安德鲁斯(Lancelot Andrewes,1555—1626),英国主教,曾参加著名的詹姆斯王《钦定本圣经》的英译工作。

the entire journal transpires at length by piece-meal. Seldom-readers are slow readers, and without this expedient, no one in the company would probably ever travel through the contents of a whole paper.

Newspapers always excite curiosity. No one ever lays one down without a feeling of disappointment.

What an eternal time that gentleman in black, at Nando's, keeps the paper! I am sick of hearing the waiter bawling out incessantly, "*The Chronicle* is in hand, Sir."

Coming in to an inn at night—having ordered your supper—what can be more delightful than to find lying in the window-seat, left there time out of mind by the carelessness of some former guest—two or three numbers of the old *Town and Country Magazine*, with its amusing *tête-à-tête* pictures—"The Royal Lover and Lady G—"; "The Melting Platonic and the Old Beau",—and such like antiquated scandal? Would you exchange it—at that time, and in that place—for a better book?

Poor Tobin, who latterly fell blind, did not regret it so much for the weightier kinds of reading—*The Paradise Lost*, or *Comus*, he could have *read* to him—but he missed the pleasure of skimming over with his own eye a magazine, or a light pamphlet.

I should not care to be caught in the serious avenues of some cathedral alone and reading *Candide*.

I do not remember a more whimsical surprise than having been once detected—by a familiar damsel—reclining at my ease upon the

---

1 即主张精神恋爱的人。此处用来，有嘲笑的意味。
2 弥尔顿早期写的一个假面舞剧脚本。

个报纸的内容，便如此这般零敲碎打地透露给听众。不常读书的人读起东西速度就慢。如果不是靠着那种办法，他们当中恐怕难得有人能够读完一整张报纸。

报纸能引起人的好奇心。可是，当人读完一张报纸，把它放下来，也总有那么一种惘然若失之感。

在南多饭店，有一位身穿黑礼服的先生，拿起报纸，一看就是老半天！我最讨厌茶房不住地吆喝："《纪事报》来啦，先生！"

晚上住进旅馆，晚餐也定好了，碰巧在临窗的座位上发现两三本过期的《城乡杂志》（不知在从前什么时候，哪位粗心的客人忘在那里的），其中登着关于密约私会的滑稽画：《高贵的情夫与格夫人》《多情的柏拉图主义者》[1]和老风流在一起》，这都说不清是哪辈子的桃色新闻了。此时此地，还能有什么读物比这个更叫人开心呢？难道你愿意换上一本正儿八经的好书吗？

可怜的托宾最近眼睛瞎了，不能再看《失乐园》《考玛斯》[2]这一类比较严肃的书籍了，他倒不觉得多么遗憾——这些书，他可以让别人念给他听。他感到遗憾的乃失去了那种一目十行飞快地看杂志和看轻松小册子的乐趣。

我敢在某个大教堂里森严的林荫道上，一个人读《老实人》[3]，被人当场抓住。我也不怕。

可是，有一回，我正自心旷神怡地躺在樱草山的草地上读书，一位熟识的小姐走过来（那儿本是她芳踪常

---

3 法国著名启蒙思想家和作家伏尔泰（Voltaire，1694—1778）所写的一部哲理小说。伏尔泰一生抨击教会的伪善和专制，为正人君子所畏忌。因此兰姆才有那种说法。

107

grass, on Primrose Hill (her Cythera), reading—*Pamela*. There was nothing in the book to make a man seriously ashamed at the exposure; but as she seated herself down by me, and seemed determined to read in company, I could have wished it had been—any other book. We read on very sociably for a few pages; and, not finding the author much to her taste, she got up, and—went away. Gentle casuist, I leave it to thee to conjecture, whether the blush (for there was one between us) was the property of the nymph or the swain in this dilemma. From me you shall never get the secret.

I am not much a friend to out-of-doors reading. I cannot settle my spirits to it. I knew a Unitarian minister, who was generally to be seen upon Snow Hill (as yet Skinner's Street *was not*), between the hours of ten and eleven in the morning, studying a volume of Lardner. I own this to have been a strain of abstraction beyond my reach. I used to admire how he sidled along, keeping clear of secular contacts. An illiterate encounter with a porter's knot, or a bread basket, would have quickly put to flight all the theology I am master of, and have left me worse than indifferent to the five points.

There is a class of street-readers, whom I can never contemplate without affection—the poor gentry, who, not having wherewithal to buy or hire a book, filch a little learning at the open stalls—the owner, with his hard eye, casting envious looks at them all the while, and thinking

---

1 英国小说家塞缪尔·理查森(Samuel Richardson，1689—1761)的小说，描写一个年轻女仆被她女主人的浪荡少爷所追求，最后终于正式结婚的故事。

往之地),一瞧,我读的却是《帕梅拉》[1]——叫人没躲没闪,心里有一种说不出的滋味。要说呢,被人发现读这么一本书,也并没有什么叫人不好意思的地方;然而,当她坐下来,似乎下定决心要跟我并肩共读时,我却巴不得能够换上一本别的什么书才好。我们一块儿客客气气读了一两页,她觉得这位作家不怎么对她的口味,站起身来走开了。爱刨根问底的朋友,请你去猜一猜:在这种微妙的处境中,脸上出现红晕的究竟是那位仙女,还是这位牧童呢?——反正两人当中总有一个人脸红,而从我这里你休想打听到这个秘密。

我不能算是一个户外读书的热心支持者,因为我在户外精神无法集中。我认识一位唯一神教派[2]的牧师——他常在上午十点到十一点之间,在斯诺希尔(那时候还没有斯金纳大街)一边走路,一边攻读拉德纳[3]的一卷大著。我对他那种远避尘俗、孑然独行的风度常常赞叹,但我不得不承认,这种超然物外、凝神贯注的脾气与我无缘。因为,只要在无意之中瞥一眼从身旁走过的一个脚夫身上的绳结或者什么人的一只面包篮子,我就会把好不容易记住的神学常识忘到九霄云外,就连五大论点也都不知去向了。

还要说一说那些站在街头看书的人,我一想起他们就油然而生同情之心。这些穷哥儿们无钱买书,也无钱租书,只得到书摊上偷一点知识——书摊老板眼神冷冰冰的,不住拿忌恨的眼光瞪着他们,看他们到底什么时

---

2 基督教中的一派,反对三位一体说,主张神格只能由一个神代表。
3 拉德纳(Nathaniel Lardner, 1684—1768),英国神学家。

when they will have done. Venturing tenderly, page after page, expecting every moment when he shall interpose his interdict, and yet unable to deny themselves the gratification, they "snatch a fearful joy". Martin B—,[1] in this way, by daily fragments, got through two volumes of *Clarissa*, when the stall-keeper damped his laudable ambition, by asking him (it was in his younger days) whether he meant to purchase the work. M. declares, that under no circumstance in his life did he ever peruse a book with half the satisfaction which he took in those uneasy snatches. A quaint poetess of our day has moralised upon this subject in two very touching but homely stanzas.

> *I saw a boy with eager eye*
> *Open a book upon a stall,*
> *And read, as he'd devour it all;*
> *Which when the stall-man did espy,*
> *Soon to the boy I heard him call,*
> *"You, Sir, you never buy a book,*
> *Therefore in one you shall not look."*
> *The boy pass'd slowly on, and with a sigh*
> *He wish'd he never had been taught to read,*
> *Then of the old churl's books he should have had no need.*

---

1 即 Martin Burney（马丁·伯尼），兰姆的一个朋友。

候才肯把书放下。这些人战战兢兢,看一页算一页,时刻都在担心老板发出禁令,然而他们还是不肯放弃他们那求知的欲望,而要"在担惊受怕之中寻找一点乐趣"。马丁·伯[1]——就曾经采取这种办法,天天去书摊一点一点地看,看完了两大本《克拉丽莎》[2](这是他小时候的事)。突然间,书摊老板走过来,打断了他这番值得赞美的雄心壮志,问他到底打算不打算买这部书。马丁后来承认,他一生中,读任何书也没有享受到像他在书摊上惶惶不安看书时所得到的乐趣的一半。当代一位古怪的女诗人[3]根据这个题材,写了两段诗,非常感人而又质朴。诗曰:

> 我看见一个男孩站在书摊旁,
> 眼含渴望,打开一本书在看,
> 他读着、读着,像要把书一口吞下,
> 这情景却被书摊的老板瞧见——
> 他立刻向那男孩喝道:
> "先生,你从来没买过一本书,
> 那么你一本书也不要想看!"
> 那孩子慢吞吞地走开,发出长叹:
> 他真后悔不如从来不会念书,
> 那么,那个老混蛋的书也就跟自己毫不相干。

---

2 即 *Clarissa Harlowe*,理查逊的另一部小说,两卷。
3 指作者的姐姐 Mary Lamb(玛丽·兰姆)。

Of sufferings the poor have many,
Which never can the rich annoy:
I soon perceiv'd another boy,
Who look's as if he had not any
Food, for that day at least—enjoy
The sight of cold meat in a tavern larder.
This boy's case, then thought I, is surely harder,
Thus hungry, longing, thus without a penny,
Beholding choice of dainty-dressed meat:
No wonder if he wish he ne'er had learn'd to eat.

穷人家有许许多多的辛酸——
对这些,有钱人根本不必操心。
我很快又看见另外一个男孩,
他脸色憔悴,似乎一整天饮食未进。
他站在一个酒馆门前,
望着食橱里的肉块出神。
这孩子,我想,日子真不好过,
饥肠辘辘,渴望饱餐,却身无一文;
无怪他恨不得不懂什么叫作吃饭,
那样,他就无须对着美味的大菜望洋兴叹。

威廉·黑兹利特

1778—1830

19世纪初期的英国散文作家威廉·黑兹利特（William Hazlitt，1778—1830），像查尔斯·兰姆一样，在文学观点上属于浪漫主义流派。他的文学成就和兰姆处于伯仲之间，都是先从事文学批评，尔后以各自具有独特风格的随笔散文著称于世。

黑兹利特生于1778年。他的父亲是一个有激进思想的非国教派牧师。在18世纪和19世纪之交，欧洲最大的政治事件是法国革命。时代的潮流、父亲的影响，使得黑兹利特从小就成为法国革命的热烈拥护者。十三岁的时候，他向地方报纸投书，抗议英国政府怂恿暴徒焚掠有民主思想的科学家普里斯特利的住宅。他十五岁进神学院读书，父亲希望他成为一个牧师。但三年后他离开神学院时，完全和宗教分手，成为卢梭的信徒。此后，法国革命几经反复，随着雅各宾党上台、拿破仑称帝与下台，欧洲反动势力抬头，许多原来拥护法国革命的人纷纷改变政治态度。在这风云多变的时代，黑兹利特始终坚持拥护法国革命的原则不变。

十四岁到二十岁是黑兹利特广泛阅读的时期。二十岁上，他结识了英国浪漫主义诗歌的两个开创者柯尔律治和华兹华斯，思想上受到很大影响。这使他下决心以文学为自己的终身事业。此后几年，为了谋生，他曾经学画。1812年，他迁居伦敦，结交了兰姆等作家。从三十六岁起，他完全投身于写作生涯，直到1830年去世。他的主要著作是在他一生中最后十五年写出来的，包括文学、戏剧、艺术方面的评论，文学讲稿，随笔散文。

William Hazlitt

他在文学、戏剧方面的论著有《莎士比亚戏剧中的人物》《伊丽莎白时代的戏剧文学》《英国诗人论稿》《英国喜剧作家论稿》，以及《时代的精神》等书——这些论著概括了从伊丽莎白时代直到他当时的英国文学全貌。他的随笔散文则收进了《座谈》《闲话》《家常话》和《素描与随笔》等集子里。

黑兹利特的随笔散文在英国文学中享有很高的声誉。评论家常常把他的随笔和兰姆的作品相比，认为两者都是英国浪漫主义时期散文的佳作，而由于作者的个性不同，又各有独到之处。兰姆的随笔更为圆熟、丰厚，黑兹利特的随笔则更为奔放、开朗。

关于黑兹利特的为人，在较早的文学史上常说他脾气坏、爱争吵。这大概因为他一生对于法国革命拥护到底，不变初衷；而对于他的老朋友，甚至像华兹华斯、柯尔律治那样的早年崇拜对象，一旦由于形势变化而改变信仰，黑兹利特就不惜与之翻脸，并且也受到对方攻击。今天看来，这还不能算是简单的个人意气之争。对此，《牛津英国文学作品选集》的编者这样评论说：

> 终其一生，他（黑兹利特——引者）对于从他父亲那里接受过来的激进思想，一直保持着热烈的信仰；而他的朋友们，由于法国革命的种种变化而幻想破灭，放弃了青年时代的理想，这在黑兹利特眼里则被看作是一种不可原谅的变节行为。然而，与他这种尖锐态度相辅相成的，是他

William Hazlitt

在批评中的博大胸怀。在他的著作里,他尽管哀叹柯尔律治和华兹华斯的政治变化,但对于他们的天才,他仍然表示出热情而细心的赞赏。

我以为这个评语是比较公允的。

这里介绍的黑兹利特的作品《论平易的文体》是作者的名篇之一。文章提出了作者关于文体,特别是关于散文文体的见解,也总结了他自己写作散文的经验。作者既反对鄙俚无文的文体,也反对华而不实的文体,而将批评的矛头针对在19世纪业已过时而在18世纪流行过的古典主义末流的那种华丽堆砌、空洞无物的文风。黑兹利特指出:好的文学语言只能从现当代约定俗成的通用语言中选择、提炼而成,而文学语言的高下从根本上还要看它能否准确地反映事物的本来面目以及作者的真实思想感情。比较华兹华斯在《抒情歌谣集·序言》中所说,诗人写作时要"竭力使语言接近人们的真实语言","把人们的真实语言加以精选,然后再使之符合诗律节奏",可知黑兹利特的文体主张是和浪漫主义的文学原则相一致的。

黑兹利特是英国文学史上有名的文体家。他的文章以语言准确、清晰、生动、流畅、富有感染力而著称。他的优美语言是从下苦功中得来的。《论平易的文体》本身就是一篇优美的随笔散文,写得凝练、有力。

我国自古以来,关于文体和文学语言,也有许多正确的主张,像大家所熟知的"修辞立诚""言之不文,行之不远""不以词害意"等等。和黑兹利特的看法比较一下，对于树立我们今天的优良文风，不无可供借鉴之处。

On Familiar Style

It is not easy to write a familiar style. Many people mistake a familiar for a vulgar style, and suppose that to write without affectation is to write at random. On the contrary, there is nothing that requires more precision, and, if I may so say, purity of expression, than the style I am speaking of. It utterly rejects not only all unmeaning pomp, but all low, cant phrases, and loose, unconnected, *slipshod* allusions. It is not to take the first word that offers, but the best word in common use; it is not to throw words together in any combinations we please, but to follow and avail ourselves of the true idiom of the language. To write a genuine familiar or truly English style is to write as any one would speak in common conversation who had a thorough command and choice of words, or who could discourse with ease, force, and perspicuity, setting aside all pedantic and oratorical flourishes. Or, to give another illustration, to write naturally is the same thing in regard to common conversation as to read naturally is in regard to common speech. It does not follow that it is an easy thing to give the true accent and inflexion to the words you utter, because you do not attempt to rise above the level

论平易的文体

　　平易的文体并非轻易得来。不少人误识为文字俚俗便是文风平易，信笔写去即为不加雕饰。其实恰恰相反。我说的这种文体比任何文字都更加需要精确，或者说，需要语言纯净。它不但要摒除一切华而不实之词，也要摒除一切陈言套语以及那些若即若离、不相连属、胡拼乱凑的比喻。飘然自来的浮词切不可使用，而要在通行词语中选优拔萃；也不可随心所欲将各种词语任意搭配，必须在习惯用语中确有所本方可加以发挥。所谓写出一手纯正、平易的英语文体，意思是说：要像一个完全精通辞章之道的人在日常谈话中那样，说话行云流水，娓娓动人，明晰畅达，却无掉书袋、炫口才之嫌。换句话说，朴素的作文与日常谈话的关系，正和朴素的朗读与日常口语的关系相同。这并非说，只要不去超越日常口头表达的规范，你便可轻而易举地出口字正

of ordinary life and colloquial speaking. You do not assume, indeed, the solemnity of the pulpit, or the tone of stage-declamation; neither are you at liberty to gabble on at a venture, without emphasis or discretion or to resort to vulgar dialect or clownish pronunciation. You must steer a middle course. You are tied down to a given and appropriate articulation, which is determined by the habitual associations between sense and sound, and which you can only hit by entering into the author's meaning, as you must find the proper words and style to express yourself by fixing your thoughts on the subject you have to write about. Any one may mouth out a passage with a theatrical cadence, or get upon stilts to tell his thoughts; but to write or speak with propriety and simplicity is a more difficult task. Thus it is easy to affect a pompous style, to use a word twice as big as the thing you want to express: it is not so easy to pitch upon the very word that exactly fits it. Out of eight or ten words equally common, equally intelligible, with nearly equal pretensions, it is a matter of some nicety and discrimination to pick out the very one the preferableness of which is scarcely perceptible but decisive. The reason why I object to Dr. Johnson's style is that there is no discrimination, no selection, no variety in it. He uses none but "tall, opaque words", taken from the "first row of the rubric"—words with the greatest number of syllables, or Latin phrases with merely English terminations. If a fine style depended on this sort of arbitrary pretension, it would be fair to judge of an author's elegance by the measurement

---

1 即塞缪尔·约翰逊（Samuel Johnson, 1709—1784），18世纪著名英国学者和作家，属于古典主义流派。

腔圆，发音抑扬适度。当然，你无须像在教堂里讲道或在舞台上朗诵那样拿腔作势；然而，你也不可不分轻重，不讲分寸，信口哇啦哇啦，再不然就乞灵于粗俗方音，油腔滑调。中间之道才是应当采取的办法。某种疾徐适度的发音方法制约着你，而这种发音方法又受制于某种约定俗成的以音表意的关系，要想找到它只有去体察作者的本意——这就正如你要想找到恰当的字眼和风格来表达自己的意思，必须凝神细思自己要写的内容一样。用演戏似的调子朗诵一段文章，或者用夸张的方式把自己的思想表述一番，这样的事人人会做；但是，要想作文、说话恰到好处，朴实无华，可就比较难了。华丽的文章好做，只要在叙事状物之际采用夸大一倍的字眼就行；然而，要想找出确切的字眼，与那一事物铢两悉称，纤毫不差，可就不那么容易了。从十个八个同样通俗易懂，也几乎同样可供采用的字眼当中，选出某一个字眼，这个字眼的优长之处极难分辨但又至关紧要，这是要有明察秋毫的眼力的。我之所以不赞成约翰逊博士[1]的文体，原因就在于那种文体缺乏明辨，缺乏汰选，缺乏变化。他使用的全是从"朱红字体训诫"[2]中挑出来的那些"高大、晦涩的字眼"——这些字眼音缀很长，或者是加上英语词尾的拉丁词。要是这样随心所欲的矫饰就能形成优美的文体，那么只要对某位作家使用的单词长度加以计算，或者只看他如何把本国语言换成

---

[2] 指在经书或祈祷书上用红字印出的礼拜规程、教规。此处比喻约翰逊博士所爱使用的高大、堂皇、古奥的字眼。

of his words and the substitution of foreign circumlocutions (with no precise associations) for the mother-tongue.[1] How simple is it to be dignified without ease, to be pompous without meaning! Surely it is but a mechanical rule for avoiding what is low, to be always pedantic and affected. It is clear you cannot use a vulgar English word if you never use a common English word at all. A fine tact is shown in adhering to those which are perfectly common, and yet never falling into any expressions which are debased by disgusting circumstances, or which owe their signification and point to technical or professional allusions. A truly natural or familiar style can never be quaint or vulgar, for this reason, that it is of universal force and applicability, and that quaintness and vulgarity arise out of the immediate connexion of certain words with coarse and disagreeable or with confined ideas. The last form what we understand by *cant* or *slang* phrases.—To give an example of what is not very clear in the general statement. I should say that the phrase "to cut with a knife", or "to cut a piece of wood", is perfectly free from vulgarity, because it is perfectly common; but "to *cut* an acquaintance" is not quite unexceptionable, because it is not perfectly common or intelligible, and has hardly yet escaped out of the limits of slang phraseology. I should hardly, therefore, use the word in this sense without putting it in italics as a license of expression, to be received *cum grano salis*. All provincial or bye-phrases come under the same mark of reprobation—all such as

---

1 I have heard of such a thing as an author who makes it a rule never to admit a monosyllable into his vapid verse. Yet the charm and sweetness of Marlowe's lines depended often on their being made up almost entirely of monosyllables.

累赘的外来语词（不管和内容关系如何），便可判定文风的典雅了。[1]这么说来，为高雅而舍平易，因典丽而失本意，岂不是太容易了吗？要想避免文风卑下，只要机械似的在文章中一味卖弄学问，装腔作势也就是了。你在文章中连一个普通字眼也不用，自然不会犯用词粗俗之病。然而，真正的文字圆熟却表现在一方面坚持使用那些人人通用的字眼，而又回避那些在某些可厌的环境中用滥了的字眼，以及那些仅仅对于某种技术或某种行业才有意义的词语。真正平易自然的文体不可给人以怪僻或粗俗之感，因为这种文体要通行四方，说服公众，而冷僻粗俗之词却容易使人联想到某些粗野、不快或狭隘的概念。这里指的是所谓"切口"或"俚语"。笼统议论，难以说明，且举一例：像to cut with a knife（用刀子来切）或to cut a piece of wood（切开一块木头）这样的短语，完全不会给人以粗俗之感，因为它们是到处通用的；然而，to cut an acquaintance（切断和熟人的来往）这个说法，就不能说是无懈可击的了，因为它并非处处通行，人人明了，它还没有走出俚语的范围之外。因此，我将这个单词用于此种意义时，不得不写成斜体字样，以表明这是一种破格用法，在采用时要加以斟酌[2]。一切土语冷词也应在摒弃之列——因为作者把此类字

---

1 作者原注：我听说有这么一位作家，他的诗写得缺乏生气，但他还偏偏坚持一个单音词也不用。其实，马洛诗歌之妙，正由于他那些诗行常常是几乎全用单音词所构成。
2 *cum grano salis*，拉丁语，意即with a grain of salt，此处引申为"需加斟酌"。

the writer transfers to the page from his fireside or a particular *coterie*, or that he invents for his own sole use and convenience. I conceive that words are like money, not the worse for being common, but that it is the stamp of custom alone that gives them circulation or value. I am fastidious in this respect, and would almost as soon coin the currency of the realm as counterfeit the King's English. I never invented or gave a new and unauthorized meaning to any word but one single one (the term "impersonal" applied to feelings), and that was in an abstruse metaphysical discussion to express a very difficult distinction. I have been (I know) loudly accused of revelling in vulgarisms and broken English. I cannot speak to that point; but so far I plead guilty to the determined use of acknowledged idioms and common elliptical expressions. I am not sure that the critics in question know the one from the other, that is, can distinguish any medium between formal pedantry and the most barbarous solecism. As an author I endeavour to employ plain words and popular modes of construction, as, were I a chapman and dealer, I should common weights and measures.

The proper force of words lies not in the words themselves, but in their application. A word may be a fine-sounding word, of an unusual length, and very imposing from its learning and novelty, and yet in the connexion in which it is introduced may be quite pointless and irrelevant. It is not pomp or pretension, but the adaptation of the expression to the idea, that clenches a writer's meaning: as it is not the size or glossiness of the materials, but their being fitted each to its place,

眼写在纸上,是为了谈论他自己家里或某个"小圈子"的私事,再不然就是他为了某种个人方便自己生造的。我想,词汇就像货币,愈通用愈好;而且,它们也只有靠着习俗的批准才能流通、才有价值。在这个问题上,我是宁缺毋滥的——我宁愿去冒险私造国家货币,也不肯去私造国王陛下的英语[1]。我从未生造过什么单词,也不曾毫无根据地给哪个单词添加什么新的意义,只有一次例外——用impersonal(非个人的)这个词去形容感情,那还是在讨论深奥的形而上学问题时,为了表示某种非常难以界说的特征时才使用的。我知道,我曾经被人强烈谴责,说我爱用粗鄙字眼和蹩脚英语。对此我不想辩解。不过,我倒愿意自己招认:对于那些公认的习惯用语和通行省略句型,我是坚决采用的。而且,我相信,那些评论家们自己也未必能够把这两回事分得清清楚楚;就是说,在煞有介事掉书袋和不顾文理、野调无腔这两者之间还能看出点儿别的什么名堂。作为一个作家,我竭力使用那些普普通通的字眼和那些家喻户晓的语言结构,正像假如我是一个商贩,我一定使用大家通用的度量衡器具一样。

  词汇的力量不在词汇本身,而在词汇的应用。一个音节嘹亮的长字,就其本身的学术性和新奇感来说,可能是令人叹赏的;然而,把它放在某句上下文之中,说不定倒会牛头不对马嘴。这是因为要确切表达作者的意思,关键并不在文辞是否华丽、堂皇,而在于文辞是否

---

[1] 即地地道道的英语。

that gives strength to the arch; or as the pegs and nails are as necessary to the support of the building as the larger timbers, and more so than the mere showy, unsubstantial ornaments. I hate anything that occupies more space than it is worth. I hate to see a load of bandboxes go along the street, and I hate to see a parcel of big words without anything in them. A person who does not deliberately dispose of all his thoughts alike in cumbrous draperies and flimsy disguises may strike out twenty varieties of familiar everyday language, each coming somewhat nearer to the feeling he wants to convey, and at last not hit upon that particular and only one which may be said to be identical with the exact impression in his mind. This would seem to show that Mr. Cobbett is hardly right in saying that the first word that occurs is always the best. It may be a very good one; and yet a better may present itself on reflection or from time to time. It should be suggested naturally, however, and spontaneously, from a fresh and lively conception of the subject. We seldom succeed by trying at improvement, or by merely substituting one word for another that we are not satisfied with, as we cannot recollect the name of a place or person by merely plaguing ourselves about it. We wander farther from the point by persisting in a wrong scent; but it starts up accidentally in the memory when we least expected it, by touching some link in the chain of previous association.

There are those who hoard up and make a cautious display of nothing but rich and rare phraseology—ancient medals, obscure coins,

切合内容。正像在建筑中，要使拱门坚固，关键不在于材料的大小和光泽，而在于它们用在那里是否恰好严丝合缝。因此，在建筑物中，竹头木钉有时竟与大件木料同等重要，而其支撑作用肯定远远胜过那些徒有其表、不切实用的装饰部件。我最见不得那些白占地位的东西，见不得一大堆空纸盒装在车上招摇过市，也见不得那些写在纸面上的大而无当的字眼。一个人写文章，只要他不是立志要把自己的真意用重重锦绣帐幔、层层多余伪装完全遮掩起来，他总会从熟悉的日常用语中想出一二十种说法，一个比一个接近他所要表达的情感。只怕到了最后，他竟会拿不定主意要用哪一种说法才能恰如其分地表达自己的心意哩！如此说来，科贝特[1]先生所谓最先闪现脑际之词自然最好的说法未必可靠。这样出现的字眼也许很好，然而经过一次又一次推敲，还会发现更好的字眼。这种字眼，要经过围绕内容进行清醒而活泼的构思，才能够自自然然出现。碰上一个字眼不满意，只顾在那里改来换去，是不济事的；正像我们有时忘记一个人名、地名，光逼迫脑子苦思呆想无用一样。路子走偏了，愈坚持就离目标愈远。但是，沿着本来的思路，一旦想到点子上，需要的词儿说不定就会在意料不到的时候一下子出现。

有人专爱搜藏华丽奇巧的辞藻，就像珍藏着古老的奖章、年代不明的钱币和西班牙八里尔的小钱那样，郑重其

---

[1] 科贝特（William Cobbett，1763—1835），农民出身的英国政论家，属于小资产阶级激进派，散文代表作为《骑马乡行记》。

and Spanish pieces of eight. They are very curious to inspect, but I myself would neither offer nor take them in the course of exchange. A sprinkling of archaisms is not amiss, but a tissue of obsolete expressions is more fit *for keep than wear*. I do not say I would not use any phrase that had been brought into fashion before the middle or the end of the last century, but I should be shy of using any that had not been employed by any approved author during the whole of that time. Words, like clothes, get old-fashioned, or mean and ridiculous, when they have been for some time laid aside. Mr. Lamb is the only imitator of old English style I can read with pleasure; and he is so thoroughly imbued with the spirit of his authors that the idea of imitation is almost done away. There is an inward unction, a marrowy vein, both in the thought and feeling, an intuition, deep and lively, of his subject, that carries off any quaintness or awkwardness arising from an antiquated style and dress. The matter is completely his own, though the manner is assumed. Perhaps his ideas are altogether so marked and individual as to require their point and pungency to be neutralized by the affectation of a singular but traditional form of conveyance. Tricked out in the prevailing costume, they would probably seem more startling and out of the way. The old English authors, Burton, Fuller, Coryate, Sir Thomas Browne, are a kind of mediators between us and the more eccentric and whimsical modern, reconciling us to his peculiarities. I do not, however, know how far this is the case or not, till he condescends to write like one of us. I must confess that what I like best of his papers under the

---

1 这四人都是17世纪的英国散文作家，为兰姆所喜爱和模拟。

事向人炫耀。这些玩意儿拿来猎奇欣赏是很好玩的，但我却不愿在流通过程中接受它们、使用它们。文章中带上一点儿古色古香并不妨事，但若满篇古语废词，那就"仅可供摆设而不切实用"了。我并不是说，凡是在上一世纪中叶或末期曾经流行过的习语，我统统摒弃不用；我是说，在那个时期的习语中，凡是未经有定评的作家使用过的，我也尽量小心，以不用为是。词汇，像衣服一样，经过一段时间弃置不用，就会失去时效，变得相形见绌，甚至滑稽可笑。只有兰姆先生的文章，虽然模拟古老的英语文体，我仍然能够高高兴兴地读下去，原因是他和那些作家在精神上浑然相通，让人不觉其为模拟。他那内在的温情，藏在思想感情深处的禀性，那通过深邃、灵敏的直觉而获得的题材，冲淡了古色古香的文体外衣所带来的古怪、别扭之感。内容全是他自己的，风格却是模拟他人的。也许正因为他那种思想太与众不同了，才不得不采用一种特别的传统表达方式，把他那尖锐的锋芒加以收敛。因为，以他那样的思想，再用时新的服装打扮起来，恐怕就太惊世骇俗了。伯顿、富勒、科里亚特、托马斯·布朗爵士这几位古老的英国作家，[1]夹在我们和我们这位当代奇才[2]之间，似乎起着一种调解人的作用，使得我们对于他的怪癖能够不以为奇。当然，情况是否果真如此，我不敢说，那还要等他自己肯像我们普通人这样写作，才能见个分晓。但我得承认，在他使用伊利亚为笔名所发表的那些篇子

---

[2] 指兰姆。

signature of Elia (still I do not presume, amidst such excellence, to decide what is most excellent) is the account of "Mrs. Battle's Opinions on Whist", which is also the most free from obsolete allusions and turns of expression—

A well of native English undefiled.

To those acquainted with his admired prototypes, these *Essays* of the ingenious and highly gifted author have the same sort of charm and relish that Erasmus's *Colloquies* or a fine piece of modern Latin have to the classical scholar. Certainly, I do not know any borrowed pencil that has more power or felicity of execution than the one of which I have here been speaking.

It is as easy to write a gaudy style without ideas as it is to spread a pallet of showy colours or to smear in a flaunting transparency. "What do you read?" "Words, words, words."—"What is the matter?" "*Nothing*", it might be answered. The florid style is the reverse of the familiar. The last is employed as an unvarnished medium to convey ideas; the first is resorted to as a spangled veil to conceal the want of them. When there is nothing to be set down but words, it costs little to have them fine. Look through the dictionary, and cull out a *florilegium*, rival the *tulipomania*. *Rouge* high enough, and never mind the natural complexion. The vulgar, who are not in the secret, will admire the look of preternatural health

---

1 兰姆《伊利亚随笔》中的一篇文章。
2 此句引自英国著名诗人斯宾塞的长诗《仙后》第四部，原意是赞美乔叟的语言。

里(尽管对于如此妙文,我不敢妄评甲乙),我最喜爱的乃《巴特尔太太谈打牌》[1],因为,这篇纪事摆脱了陈旧的典故和辞藻,真像是——

一泓清泉,贮存着纯净、地道的英语。[2]

对于这位才思敏捷、天赋高超的作者,在了解他的文学师承关系之后,再读他这些随笔,人们所感到的魅力和兴味,恰如一个古典学者读到伊拉斯谟[3]的《对话集》或者一部优美的近代拉丁文作品。说实话,我不知道还有什么人模拟他人笔法,竟能比我现在谈到的这位作者更有气势,效果更为完满。

内容空洞、辞藻华丽的文章写来容易,因为那就如同把调色板上的颜料五颜六色任意涂抹,或者把画面涂得一片明亮,令人目眩。"你读的是什么?""词儿,词儿,词儿。"[4]"里边说的什么?"回答也许是:"空话。"华丽的文体和平易的文体截然不同——后者如实表达思想,不加粉饰;前者却拿闪光的外表把思想的空洞掩盖起来。既然除了文字以外再也没有什么可说,那么把文字写得漂漂亮亮,就不必花什么力气了。"爱花入迷"这个说法不好,打开词典,挑出"雅好群芳"来换上。"绯红"高雅之至,拿来使用,不必管人脸上到底是什么颜色。一般人不明底细,见了这样的盛颜花貌,只顾赞叹

---

3 伊拉斯谟(Desiderius Erasmus,1469—1536),欧洲文艺复兴时期的荷兰人文主义学者和作家,《对话集》是他的拉丁文作品。
4 《哈姆雷特》第二幕第二场的台词。

and vigour; and the fashionable, who regard only appearances, will be delighted with the imposition. Keep to your sounding generalities, your tinkling phrases, and all will be well. Swell out an unmeaning truism to a perfect tympany of style. A thought, a distinction is the rock on which all this brittle cargo of verbiage splits at once. Such writers have merely *verbal* imaginations, that retain nothing but words. Or their puny thoughts have dragon-wings, all green and gold. They soar far above the vulgar failing of the *Sermo humi obrepens*—their most ordinary speech is never short of a hyperbole, splendid, imposing, vague, incomprehensible, magniloquent, a cento of sounding commonplaces.—If some of us, whose "ambition is more lowly", pry a little too narrowly into nooks and corners to pick up a number of "unconsidered trifles", they never once direct their eyes or lift their hands to seize on any but the most gorgeous, tarnished, thread-bare, patchwork set of phrases, the left-off finery of poetic extravagance, transmitted down through successive generations of barren pretenders. If they criticize actors and actresses, a huddled phantasmagoria of feathers, spangles, floods of light, and oceans of sound float before their morbid sense, which they paint in the style of Ancient Pistol. Not a glimpse can you get of the merits or defects of the performers: they are hidden in a profusion of barbarous epithets and wilful rhodomontade. Our hypercritics are not thinking of these little *fantoccini* beings—

> *That strut and fret their hour upon the stage*—

---

1 莎士比亚《亨利四世》中的一个人物，爱吵吵嚷嚷、乱引诗文。

不止；那些赶时髦的人，以浮光掠影为满足，对此等瞒骗文字更是欣然接受。这么一来，写文章时只要语言响亮，内容模糊，就能万事大吉。结果废话大大膨胀，造成文风臃肿。然而，思想，或者说，明辨力，是一块试金石，在这上面，一切脆弱的冗词赘语都要碰得粉碎的。那样的作家只有语言方面的想象力，除了辞藻以外他们再也抓不住什么了。或者说，他们那孱弱的思想长上了蜻蜓似的金碧辉煌的翅膀。他们翱翔于芸芸众生之上，对于"土生土长的语言"不屑一顾——他们的语言至低也带上夸张修辞法，那是漂亮、气派、含糊，叫人不懂却又堂皇典雅，总之，是一堆铿然锵然的陈词滥调。如果说，像我们这样"胸无大志"的人专爱盯住角角落落，打听那些"无人关心的小事"，那么他们一睁眼、一抬手就会老去光顾那些华丽的、晦涩的、陈腐的、拼拼凑凑的连篇空话——那像陈年留下来的锦绣碎片一样，是经过一代一代无才思的冒牌作家承袭下来的诗歌破烂儿。如果让他们写戏评，他们那病态的感官只能看到舞台上羽毛飞舞，金片闪烁，灯光似波涛翻滚，人声如海洋鼎沸。于是，他们就拿出旗官皮斯托尔[1]那样说话的腔调儿，如此这般描绘一番。至于演员表演的长短，你却休想窥见半点儿——它们完全被一派大言狂语所淹没了。我们的胡批乱评家不肯去想一想那些可怜的小戏子——

　　他们台上指手画脚，辛辛苦苦做戏。[2]

---

[2] 改编自莎士比亚《麦克白》第五幕第五场。

but of tall phantoms of words, abstractions, *genera* and species, sweeping clauses, periods that unite the Poles, forced alliterations, astounding antitheses—

And on their pens Fustian sits plumed.

If they describe kings and queens, it is an Eastern pageant. The Coronation at either House is nothing to it. We get at four repeated images—a curtain, a throne, a sceptre, and a footstool. These are with them the wardrobe of a lofty imagination; and they turn their servile strains to servile uses. Do we read a description of pictures? It is not a reflection of tones and hues which "nature's own sweet and cunning hand laid on", but piles of precious stones, rubies, pearls, emeralds, Golconda's mines, and all the blazonry of art. Such persons are in fact besotted with words, and their brains are turned with the glittering but empty and sterile phantoms of things. Personifications, capital letters, seas of sunbeams, visions of glory, shining inscriptions, the figures of a transparency, Britannia with her shield, or Hope leaning on an anchor, make up their stock-in-trade. They may be considered as *hieroglyphical* writers. Images stand out in their minds isolated and important merely in themselves, without any groundwork of feeling—there is no context in their imaginations. Words affect them in the same way, by the mere

---

1 印度的金刚石产地，引申为"宝藏""富源"。

在这些作者心目中，只有堂皇的词汇影子、抽象概念、门类概念和种属概念，只有以气势凌人的子句，只有几乎能把南北极连起来的掉尾长句，牵强的头韵，惊人的对仗——

浮夸踞笔端，搔首自得意。

如果让他们描写君主和皇后，他们一定会写得像东方的赛会一般豪华，连国王在议院的加冕典礼也无法与之相比。读者只能反复看到四样东西：帐幔，宝座，王笏，脚凳——这些，对于作者来说，就是崇高想象的全部依据，翻来覆去运用，直到用滥为止。另外，难道我们没有读过这一类的图画评论吗？它根本不去反映"大自然的妙手涂抹"所造成的光影和色彩，而是满纸宝石、红玉、珍珠、绿翠、戈尔孔达[1]的宝藏，一派人工造成的珠光宝气。这种人被辞藻弄糊涂了，他们头脑里总是转悠着那些亮闪闪、空洞洞的事物假象。拟人化、大写字母、阳光的海洋、光荣的幻景、闪光的题词、鲜丽的藻饰、拿着盾牌的不列颠女神[2]、倚锚而立的希望女神——这些就是他们的看家本领。他们可以叫作"象形文字作家"[3]。在他们心中，意象脱离感情基础，可以独立存在，不受制约——他们的想象力可以不顾内容的连贯，任意驰骋。词汇打动他们，只是由于声

---

2 象征英国的带有盾牌的女神。
3 意即专门写文字华丽、内容晦涩的作品的作家。

135

sound, that is, by their possible, not by their actual application to the subject in hand. They are fascinated by first appearances, and have no sense of consequences. Nothing more is meant by them than meets the ear: they understand or feel nothing more than meets their eye. The web and texture of the universe, and of the heart of man, is a mystery to them: they have no faculty that strikes a chord in unison with it. They cannot get beyond the daubings of fancy, the varnish of sentiment. Objects are not linked to feelings, words to things, but images revolve in splendid mockery, words represent themselves in their strange rhapsodies. The categories of such a mind are pride and ignorance—pride in outside show, to which they sacrifice everything, and ignorance of the true worth and hidden structure both of words and things. With a sovereign contempt for what is familiar and natural, they are the slaves of vulgar affectation—of a routine of high-flown phrases. Scorning to imitate realities, they are unable to invent anything, to strike out one original idea. They are not copyists of nature, it is true; but they are the poorest of all plagiarists, the plagiarists of words. All is far-fetched, dear-bought, artificial, oriental in subject and allusion; all is mechanical, conventional, vapid, formal, pedantic in style and execution. They startle and confound the understanding of the reader by the remoteness and obscurity of their illustrations; they soothe the ear by the monotony of the same everlasting round of circuitous metaphors. They are the *mock-school* in poetry and prose. They flounder about between fustian in expression and bathos in sentiment. They tantalize the fancy, but never reach the head nor touch the heart. Their Temple of Fame is like

音响亮，只是由于它们与内容或许有关，而不是因为它们能够贴切表达内容。他们对于词汇一见倾心，并不考虑后果——只要听来顺耳，看来悦目，此外他们什么也不管、不问、不理。宇宙的构造、人心的素质，对他们来说，都是漆黑一团——他们无法与之同声相应，息息相通。他们只能在胡思乱想、粉饰感情中度日，无力自拔。在他们的奇文中，物体脱离了感情，形象自顾自地在那里光怪陆离地旋转；辞藻脱离了事物，独来独往，狂飞乱舞。这样一种精神状态的特点是狂妄与无知：表面看来狂妄，因为他们牺牲一切，不以为意；实质上对于语言的真正价值和事物的内在构造却是全然无知。他们以最高的轻蔑对待一切平易自然的事物，却做了粗鄙的矫揉造作和陈腐的夸夸其谈的奴隶。他们不屑于模拟现实，又无力进行任何创造，提不出一点新意。他们当然不肯做大自然的记录者，却做了最拙劣的剽窃家——剽窃前人的辞藻。在他们那里，从题材到典故，一切都是牵强附会、华美离奇、匠气十足、得不偿失；从文风到手法，也都是机械呆板、陈陈相因、索然寡味、拘泥形式、装腔作势。他们那些朦朦胧胧、令人费解的例证搅乱了读者的理解力；他们在读者耳边一遍又一遍重复着那些单调无味、迂回含糊的比喻。他们属于诗坛文苑中的蹩脚模拟派。他们使出浑身解数，也走不出夸大其词或无病呻吟的范围。他们逗弄着读者的想象力，但永远不能启发他们的头脑，感动他们的心灵。他们的荣誉

a shadowy structure raised by Dulness to Vanity, or like Cowper's description of the Empress of Russia's palace of ice, "as worthless as in show 'twas glittering"!

It smiled, and it was cold!

的殿堂,是由愚蠢为虚荣而树立的一座虚无缥缈的建筑物——那就像柯珀[1]诗里所描写的俄国女皇的冰宫,"外表光彩夺目,实际一文不值":

它笑容可掬,但却冷酷无情!

---

[1] 柯珀(William Cowper, 1731—1800),英国诗人,诗句引自他的诗歌《任务》。

托马斯·德·昆西

1785—1859

托马斯·德·昆西（Thomas De Quincey, 1785—1859）是与兰姆、黑兹利特、亨特大致同时的另一英国散文名家。他于1785年生于曼彻斯特一个商人家庭，七岁父死，由监护人送入语法学校念书。他小时早熟，在校不仅熟读了英国文学作品，而且把希腊文、拉丁文也学得很好，能用拉丁文写诗，还能流利地讲希腊语。他的另一特点是性格内向，从小就是一个"梦想家"。十七岁时，他感到学校生活沉闷，离校出走，流浪到了伦敦，在下层过了一段挨饿受冻的日子，后为其家人送到牛津大学上学。此时，他个人攻读的项目又增加了希伯来文和德国哲学、文学。在牛津，他患神经痛，接受医生建议，以鸦片为药剂，以致染上嗜好，终身未能戒除，对他的精神生活有很大影响。

德·昆西没等毕业即离开牛津，结识了当时浪漫主义诗歌首领柯尔律治和华兹华斯，并追随他们，在英国西北部著名的湖区居住了十二年(1809—1821)，并在那里娶妻生子。1821年，他移居伦敦，发表了代表作《一个英国吸食鸦片者的自述》。1829年，他搬到爱丁堡，在那里生活、写作，直到1859年去世。

德·昆西的文学活动以浪漫主义为准绳，属于以华兹华斯和柯尔律治为代表的早期英国浪漫主义的流派。他学识广博，著作涉及哲学、历史、政治经济学和文学等方面。一方面，由于他性格内向，感受敏锐，想象力丰富，耽于幻想，青年时代又有一段暂时脱离绅士家庭常轨的生活经历，这就产生了《一

Thomas De Quincey

个英国吸食鸦片者的自述》等一组以个人自传、抒情、幻想交织一起为内容的散文作品，即他自己说的"热情洋溢的散文"。另一方面，他还写了一批文学批评论文，以明晰的文笔分析他人的作品，阐述自己的文学主张，最著名的是《论<麦克白>一剧中的敲门声》。现在所介绍的《知识的文学与力量的文学》一文也属于后一类。

此文中，作者把文学分为"知识的文学"与"力量的文学"两种，前者以知识教育人，后者以激情感染人。作者所心折的在于后者，认为前者受时间推移之影响（即我们今天所谓"知识换代"）而容易变得陈旧落后，而后者一旦得以流传后世，则可长期甚至永远感染读者。这话如果是针对那些世界文学杰作而言，自然也有一定道理。不过，凡是造福于人类的科学（社会科学以及自然科学）著作，在历史上也同样是不朽的。区别仅仅在于：文学作品由于它们的语言特点和艺术魅力，可以雅俗共赏，读者面广泛；而要读懂高深的科学著作，则非具备相当的专业基础知识不可。浪漫主义作家重直觉，重感情，重个性，重兴趣，以个人欣赏的印象为准进行文学批评，有时似乎有贬低理论著作的倾向。德·昆西在此文中的观点如此，兰姆在《读书漫谈》中也流露过类似看法。只有黑兹利特在《论青年的不朽之感》中却维护科学家牛顿的历史地位，而嘲笑那些贬低牛顿的人。用我们今天所熟悉的语言来说，浪漫主义作家们在某种程度上，只把形象思维的成果看得很高，却把逻辑思维的成果看得过低。

The Literature of Knowledge and the Literature of Power

What is it that we mean by *literature*? Popularly, and amongst the thoughtless, it is held to include everything that is printed in a book. Little logic is required to disturb that definition. The most thoughtless person is easily made aware that in the idea of literature one essential element is some relation to a general and common interest of man—so that what applies only to a local, or professional, or merely personal interest, even though presenting itself in the shape of a book, will not belong to literature. So far the definition is easily narrowed; and it is as easily expanded. For not only is much that takes a station in books not literature, but inversely, much that really is literature never reaches a station in books. The weekly sermons of Christendom, that vast pulpit literature which acts so extensively upon the popular mind—to warn, to uphold, to renew, to comfort, to alarm—does not attain the sanctuary of libraries in the ten-thousandth part of its extent. The drama again—as, for instance, the finest part of Shakespeare's plays in England, and all leading Athenian plays in the noontide of the Attic stage—operated

知识的文学与力量的文学

我们说的文学,到底指的是什么呢?不用心思的人通常认为,它统指一切印在书上的东西。这样一个定义,用不着什么逻辑就能推翻。因为,再粗心的人也很容易看出:在文学这个概念里,一个基本要素是和人类普遍的、共同的某项利益有关——因此,那些仅仅适用于某一地区、某一职业或者某一狭隘个人利益的东西,即使以书本形式公之于世,也不能算是文学。如此说来,定义的内涵不难加以收缩——不过,它也同样不难加以扩充。因为,一方面,许多业已跻身书籍之林的东西并不能算是文学;另一方面,也有许多的确属于文学的东西却未印成书本。譬如说,基督教国家里每周必有的布道词,那规模庞大的教坛文学——它告诫着、鼓舞着、提醒着、警告着人们,广泛地影响着民众的心灵,但是在它当中能够在那书籍的圣堂里占有一席之地的,却达不到它那总数的万分之一。还有戏剧——例如,英国莎士比亚最优秀的剧作,以及在雅典鼎盛时期的希腊戏剧代表之作,在它们作为供阅读的剧本发表之前,早

as a literature on the public mind, and were (according to the strictest letter of that term) *published* through the audiences that witnessed their representation some time before they were published as things to be read; and they were published in this scenical mode of publication with much more effect than they could have had as books during ages of costly copying or of costly printing.

Books, therefore, do not suggest an idea coextensive and interchange-able with the idea of literature; since much literature, scenic, forensic, or didactic (as from lecturers and public orators), may never come into books, and much that does come into books may connect itself with no literary interest. But a far more important correction, applicable to the common vague idea of literature, is to be sought not so much in a better definition of literature as in a sharper distinction of the two functions which it fulfills. In that great social organ which, collectively, we call literature, there may be distinguished two separate offices, that may blend and often do so, but capable, severally, of a severe insulation, and naturally fitted for reciprocal repulsion. There is, first the literature of *knowledge*, and secondly, the literature of *power*. The function of the first is to *teach*; the function of the second is to *move*; the first is a rudder, the second an oar or a sail. The first speaks to the *mere* discursive understanding; the second speaks ultimately, it may happen, to the higher understanding or reason, but always through affections of pleasure and sympathy. Remotely, it may travel toward an object

---

1 在印刷术发明以前，书籍靠手抄本流传，书价自然是昂贵的；后来，印刷术刚发明时，由雕版而排印，早期印数不多，书价也不便宜，故云。

就在亲眼看到演出的观众面前发表过（从"发表"一词最严格的字面意义来说），作为一种文学力量在公众心灵上产生过影响；而且，这种通过舞台形式的发表，较之后来它们成为传抄的或印刷的珍贵书册，[1]影响要大得多。

这么说来，书籍和文学这两个概念并不表示着同样久远的含义，也不可以互相替代；因为，不少属于文学的东西，包括戏剧、论辩和教诲（例如讲学、演说之类）[2]也许从不收入书本，而许多印成书本的东西又可能和文学趣味丝毫无涉。但是，为了纠正关于文学所普遍存在的这种模糊观念，与其设法为文学寻求一个贴切的定义，倒不如把文学所起的两种作用划分个清清楚楚。在那从总体来说我们叫作文学的重大社会官能中，可以分辨出两种不同的职司——它们之间常常混淆不清，然而分别论之，又是截然不同，而且天然互相排斥的。这就是说，一方面既有知识的文学，另一方面又有力量的文学。前者旨在教育，后者旨在感染；前者是舵，后者是桨或帆。前者仅仅诉诸人的推论的悟性，后者则往往而且总是通过人的喜乐之情、恻隐之心，从根本上诉诸人的高级悟性即理性。远远望去，它似乎是穿过培根爵士

---

2 德·昆西把戏剧演出、法庭辩诉、其他辩论以及牧师讲道和学术讲演都算作口头文学而包括在文学范围之内。

seated in what Lord Bacon calls "dry light"; but proximately it does and must operate—else it ceases to be a literature of *power*—on and through that *humid* light which clothes itself in the mists and glittering *iris* of human passions, desires, and genial emotions. Men have so little reflected on the higher functions of literature as to find it a paradox if one should describe it as a mean or subordinate purpose of books to give information. But this is a paradox only in the sense which makes it honourable to be paradoxical. Whenever we talk in ordinary language of seeking information or gaining knowledge, we understand the words as connected with something of absolute novelty. But it is the grandeur of all truth which can occupy a very high place in human interests that it is never absolutely novel to the meanest of minds; it exists eternally by way of germ or latent principle in the lowest as in the highest, needing to be developed, but never to be planted. To be capable of transplantation is the immediate criterion of a truth that ranges on a lower scale.

Besides which, there is a rarer thing than truth—namely *power*, or deep sympathy with truth. What is the effect, for instance, upon society, of children? By the pity, by the tenderness, and by the peculiar modes of admiration which connect themselves with the helplessness, with the innocence, and with the simplicity of children, not only are the primal affections strengthened and continually renewed, but the qualities which are dearest in the sight of heaven—the frailty, for instance, which appeals to forbearance, the innocence which symbolizes the heavenly,

---

1 语出培根《谈友谊》一文，指不受感情所影响的纯粹理智之光。

所谓"明净的理智之光"[1]而到达某一客体；近处看来，才知它只有透过人的七情六欲、喜怒哀乐所交织成的茫茫迷雾、闪闪彩虹，借助于在那明灭之间、带着一点蒙蒙水气的幽光，才能发挥它本来应有的作用[2]——否则，它就不成其为力量的文学了。大家对于文学的这种高尚作用想得太少，所以，有人若把提供知识说成不过是书籍的一种平庸而次要的作用，大家就认为那是一种自相矛盾的奇谈。但是，奇谈归奇谈，这句似乎自相矛盾的话里仍有大可玩味之处。当我们用通常的语言谈到寻求知识、获得学问的时候，我们总是把这句话和某种完全新奇的事物联系起来。然而，在人类事业中能够占有崇高地位的一切真理，其所以伟大，就在于它哪怕对于最微贱者来说，也绝不是完全新奇的；它在最高贵者和最卑贱者的心灵中，作为一种思想的萌芽、潜藏心底的天然原则，都永恒存在着；它需要不断地发展，但永远不会被取而代之。因为，能被其他东西所取代乃是判断某种低级真理的一条无可怀疑的准绳。

此外，还有一种东西比真理更为神奇——那就是力量，或者说，对真理的深切感应。譬如，想一想儿童对于社会的影响吧。由于儿童的幼弱无依、天真无邪、纯朴无伪而引起的种种特殊的赞叹怜爱之情，不仅使人的至情至性不断地得到巩固和更新；而且，由于脆弱唤醒了宽容，天真象征着天堂，纯朴远离于世俗，因此，这

---

2 这个比喻的意思是说：带着湿气的光穿过云层就能形成彩虹；同样，人的高级悟性只有通过七情六欲等等情感的激荡才能发挥到极为敏锐的程度，其力量要远远超过仅仅靠理智来推论的精神力量。

and the simplicity which is most alien from the worldly—are kept up in perpetual remembrance, and their ideals are continually refreshed. A purpose of the same nature is answered by the higher literature, viz., the literature of power. What do you learn from *Paradise Lost*? Nothing at all. What do you learn from a cookery-book? Something new, something that you did not know before, in every paragraph. But would you therefore put the wretched cookery-book on a higher level of estimation than the divine poem? What you owe to Milton is not any knowledge, of which a million separate items are still but a million of advancing steps on the same earthly level; what you owe is *power*—that is, exercise and expansion to your own latent capacity of sympathy with the infinite, where every pulse and each separate influx is a step upward, a step ascending as upon a Jacob's ladder from earth to mysterious altitudes above the earth. All the steps of knowledge, from first to last, carry you further on the same plane, but could never raise you one foot above your ancient level of earth; whereas the very *first* step in power is a flight—is an ascending movement into another element where earth is forgotten.

Were it not that human sensibilities are ventilated and continually called out into exercise by the great phenomena of infancy, or of real life as it moves through chance and change, or of literature as it recombines these elements in the mimicries of poetry, romance, etc., it is certain that, like any animal power or muscular energy falling into disuse, all such sensibilities would gradually droop and dwindle. It is in relation

---

1 指弥尔顿的长诗《失乐园》。

些在上帝面前最可宝贵的品质也就经常受到忆念，对它们的理想便可不断地重温。高级的文学，即力量的文学，作用与此相类。从《失乐园》你能学到什么知识呢？什么也学不到。从一本食谱里又能学到什么呢？从每一段都能学到你过去所不知道的某种新知识。然而，在评定甲乙的时候，难道你会因此就把这本微不足道的食谱看得比那部超凡入圣的诗篇[1]还高明吗？我们从弥尔顿那里学来的并不是什么知识，因为知识，哪怕有一百万条，也不过是在尘俗的地面上开步一百万次罢了；而弥尔顿所给予我们的是力量——也就是说，运用自己潜在的感应能力，向着无限的领域扩张。在那里，每一下脉动、每一次注入，都意味着上升一步，好似沿着雅各的天梯[2]，从地面一步一步登上那奥秘莫测的苍穹。知识的一切步伐，从开始到终结，只能在同一水平面上将人往前运载，但却无法使人从原来的地面上提高一步；然而，力量所抬出的第一步就是飞升，就是飞向另一种境界——在那里，尘世的一切全被忘却。

人，经历了幼年时代，又经历了现实生活的种种机运变化，并从诗歌、传奇等等之中看到文学对于生活的模拟、对于事事物物的重新组合——有了这些重大的特殊经历，人的感应能力才能得到净化，并在外界启迪下不断得到发挥；否则，就像人的元气和膂力废弃不用一样，这些感应能力同样也会渐渐枯萎而退化。力量的文

---

2 典出《旧约·创世记》第二十八章第十二节：雅各做梦，看见有一个梯子从地面直通天上，在梯子上有天使来来往往。

to these great *moral* capacities of man that the literature of power, as contradistinguished from that of knowledge, lives and has its field of action. It is concerned with what is highest in man; for the Scriptures themselves never condescended to deal by suggestion or co-operation with the mere discursive understanding. When speaking of man in his intellectual capacity, the Scriptures speak not of the understanding, but of "the understanding heart"—making the heart, i.e., the great *intuitive* (or non-discursive) organ, to be the interchangeable formula for man in his highest state of capacity for the infinite. Tragedy, romance, fairy tale, or epopee, all alike restore to man's mind the ideals of justice, of hope, of truth, of mercy, of retribution, which else (left to the support of daily life in its realities) would languish for want of sufficient illustration.

What is meant, for instance, by *poetic justice*? It does not mean a justice that differs by its object from the ordinary justice of human jurisprudence, for then it must be confessedly a very bad kind of justice; but it means a justice that differs from common forensic justice by the degree in which it attains its object—a justice that is more omnipotent over its own ends, as dealing, not with the refractory elements of earthly life, but with the elements of its own creation, and with materials flexible to its own purest preconceptions. It is certain that, were it not for the literature of power, these ideals would often remain amongst us as mere arid notional forms; whereas, by the creative forces of man put forth in literature, they gain a vernal life of restoration, and germinate into vital activities. The commonest novel, by moving in alliance with human fears and hopes, with human instincts of wrong and right,

学与知识的文学判然有别之处即在于，它正是以人的这些巨大的精神能力作为存在的依托、活动的领域。它所涉及的乃是人至高无上的情性。譬如说，《圣经》就从来不肯降低身份，通过暗示或调和的方式去讨论什么推论的悟性。在《圣经》里提到人的智力的时候，从不用悟性这一字眼，而说成是"敏悟的心"——把心这一重要的直觉的(非推论的)器官，当作人以及至情至性通向无限的交流媒介。悲剧、传奇、童话、史诗，都能够使得正义、希望、真理、仁爱、复仇等等理想在人的心灵中复活；不然的话，如果这些理想仅仅靠着日常的实际生活来维持其存在，它们就会由于缺少足够的例证而枯萎下去。

譬如说，诗歌中的裁判[1]又是什么意思呢？从目的来说，它与人类一般法律意义上的裁判并无二致；否则，它就等于宣告自己是一种不正当的裁判了。只是，它这种裁判和普通法庭的裁判比起来达到目的的程度不同——诗歌，对于裁判的结局是无所不能的，因为它所要处理的并非世俗生活中难以驾驭的种种力量，而是它自己所创造出的事事物物，那些完全可以按照它的预想灵活安排的素材。实在说，世界上要是没有了力量的文学，一切理想便只好以枯燥概念的形式保存在人们当中；然而，一旦在文学中为人的创造力所点化，它们就重新获得了青春朝气，萌发出活泼泼的生机。最普通的小说，只要内容能够触动人的恐惧和希望、人对是非的本能直觉，便给予它们

---

[1] 诗歌中的裁判，又译"诗歌中的正义"，指在戏剧中对主人公生死祸福、是非好歹的命运安排。欧洲的戏剧，从古希腊罗马到莎士比亚时代，都是诗剧或戏剧诗，故云。

sustains and quickens those affections. Calling them into action, it rescues them from torpor. And hence the pre-eminency over all authors that merely *teach*, of the meanest that *moves*, or that teaches, if at all, indirectly by moving. The very highest work that has ever existed in the literature of knowledge is but a provisional work—a book upon trial and sufferance, and *quamdiu bene se gesserit*. Let its teaching be even partially revised, let it be but expanded—nay, even let its teaching be but placed in a better order—and instantly it is superseded. Whereas the feeblest works in the literature of power, surviving at all, survive as finished and unalterable amongst men. For instance, *The Principia* of Sir Isaac Newton was a book *militant* on earth from the first. In all stages of its progress it would have to fight for its existence: first, as regards absolute truth; secondly, when that combat was over, as regards its form or mode of presenting the truth. And as soon as a Laplace, or anybody else, builds higher upon the foundations laid by this book, effectually he throws it out of the sunshine into decay and darkness; by weapons won from this book he superannuates and destroys this book, so that soon the name of Newton remains as a mere *nominis umbra*, but his book, as a living power, has transmigrated into other forms. Now, on the contrary, *The Iliad*, the *Prometheus* of Aeschylus,

---

1 拉普拉斯(Pierre-Simon Laplace, 1749—1827), 法国天文学家和数学家。
2 德·昆西的这种说法，稍嫌夸张。文艺与科学各有其用，同样造福于人类，无高低之分。伟大的科学家和伟大的文学家、艺术家，应当受到人们同样的尊敬和爱戴。浪漫主义作家和批评家有重视感情作用而轻视理性的倾向。诚然，文学艺术作品通过直感而影响人们思想感情的力量的确很大，但轻视科学家、轻视理性的作用是不对的。

以支持和鼓舞,促使它们活跃,将这些情性从迟钝状态中解放出来。这也正是那些极其平凡的作者,只因能够感染读者,或者虽然意在教育,却采取感染人的方式来间接进行,因而远远胜过所有那些只会教育人的作者的根源所在。从知识的文学中所存留下来的登峰造极之作充其量不过是某种暂时需要的书——人们对它抱着宽容的态度加以试用,"且看结果如何"。一旦有人对它那教诲的内容进行局部性的修改,或者稍加增订——不,甚至只要有人把它的内容次序加以重新调整——它也就立刻被人弃置一旁。反之,在力量的文学中,即使并非高明之作,只要得以流传于世,总是作为一旦定稿、永不改动的作品,在读者当中流传的。譬如说吧,牛顿爵士的《数学原理》在问世之际本是一部富于战斗性的著作。在发表过程中的各个阶段,它都得为自己的生存权进行斗争:开始,为了绝对真理问题;那场战斗结束,继之又为了著作的形式和真理的表达方式。但是,一旦出了个拉普拉斯[1]或者另外什么人,在这部著作所奠定的基础上做出更高的贡献,从实际上将它从阳光灿烂之处摈斥于衰微暗淡之所,这就利用这部著作所提供的武器,使得它自己归于老朽无用之列。于是,牛顿之名虽然还能作为一种"盛名的幻影"存留人间;他的著作,作为一种生命力量,经过转化,却已经面貌全非了。[2]然而,与此相反,《伊利亚特》、埃斯库罗斯[3]的《普罗米修斯》、《奥赛罗》或《李尔王》、

---

3 埃斯库罗斯(Aeschylus,前556—前525),古希腊悲剧家。

the *Othello* or *King Lear*, the *Hamlet* or *Macbeth*, and the *Paradise Lost*, are not militant, but triumphant forever, as long as the languages exist in which they speak or can be taught to speak. They never *can* transmigrate into new incarnations. To reproduce *these* in new forms, or variations, even if in some things they should be improved, would be to plagiarize. A good steam engine is properly superseded by a better. But one lovely pastoral valley is not superseded by another, nor a statue of Praxiteles by a statue of Michelangelo. These things are separated not by imparity, but by disparity. They are not thought of as unequal under the same standard, but as different in *kind*, and, if otherwise equal, as equal under a different standard. Human works of immortal beauty and works of nature in one respect stand on the same footing: they never absolutely repeat each other, never approach so near as not to differ, and they differ not as better and worse, or simply by more and less—they differ by undecipherable and incommunicable differences, that cannot be caught by mimicries, that cannot be reflected in the mirror of copies, that cannot become ponderable in the scales of vulgar comparison.

All works in this class, as opposed to those in the Literature of Knowledge, first, work by far deeper agencies, and, secondly, are more permanent; in the strictest sense they are "Eternal possessions": and what evil they do, or what good they do, is commensurate with the national language, sometimes long after the nation has departed. At this

《哈姆雷特》或《麦克白》，以及《失乐园》，尽管并非什么战斗性的著作，只要它们所采用或可以采用的语言一日不灭，却是永远所向无敌的。它们不可能转变成为什么新的化身。对于这样一些作品，如果竟要通过什么新鲜形式或者某些更动来进行改变，即使一些细节也许能够提高，终不免迹近剽窃。一架性能良好的蒸汽机被另一架更为完善的蒸汽机所取而代之——这是正常的事。但是，一座富有田园风光的山谷决不会为另一座山谷所取代，正像普拉克西特列斯[1]的一座雕像决不会为米开朗琪罗的一座雕像所取代一样。把这些东西区别开的并不是差异，而是悬隔。衡量时，你不能拿着同一标准在它们之间分个高低，因为它们品类不一；如果说它们不相上下，也只是因为根据不同的尺度它们各有千秋。具有不朽之美的人类创作和大自然的创造在这一立足点上是完全一致的：它们之间绝不会互相重复雷同，绝不会近似得失去差别，而且，它们之间的差别并不在于好坏之分或者简单的多少之分——因为那差别是微妙得难于分辨，无法以语言表达，既模拟不出，又无法通过摹本像镜子一样反映出来，更不能放在粗俗类比的天平上来加以称量。

凡属这一类的作品，与知识的文学作品相比之下，不同之处在于：一、它们借助于远为深邃的力量而发挥其作用；二、它们更能垂之久远，从最严格的意义上来说，它们属于"永恒的财富"——它们对人们所起的坏作用、好作用，都将与本民族的语言一同延续，有时甚

---

[1] 普拉克西特列斯是公元前4世纪的古希腊雕塑家。

hour, five hundred years since their creation, the tales of Chaucer, never equaled on this earth for their tenderness and for life of picturesqueness, are read familiarly by many in the charming language of their natal day, and by others in the modernizations of Dryden, of Pope, and of Wordsworth. At this hour, one thousand eight hundred years since their creation, the pagan tales of Ovid, never equaled on this earth for the gayety of their movement and the capricious graces of their narrative, are read by all Christendom. This man's people and their monuments are dust, but *he* is alive; he has survived them, as he told us that he had it in his commission to do, by a thousand years, "and shall a thousand more".

All the literature of knowledge builds only ground-nests, that are swept away by floods, or confounded by the plow; but the literature of power builds nests in aerial altitudes of temples sacred from violation, or of forests inaccessible to fraud. This is a great prerogative of the *power* literature, and it is a greater which lies in the mode of its influence. The *knowledge* literature, like the fashion of this world, passes away. An encyclopedia is its abstract; and, in this respect, it may be taken for its speaking symbol—that before one generation has passed, an encyclopedia is superannuated; for it speaks through the dead memory and unimpassioned understanding, which have not the repose of higher faculties, but are continually enlarging and varying their phylacteries. But all literature properly so called—literature *par*

---

1 奥维德(Ovid, 前43—后17), 古罗马著名诗人。

至延续到该民族消失很久之后。此时此刻,在乔叟的故事写成五百年之后,这些作品中的温厚笔调和栩栩如生的描绘仍然是举世无俦,它们的原文仍同问世之初那样使许多读者感到亲切动人;而另一些人则津津有味地欣赏着德莱顿、蒲柏和华兹华斯的近代改订本。此时此刻,在奥维德[1]的故事写成一千八百年之后,这些异教的作品中欢快活泼的节奏、行云流水般的情节,仍然举世无双,仍然在一切基督教国家中为人所爱读。这位作家的同胞连同他们的坟墓早已化为尘埃,然而,只有他还活着——正如他自己说的,他责无旁贷,要在他们身后活上一千年,而且,"还要再活一千年"。

一切知识的文学都在地面上筑巢,结果不被洪水所冲掉,就是被耕犁所掀翻;只有力量的文学却在那巍巍苍穹间的圣殿之内,或在那高入云际的森林之巅营造自己的安身之处,那是神圣不可侵犯、也是欺诈所无法企及的。这是力量的文学所独有的重大特权,而它影响人类的方式尤为特殊。知识的文学,如时尚一样,与时俱逝。百科全书正是此种文学的缩影,从这方面来看,似乎可以说是它活生生的象征:一个世代尚未过去,一部百科全书就陈旧过时了。因为,在它那里面所讲的不外是虽然存留在记忆中却已失去新意的东西,以及不带任何感情色彩的推理。凡此,犹如经匣[2]中的教条,即使补充几句、略变花样,仍无法使得人的高尚精神恬然宁息。但是,一切当之无愧的文学——"最优秀的文

---

2 指古犹太人在祷告时系在额头上和臂上的装经文的皮制小匣。

excellence—for the very reason that it is so much more durable than the literature of knowledge, is (and by the very same proportion it is) more intense and electrically searching in its impressions. The directions in which the tragedy of this planet has trained our human feelings to play, and the combinations into which the poetry of this planet has thrown our human passions of love and hatred, of admiration and contempt, exercise a power for bad or good over human life that cannot be contemplated, when stretching through many generations, without a sentiment allied to awe. And of this let everyone be assured—that he owes to the impassioned books which he has read many a thousand more of emotions than he can consciously trace back to them. Dim by their origination, these emotions yet arise in him, and mould him through life, like forgotten incidents of his childhood.

学"——由于它比知识的文学远能垂之永久，它的影响与此形成相应比例，也就远为深邃，而像电光石火一般无空不入。一方面，我们这个星球上的悲剧培养着人的感情，使之朝着某些方向发展；另一方面，我们这个星球上的诗歌又把人的爱与憎、赞美与鄙薄等激情组成种种的结合。这样共同形成强大的力量，对人类生活产生了或消极、或积极的作用，而这些作用往往会延续许许多多世代，令人考虑之下不能不感到肃然起敬。总之，有一点可以确信：一个人从他读过的那些充满激情的文学作品中所感染到的种种喜怒哀乐之情，比他自己所能清楚意识到的要多出何止成千上万。这种种感情，虽然来源难于说清，却在他心中不断涌起，在他一生中塑造着他的灵魂，正像已被遗忘了的儿童时代的往事。

夏洛特·勃朗特

1816—1855

勃朗特三姊妹是19世纪中期的英国作家。姊妹三人都有文学才能，都写出长篇小说留传后世，在文学史上占有一席地位。她们出身贫苦，一生为谋生奔忙，而又找不到安定的职业；且由于长年的艰苦生活，都患有疾病。艾米莉与安妮一生未婚，二十多岁去世。夏洛特在三十八岁才结婚，不到一年就去世。她们的生涯是英国文学史上最令人同情的篇页之一。

她们的创作活动，是在非常不顺利的条件下进行的。除了她们是"小人物"、作品受人漠视以外，当时还存在一种歧视女作家的社会习惯势力，上流社会对于妇女从事文学创作(特别是写小说)常常予以鄙视，这给勃朗特姊妹造成一种精神压力。因此，她们写出作品要发表时，不得不分别取了三个类似男子的假名：柯勒·贝尔(夏洛特)，埃利斯·贝尔(艾米莉)，阿克顿·贝尔(安妮)。

就文学成就而论，夏洛特·勃朗特(Charlotte Brontë, 1816—1855)的《简·爱》从19世纪以来一直被公认为现实主义的名著。艾米莉·勃朗特的《呼啸山庄》很长时期受到社会的冷淡对待，但从20世纪以来，对这部小说的社会意义和艺术成就的评价愈来愈高。30年代的英国进步评论家福克斯(Ralph Fox)称它是19世纪"维多利亚时代"所产生的"三大巨著"之一，原因在于它代表受压抑的下层人民对资本主义社会发出了强烈的抗议。

《埃利斯·贝尔与阿克顿·贝尔生平纪略》一文是夏洛特·勃朗特为艾米莉和安妮的小说再版写的一篇回忆录。文章

Charlotte Brontë

回顾了她们姊妹三人在文学创作中艰苦奋斗的经过,感情真挚动人之处可与我国宋代女诗人李清照所写的《金石录后序》媲美。这篇《纪略》是了解勃朗特姊妹的生平和创作的第一手材料,作为一篇情文并茂的散文作品,也是值得一读的。

Biographical Notice of Ellis and Acton Bell

It has been thought that all the works published under the names of Currer, Ellis, and Acton Bell, were, in reality, the production of one person. This mistake I endeavoured to rectify by a few words of disclaimer prefixed to the third edition of *Jane Eyre*. These, too, it appears, failed to gain general credence, and now, on the occasion of a reprint of *Wuthering Heights*, I am advised distinctly to state how the case really stands.

Indeed, I feel myself that it is time the obscurity attending those two names—Ellis and Acton—was done away. The little mystery, which formerly yielded some harmless pleasure, has lost its interest; circumstances are changed. It becomes, then, my duty to explain briefly the origin and authorship of the books written by Currer, Ellis, and Acton Bell.

About five years ago, my two sisters and myself, after a somewhat prolonged period of separation, found ourselves reunited, and at home. Resident in a remote district, where education had made little progress, and where, consequently, there was no inducement to seek social intercourse beyond our own domestic circle, we were wholly dependent

埃利斯·贝尔与阿克顿·贝尔生平纪略

长期以来,在柯勒、埃利斯和阿克顿·贝尔的署名下所发表的作品,一直被认为统统不过是某一个人的化名之作。对此误解,我曾在《简·爱》第三版书前以寥寥数语予以否认和纠正,但那番话看来并未得到大家相信。所以,当此《呼啸山庄》重印之际,我接受建议,愿将事实真相加以澄清。

而且,我个人也深深感到:笼罩着埃利斯和阿克顿这两个名字的迷茫之雾,现在确实应该驱散了。那种小小的秘密,往日曾给我们一点点善良无害的快乐,由于时过境迁,早已失去了原来的兴味。今天,我责无旁贷,理应对于柯勒、埃利斯和阿克顿·贝尔所写各书的来历和著作权,加以简短说明。

约当五年以前,我的两个妹妹和我,在相当长时期的分别之后,又在家中重新会面。住在偏远之地,教育素不发达,故于亲人团聚以外,殊乏拜客访友之趣;日

on ourselves and each other, on books and study, for the enjoyments and occupations of life. The highest stimulus, as well as the liveliest pleasure we had known from childhood upwards, lay in attempts at literary composition; formerly we used to show each other what we wrote, but of late years this habit of communication and consultation had been discontinued; hence it ensued that we were mutually ignorant of the progress we might respectively have made.

One day, in the autumn of 1845, I accidentally lighted on a MS. volume of verse in my sister Emily's handwriting. Of course, I was not surprised, knowing that she could and did write verse. I looked it over, and something more than surprise seized me—a deep conviction that these were not common effusions, nor at all like the poetry women generally write. I thought them condensed and terse, vigorous and genuine. To my ear, they also had a peculiar music—wild, melancholy, and elevating.

My sister Emily was not a person of demonstrative character, nor one on the recesses of whose mind and feelings even those nearest and dearest to her could, with impunity, intrude unlicensed; it took hours to reconcile her to the discovery I had made, and days to persuade her that such poems merited publication. I knew, however, that a mind like hers could not be without some latent spark of honourable ambition, and refused to be discouraged in my attempts to fan that spark to flame.

Meantime, my younger sister quietly produced some of her own compositions, intimating that, since Emily's had given me pleasure, I might like to look at hers. I could not but be a partial judge, yet I thought that these verses, too, had a sweet sincere pathos of their own.

常心之所乐、情之所寄，唯有姊妹间相亲相依，唯有读书一事而已。好在我们自孩童时代以来所极感振奋、乐此不疲之事尚有文学习作。往日我们常将自己作品互相传阅，但后来几年此种交流、磋商业已中断，因而姊妹间对于各自写作进展情况不免隔膜。

1845年秋季的一天，我偶尔看到二妹艾米莉手写的一卷诗稿。当然，对此我并不觉得奇怪，因为我知道她赋有诗才且不断写诗。然而披览之后，我仍不禁深为震惊，感到这些诗歌绝非平平之作。它们毫无通常所谓的脂粉气息，而是精炼、简洁、刚健、率真。在我耳中，这些诗歌具有一种特殊的音韵之美——它们粗犷、忧郁、崇高。

艾米莉生性含而不露。埋藏在她心底的感情秘密，虽是至亲至近之人，非经许可也不得贸然侵犯。因此，仅仅诗稿被我发现一事，就需我解释几个小时，她才释然于怀；而使她相信这些诗歌确有发表价值，又费我整整几天。然而我认为，像她那样性格的人，在内心深处绝不会没有潜伏着远大抱负的星星之火；不把这星星之火煽成熊熊火焰，我决不罢休。

与此同时，我的小妹也悄悄拿出了她的创作，并且吐露说：既然我对艾米莉的作品感到高兴，或许对她的作品也肯一顾。要我来对这些诗歌下个断语，恐怕不免有偏爱之嫌，然而我还是要说，她的这些诗也具有自己真挚可爱的凄婉情趣。

We had very early cherished the dream of one day becoming authors. This dream, never relinquished even when distance divided and absorbing tasks occupied us, now suddenly acquired strength and consistency: it took the character of a resolve. We agreed to arrange a small selection of our poems, and, if possible, get them printed. Averse to personal publicity, we veiled our own names under those of Currer, Ellis, and Acton Bell; the ambiguous choice being dictated by a sort of conscientious scruple at assuming Christian names positively masculine, while we did not like to declare ourselves women, because—without at that time suspecting that our mode of writing and thinking was not what is called "feminine"—we had a vague impression that authoresses are liable to be looked on with prejudice; we had noticed how critics sometimes use for their chastisement the weapon of personality and, for their reward, a flattery which is not true praise.

The bringing out of our little book was hard work. As was to be expected, neither we nor our poems were at all wanted; but for this we had been prepared at the outset; though inexperienced ourselves, we had read the experience of others. The great puzzle lay in the difficulty of getting answers of any kind from the publishers to whom we applied. Being greatly harassed by this obstacle, I ventured to apply to the Messrs. Chambers, of Edinburgh, for a word of advice; *they* may have forgotten the circumstances, but *I* have not, for from them I received a brief and business-like, but civil and sensible reply, on which we acted, and at last made a way.

The book was printed: it is scarcely known, and all of it that merits to be known are the poems of Ellis Bell. The fixed conviction

我们姊妹早在幼小时候就抱着有朝一日成为作家的梦想。后来虽则三人天各一方，且又重务缠身，但此心此志从未抛却；如今一旦重新获得力量，便分外坚定，并形成决心。我们决定编选一本小小的诗集，并尽可能将其出版。不想把自己身份公之于众，我们采用了柯勒·贝尔、埃利斯·贝尔和阿克顿·贝尔的假名，将自己真名隐去；而选取这种模棱两可的名字，乃由于一方面不愿公开自己的女性身份，同时出于谨慎的顾虑，也不愿采用那些一望而知即是男性的名字。其所以如此，又是因为——尽管我们自知自己的笔法和思路并无一般所谓的"女儿气"——我们有一种笼统印象，就是：人们看待女作家往往怀着偏见，批评家有时拿性别当作惩罚的武器，有时又以此作为吹捧的因由——而吹捧当然不是真实的赞扬。

我们这本小书，出版实非易事。正如事前所料，不论我们这三个作者或是我们的诗歌，都不受人欢迎。不过，对此我们早有准备，因为我们自己虽是生手，却也读过他人的甘苦之谈。最使我们困惑不解的莫过于向出版商提出的请求都音信杳然。为此烦困之余，我只得向爱丁堡的钱伯斯公司诸先生冒昧投书，讨个主意。对于此事，他们或已忘在脑后，我却记忆犹新，因为从他们那里我收到了一个短短的、事务性的，同时也是有礼貌的、切切实实的答复。我们遵嘱而行，出书的事才算有了眉目。

诗集出来了，但知音寥寥，而其中确值得为人所知的作品乃是埃利斯·贝尔的诗歌——对于这些诗的价

I held, and hold, of the worth of these poems has not indeed received the confirmation of much favourable criticism; but I must retain it notwithstanding.

Ill-success failed to crush us: the mere effort to succeed had given a wonderful zest to existence; it must be pursued. We each set to work on a prose tale: Ellis Bell produced *Wuthering Heights*, Acton Bell *Agnes Grey*, and Currer Bell also wrote a narrative in one volume. These MSS. were perseveringly obtruded upon various publishers for the space of a year and a half; usually, their fate was an ignominious and abrupt dismissal.

At last *Wuthering Heights* and *Agnes Grey* were accepted on terms somewhat impoverishing to the two authors; Currer Bell's book found acceptance nowhere, nor any acknowledgment of merit, so that something like the chill of despair began to invade his heart. As a forlorn hope, he tried one publishing house more—Messrs. Smith, Elder and Co. Ere long, in a much shorter space than that on which experience had taught him to calculate—there came a letter, which he opened in the dreary expectation of finding two hard, hopeless lines, intimating that Messrs. Smith, Elder and Co. "were not disposed to publish the MS.," and, instead, he took out of the envelope a letter of two pages. He read it trembling. It declined, indeed, to publish that tale, for business reasons, but it discussed its merits and demerits so courteously, so considerately, in a spirit so rational, with a discrimination so enlightened, that this very refusal cheered the author better than a vulgarly expressed acceptance would have done. It was added, that a work in three volumes would meet with careful attention.

I was just then completing *Jane Eyre*, at which I had been working

值，我过去、现在都确信不疑；尽管此种信念尚未得到批评界的认可，我却坚持不变。

失败没有压垮我们，仅仅为了成功而奋斗本身就给人生以极大乐趣。一定要坚持下去。我们每人动手写一部小说：埃利斯·贝尔写了《呼啸山庄》，阿克顿·贝尔写了《阿格尼丝·格雷》，柯勒·贝尔也写了一部一卷本的作品[1]。这三部稿子，在一年半当中接连闯入一家又一家出版社——它们所遭受的命运往往是在寄出不久就又灰溜溜地给退回来了。

最后，《呼啸山庄》和《阿格尼丝·格雷》被人接受了，但出版条件对两位作者相当苛刻。柯勒·贝尔的书仍然到处碰壁，无人赏识。绝望，犹如一股寒流，侵袭她的内心。作为无望中之希望，她把稿子寄给另一家出版社——老史密斯公司。不久，比她根据以往经验所估计的时间要快得多，回信来了。她无精打采地把信拆开，预料内容不过是两行冷冰冰、毫无希望的字句，通知说老史密斯公司"对大作不拟刊用"，然而这次她却从信封里拿出两页信纸。她捧读时不禁心悸手颤。信中说鉴于营业上的原因，公司不打算出版此书；但接着信里分析了稿子的优点和缺点，措辞如此礼貌，考虑如此周到，态度如此合理，识见如此通达，这样的退稿真比粗俗的采纳更使作者感到快慰。信里还说若能有一部三卷本的作品，将会受到重视。

这时我正在完成《简·爱》一书。当我那部一卷本

---

[1] 指小说《教师》。

while the one-volume tale was plodding its weary round in London: in three weeks I sent it off; friendly and skilful hands took it in. This was in the commencement of September 1847; it came out before the close of October following, while *Wuthering Heights* and *Agnes Grey*, my sisters' works, which had already been in the press for months, still lingered under a different management.

They appeared at last. Critics failed to do them justice. The immature but very real powers revealed in *Wuthering Heights* were scarcely recognised; its import and nature were misunderstood; the identity of its author was misrepresented; it was said that this was an earlier and ruder attempt of the same pen which had produced *Jane Eyre*. Unjust and grievous error! We laughed at it at first, but I deeply lament it now. Hence, I fear, arose a prejudice against the book. That writer who could attempt to palm off an inferior and immature production under cover of one successful effort, must indeed be unduly eager after the secondary and sordid result of authorship, and pitiably indifferent to its true and honourable meed. If reviewers and the public truly believed this, no wonder that they looked darkly on the cheat.

Yet I must not be understood to make these things subject for reproach or complaint; I dare not do so; respect for my sister's memory forbids me. By her any such querulous manifestation would have been regarded as an unworthy and offensive weakness.

It is my duty, as well as my pleasure, to acknowledge one exception to the general rule of criticism. One writer[1], endowed with the keen

---

1 See the *Palladium Magazine* for September 1850.

的小说稿在伦敦颠连奔波之日，也正是我自己在家写作《简·爱》之时。接信三周之后，我寄出了《简·爱》。友好、老练之手接受了它——这是1847年9月初的事。不到10月底，它便问世了。与此同时，我两个妹妹的作品，《呼啸山庄》和《阿格尼丝·格雷》虽已付梓，却仍在另一家出版社耽搁了数月之久。

它们后来也出版了。批评家没有给它们以公正待遇。在《呼啸山庄》中所显示的虽嫌粗糙却是头角峥嵘的才华，几乎无人赏识。它的含义和主旨受到了误解，作者是谁也被弄错——这本书竟被说成是《简·爱》作者的一部早期拙劣之作。这是多么不公平、多么可悲的错误啊！那时我们姊妹说起此事当作笑话，如今却只剩下我一人为此深深悲痛了。而且，我担心，从那时起就对这部书产生了一种偏见。一个作者，既然能够想方设法在一部成功作品的掩护下，把自己低劣、粗糙的作品推销出去，当然肯定会因为急于成名，利欲熏心，而将作家的真正的光荣报偿撇在一边的。一旦论客和公众有了这种成见，他们对于这一欺世盗名之人抱着阴暗的看法，倒也不足为奇。

然而，千万不要误解我要为这些事而责怪、抱怨任何人。我绝不敢如此——对亡妹的敬意不允许我那样做。在她看来，任何怨天尤人都是可耻、可厌的懦弱表现。

但我有责任也乐于指出：在评论界的一般通例中却也出现了一个例外。一位对于天才具有明察的眼力并且声息相通的作者（见《雅典娜》杂志1850年9月号）看

vision and fine sympathies of genius, has discerned the real nature of *Wuthering Heights*, and has, with equal accuracy, noted its beauties and touched on its faults. Too often do reviewers remind us of the mob of Astrologers, Chaldeans, and Soothsayers gathered before the "writing on the wall", and unable to read the characters or make known the interpretation. We have a right to rejoice when a true seer comes at last, some man in whom is an excellent spirit, to whom have been given light, wisdom, and understanding, who can accurately read the "MENE, MENE, TEKEL, UPHARSIN" of an original mind (however unripe, however inefficiently cultured and partially expanded that mind may be); and who can say with confidence, "This is the interpretation thereof."

Yet even the writer to whom I allude shares the mistake about the authorship, and does me the injustice to suppose that there was equivoque in my former rejection of this honour (as an honour I regard it). May I assure him that I would scorn in this and in every other case to deal in equivoque; I believe language to have been given us to make our meaning clear, and not to wrap it in dishonest doubt.

The Tenant of Wildfell Hall, by Acton Bell, had likewise an unfavourable reception. At this I cannot wonder. The choice of subject was an entire mistake. Nothing less congruous with the writer's nature could be conceived. The motives which dictated this choice were pure, but, I think, slightly morbid. She had, in the course of her life, been called on to contemplate, near at hand, and for a long time, the terrible effects of talents misused and faculties abused; hers was naturally a

---

1 典出《旧约·但以理书》第五章：巴比伦伯沙撒王在宴会中，忽见一只手在壁上写出一些字迹，其臣下无人能认。最后先知但以理来，才读出文字并给以确解——原来是上帝对巴比伦国王的警告。

出了《呼啸山庄》的真义所在，并且准确地论列其妙处，指点其瑕疵。不过，大部分论客却往往叫人想起那一大群围观"壁上字迹"的占星学家、迦勒底人和预言家——他们读不懂文字，提不出解说。[1]因此，我们有权高兴：最后终于来了一位真正的先知，一个杰出的人物，他赋有眼光、智慧、见识，他能准确无误地读懂一个与众不同的心灵——尽管它不够成熟、教养不足、发展偏颇——所留下的"弥尼，弥尼，提客勒，乌法珥新"，[2]并且坚定地宣告："真义就是如此。"

然而，即使是我所提到的那位作者，也未能避免许多人在作者问题上所犯的错误：他认为我以往所以要推辞这一荣誉（我是把写作此书看作荣誉的）仅仅是含糊其词——这实在委屈了我。我愿向他保证：我不但在这件事情而且在任何事情上都不屑于含糊其词。我相信：我们有了语言，是为了说清楚自己的心意，而不是为了用不正派的暧昧之词把它遮掩起来。

阿克顿·贝尔的《野丘山庄的房客》也不受人们的欢迎。对此我倒并不感到惊奇。首先，题材的选择就完全错了——简直想象不出比这个更与作者性格不合拍的题材了。支配这样选材的动机虽然纯洁无疵，但在我看来总有那么一点儿病态因素在内。作者在一生中曾在自己身边长期观察到天才错用和才能滥用所产生的可怕后果；[3]而她又是一种敏于感受、寡言少语、郁郁寡欢的性

---

[2] 即前注所述的"壁上字迹"，引申为"难解之谜"。

[3] 三姊妹的唯一兄弟布兰威尔，本是一个有才能的少年，参加过她们的初期文学创作活动，且擅长绘画。传世的有他画的三姊妹画像，但后来却因爱情纠葛走上了颓唐酗酒的道路，早早死去。

sensitive, reserved, and dejected nature: what she saw sank very deeply into her mind; it did her harm. She brooded over it till she believed it to be a duty to reproduce every detail (of course with fictitious characters, incidents, and situations) as a warning to others. She hated her work, but would pursue it. When reasoned with on the subject, she regarded such reasoning as a temptation to self-indulgence. She must be honest: she must not varnish, soften, or conceal. This well-meant resolution brought on her misconstruction, and some abuse, which she bore, as it was her custom to bear whatever was unpleasant, with mild, steady patience. She was a very sincere and practical Christian, but the tinge of religious melancholy communicated a sad shade to her brief, blameless life.

Neither Ellis nor Acton allowed themselves for one moment to sink under want of encouragement; energy nerved the one, and endurance upheld the other. They were both prepared to try again; I would fain think that hope and the sense of power was yet strong within them. But a great change approached: affliction came in that shape which to anticipate is dread; to look back on, grief. In the very heat and burden of the day, the labourers failed over their work.

My sister Emily first declined. The details of her illness are deep-branded in my memory, but to dwell on them, either in thought or narrative, is not in my power. Never in all her life had she lingered over any task that lay before her, and she did not linger now. She sank rapidly. She made haste to leave us. Yet, while physically she perished, mentally she grew stronger than we had yet known her. Day by day, when I saw with what a front she met suffering, I looked on her with an anguish of wonder and love. I have seen nothing like it; but, indeed, I have never

格,她在眼里所看到的一切都深深刻印在她的心上——这就首先使她自己受了伤。她闷闷不乐地对这些反复思索,终于断定自己有责任将它们如实摹写下来(自然要将人物、事件、情节加以杜撰),以作他人之戒。她恨自己的作品,但又非写下去不可。若有人劝她放弃这一题材,她就把这种劝告当作引诱她自我放纵。她要做一个诚实的作者:不粉饰,不调和,不隐瞒。这种出于善良愿望的决心,给她带来了误解和攻击——对这个,她按照自己容忍一切不愉快事情的习惯,都默默地、平静地加以容忍了。她是一个诚挚的、平凡的基督教徒,宗教的忧郁情调给她那短短的、洁白的一生罩上一层凄婉的外衣。

埃利斯和阿克顿都不容许自己因为无人鼓励而片刻消沉。魄力给前者以勇气,忍耐给后者以支持。她们二人决心再试锋芒,我也欣然以为她们才华正富,来日方长。岂料巨变袭来,摧折骤至,令人思之可怖,忆之神伤:当烈日方中、农事正忙之时,耕耘者却在劳动中倒下了。

艾米莉首先病倒。她患病的详情依然历历在我脑际,然而要一一回顾,用文字加以细述,我是无论如何也无此力量了。她在一生中不论做任何事情从不拖拖拉拉,这一回她也不延宕。她的病情恶化得很快。她急急忙忙离开我们。然而当她身体濒临灭亡之际,她的精神却比平日格外刚强。日复一日,眼见她带着何等的气概去迎接苦难,我看着看着,心里不禁涌起一种又惊奇、又爱怜的痛楚之感。我没有见过可以与此相比的事——

seen her parallel in anything. Stronger than a man, simpler than a child, her nature stood alone. The awful point was, that while full of ruth for others, on herself she had no pity; the spirit was inexorable to the flesh; from the trembling hand, the unnerved limbs, the faded eyes, the same service was exacted as they had rendered in health. To stand by and witness this, and not dare to remonstrate, was a pain no words can render.

Two cruel months of hope and fear passed painfully by, and the day came at last when the terrors and pains of death were to be undergone by this treasure, which had grown dearer and dearer to our hearts as it wasted before our eyes. Towards the decline of that day, we had nothing of Emily but her mortal remains as consumption left them. She died December 19, 1848.

We thought this enough: but we were utterly and presumptuously wrong. She was not buried ere Anne fell ill. She had not been committed to the grave a fortnight, before we received distinct intimation that it was necessary to prepare our minds to see the younger sister go after the elder. Accordingly, she followed in the same path with slower step and with a patience that equalled the other's fortitude. I have said that she was religious, and it was by leaning on those Christian doctrines in which she firmly believed that she found support through her most painful journey. I witnessed their efficacy in her latest hour and greatest trial, and must bear my testimony to the calm triumph with which they brought her through. She died May 28, 1849.

What more shall I say about them? I cannot and need not say much more. In externals, they were two unobtrusive women; a

不过，说实在话，我也没有见过任何可以与她相比的人。比一个男子还要刚强，比一个小孩还要单纯——她的性格是举世无俦的。可怕之处还在于：尽管她对别人满怀柔肠，她对自己却毫无怜悯——她的精神对于自己的肉体毫不留情，强迫她那颤抖的手、无力的四肢、失神的眼睛仍像健康时那样工作。站在一旁眼睁睁看着这一切，而又不敢劝阻，内心之苦痛实非言语所能形容。

交织着希望和恐惧的两个月，就这样痛苦地挨过去了。那一天终于来临，死亡的恐怖和痛苦就要降临到这一人间奇才身上。当她在我们眼前一点点衰竭下去的时候，我们心里只觉得她愈发、愈发地可爱了。到那一天末尾，我们就失去了艾米莉——除了她那被肺病耗干的遗体。她死于1848年12月19日。

我们想这就足够了——但这样想真是大错特错。艾米莉还未埋葬，安妮就病了。艾米莉入土不到半个月，我们就接到明明白白的通知：要准备看到小妹也随她姐姐而去。接着，她真的走上了同一条道路，只不过那步子要缓慢一点，而她所表现出的忍耐恰与那一个的刚强相等。我刚才说过，她是虔诚的。她所笃信的基督教义支持她走完了这一段痛苦的路程。我亲眼看见了教义在她生命的最后时刻所起的作用，我可以证明它们如何帮助她安静地通过了这个最大的考验。她在1849年5月28日去世了。

关于她们我还能说些什么呢？我实在无话可说，也不必多说了。从表面看，她们是两个毫不引人注目的姑

perfectly secluded life gave them retiring manners and habits. In Emily's nature the extremes of vigour and simplicity seemed to meet. Under an unsophisticated culture, inartifical tastes, and an unpretending outside, lay a secret power and fire that might have inflamed the brain and kindled the veins of a hero; but she had no worldly wisdom: her powers were unadapted to the practical business of life: she would fail to defend her most manifest rights, to consult her most legitimate advantage. An interpreter ought always to have stood between her and the world. Her will was not very flexible, and it generally opposed her interest. Her temper was magnanimous, but warm and sudden; her spirit altogether unbending.

Anne's character was milder and more subdued; she wanted the power, the fire, the originality of her sister, but was well endowed with quiet virtues of her own. Long-suffering, self-denying, reflective, and intelligent, a constitutional reserve and taciturnity placed and kept her in the shade, and covered her mind, and especially her feelings, with a sort of nun-like veil, which was rarely lifted. Neither Emily nor Anne was learned; they had no thought of filling their pitchers at the well-spring of other minds; they always wrote from the impulse of nature, the dictates of intuition, and from such stores of observation as their limited experience had enabled them to amass. I may sum up all by saying, that for strangers they were nothing, for superficial observers less than nothing; but for those who had known them all their lives in the intimacy of close relationship, they were genuinely good and truly great.

This notice has been written because I felt it a sacred duty to wipe the dust off their gravestones, and leave their dear names free from soil.

娘，久处穷乡僻壤使她们养成了腼腆的态度和缄默的习惯。在艾米莉身上，刚强的魄力与质朴的性格似乎汇合在一起了。在她那天真无邪的情性、质朴无华的爱好与坦白率真的态度之下，隐藏着一股魄力、一团烈火——那是足以激励着英雄的头脑、点燃起英雄的热血的。然而，对于处世之道她却一无所知，她的聪明才智在生活的实际事务上毫无用处——她不懂得怎样保护自己最明显的权利，也不知道如何去考虑她最合法的利益。在她和社会之间，经常需要有那么一个解说人员。她的决心是不容易改变的，而这决心又往往违背着她自己的利益。她的脾气既宽宏大量，又热情激烈。她的性格是宁折不弯的。

　　安妮的性格却是温和而柔顺。她缺乏她姐姐的那种气魄、火气和独创性，然而她自有她自己那种文静的美德。她聪明，然而总是忍耐、克制、苦思冥想。气质上的含蓄内倾、沉默寡言，总是把她摆到一个不引人注意的地位；她的思想，尤其是她的感情，似乎被一幅修女的面纱遮盖着——这面纱很少揭开。不论艾米莉或安妮都不是博学之士——她们无意到别人的思想源泉那里把自己的水罐装满。她们写作，总是根据自己内心的冲动，根据自己感受的指使，根据自己那有限经验所容许她们贮存的观察所得。总括一句，我可以这么说：对于陌生者，她们是微不足道的人；对于浅薄的人，也许不值一顾；然而，对于那些了解她们生平的亲人来说，她们是真正优秀的人，也是真正伟大的人。

　　写此纪略，是因为我觉得自己负有神圣的责任擦去她们墓碑上的灰尘，不让她们可爱的名字沾上任何污点。

罗伯特·路易斯·史蒂文森

1850—1894

在我国，罗伯特·路易斯·史蒂文森(Robert Louis Stevenson, 1850—1894)是以小说作家和诗人而驰名的。他的探险小说《金银岛》几乎是家喻户晓了，而初学英语的小学生也无不背过他的诗《雨》("Rain")。其实，他也是19世纪后期一位重要的英国散文作家。

史蒂文森生于苏格兰首府爱丁堡。他的祖父和父亲都是修造灯塔的工程师。他自己也学过这一专业，但从小身体不好，改学法律，后来又专心致力于他所心爱的文学写作。他身患肺病，为了求得健康，不得不在英国、南欧、美国以及南太平洋诸岛之间奔波、迁移，最后定居于萨摩亚岛，在四十四岁时死于该地。在写作生涯中，他先写游记、随笔、短篇小说，后写长篇小说，也写诗歌，还写过剧本。在不算太长又是疾病缠绵的一生中，他工作得非常勤奋。

在文学史上，史蒂文森被称为英国新浪漫主义流派的代表。除了小说创作，他也写过大量的散文作品，包括游记、随笔、评论、信札。他在散文作品中直抒胸臆，从中我们可以看出他对于疾病与死亡的坚韧斗争和乐观态度，他对于儿童的热爱、对于下层小人物的同情，他对于深入麻风病区救死扶伤的自愿献身者的大声疾呼的支持，他对于受殖民统治者欺压的土著民族的援助，以及他对于资产阶级社会中那冷冰冰的"正经的赚钱世界"的厌恶不满。自然，他是生活在和我们不同的时代、不同的社会条件下的一个作家，在某些问题上和我们现在的看法不同；加之一生和疾病搏斗，文章中有时也不免流露出一些消极、空幻的情绪。

此处选译史蒂文森的随笔《为闲人一辩》，作者在这里说的

Robert Louis Stevenson

"闲人",并非真的游手好闲、无所事事,倒是"大有作为,只是所做之事不为统治阶级的教条所认可"而已。换句话说,作者之写此文,乃有所为而发,是为了表示他对于资产阶级社会中冷酷无情、唯利是图的生活方式的不满,认为倘若蝇营狗苟,追逐金钱名利,还不如于温饱之余图个一身清闲。原来,作者在这里说的"闲人"类似我国历史上曾有过的"懒道人""拙叟""痴翁"之类,自有怀抱,而隐遁于"懒""拙"之中,不欲在浊世中逐臭自污。

关于这篇随笔,还有一个典故:作者曾给他的女朋友(后来成为他的妻子)锡特威尔夫人写信说,他写了"一篇叫作《为闲人一辩》(实际上是为鄙人一辩)的文章"。可见,这里的"闲人"乃是史蒂文森的"夫子自道"。按:史蒂文森在他的《我怎样学习写作》一文中写道:"在我的整个青少年时代,别人都指指点点,说我是一个懒坏子;可是我在背地里一直在忙着自己的事业,那就是学习写作。"原来,"闲人"一词,既是作者自嘲,也是他的自辩。其实,史蒂文森绝非闲人:不但不闲,而且勤奋异常,他那二三十卷的全集"著作等身",就是证据。那么,《为闲人一辩》在某种程度上又是对于那种束缚青少年学习主动性和独立思考能力的刻板的教育方式的一种嘲讽。

正如其他的英国随笔作者一样,史蒂文森的随笔中不乏隽永的幽默意味。另外,他还是一个刻意求工的文体家。他从模仿其他散文作家的文体开始,经过不断艰苦学习,终于写出了自己清新活泼、吸引读者高高兴兴读下去的那种独特的风格。这是读者都可以体会到的。

An Apology for Idlers

Boswell: *We grow weary when idle.*
Johnson: *That is, sir, because others being busy, we want company; but if we were idle, there would be no growing weary; we should all entertain one another.*

Just now, when every one is bound, under pain of a decree in absence convicting them *lèse*-respectability, to enter on some lucrative profession, and labour therein with something not far short of enthusiasm, a cry from the opposite party who are content when they have enough, and like to look on and enjoy in the meanwhile, savours a little of bravado and gasconade. And yet this should not be. Idleness so called, which does not consist in doing nothing, but in doing a great deal not recognised in the dogmatic formularies of the ruling class, has as good a right to state its position as industry itself. It is admitted

为闲人一辩

博斯韦尔： 我们一闲，就觉得闷得慌。
约翰逊： 先生，那是因为别人都在忙着，没人给我们做伴儿；要是你我都闲着，就不会发闷——咱们可以在一起找一点儿娱乐。[1]

当今之世，每个人都不得不从事某种赚钱的职业，在其中不冷不热地应付着苦差，不然的话，就好像有一道无形的法令约束，要裁判他们为大不体面之罪；这时候，倘有人反其道而行之，发出呼声，说是生活有着即可心满意足，情愿冷眼旁观、聊以自愉，就显得有点儿故意逞强、大言不惭的味道。然而，这却于理不合。所谓闲散也者，只要不是无所事事，而是大有作为，只是所做之事不为统治阶级的教条规定所认可，那就和勤勉工作一样，也有充分权利来陈述自己的立场。大家知道，当人正在为了赢得

---

1 引自詹姆斯·博斯韦尔所著的《约翰逊博士传》(James Boswell: *The Life of Samuel Johnson*)。

that the presence of people who refuse to enter in the great handicap race for sixpenny pieces, is at once an insult and a disenchantment for those who do. A fine fellow (as we see so many) takes his determination, votes for sixpences, and in the emphatic Americanism, "goes for" them. And while such a one is ploughing distressfully up the road, it is not hard to understand his resentment, when he perceives cool persons in the meadows by the wayside, lying with a handkerchief over their ears and a glass at their elbow. Alexander is touched in a very delicate place by the disregard of Diogenes. Where was the glory of having taken Rome for those tumultuous barbarians, who poured into the Senate House, and found the Fathers sitting silent and unmoved by their success? It is a sore thing to have laboured along and scaled the arduous hilltops, and when all is done find humanity indifferent to your achievement. Hence physicists condemn the unphysical; financiers have only a superficial toleration for those who know little of stocks; literary persons despise the unlettered; and people of all pursuits combine to disparage those who have none.

But though this is one difficulty of the subject, it is not the greatest. You could not be put in prison for speaking against industry, but you can be sent to Coventry for speaking like a fool. The greatest difficulty with most subjects is to do them well; therefore, please remember this is an apology. It is certain that much may be judiciously argued in favour

---

1 公元前5世纪的古希腊犬儒学派的哲学家。据说他和赫赫有名的亚历山大大帝见面时，后者问他有何要求，他说："Yes, stand out of my sunshine." 亚历山大离开时说："If I were not Alexander, I would be Diogenes."

六便士的小银币而举行大规模的障碍赛跑,如果有人拒绝下注,那对于参加者无异于侮辱、泼冷水。一位漂漂亮亮的人物(这种人我们见得可多了)下定决心要挣这六便士银币,或者,用美国人的说法,他"为它干上啦!"当这位先生正在跑道上疲于奔命,却一眼瞥见路边有人在草地上仰面而卧,耳边垫着一条手帕,肘旁放着一只杯子,颇为悠然自得,他那心里的不高兴也就可想而知了。第欧根尼[1]的冷漠不理使得亚历山大伤透了脑筋。狂吼乱叫的蛮子占领了罗马,一窝蜂地拥进了元老院[2],却看见那些老头子们声色不动,默然危坐,那么,胜利的光荣又安在哉?费尽力气攀上陡峭的峰顶,大功告成了,却发现人类对于自己的成就一点儿也不感兴趣,自然是一件伤心的事。所以,物理学家宣告不懂物理学的人为不可救药,金融家对于那些竟不知股票为何物的人只好保持一种勉强的容忍,文学家看不起那些胸无点墨的人,而各行各业的人一齐骂那些没有正业的闲汉。

　　这就是谈论这个题目的困难之处,但它还不算最大的困难。发发议论反对黾勉从公自然不致被人投入监狱,不过,像傻瓜一样信口开河却会使自己孤立。谈任何题目的最大困难在于保持分寸适当;因此,请不要忘记:我这篇文章是一种辩白。的确,主张勤奋办事完全

---

2 指古罗马的决策集团"元老院"。

of diligence; only there is something to be said against it, and that is what, on the present occasion, I have to say. To state one argument is not necessarily to be deaf to all others, and that a man has written a book of travels in Montenegro, is no reason why he should never have been to Richmond.

It is surely beyond a doubt that people should be a good deal idle in youth. For though here and there a Lord Macaulay may escape from school honours with all his wits about him, most boys pay so dear for their medals that they never afterwards have a shot in their locker, and begin the world bankrupt. And the same holds true during all the time a lad is educating himself, or suffering others to educate him. It must have been a very foolish old gentleman who addressed Johnson at Oxford in these words: "Young man, ply your book diligently now, and acquire a stock of knowledge; for when years come upon you, you will find that poring upon books will be but an irksome task." The old gentleman seems to have been unaware that many other things besides reading grow irksome, and not a few become impossible, by the time a man has to use spectacles and cannot walk without a stick. Books are good enough in their own way, but they are a mighty bloodless substitute for life. It seems a pity to sit like the Lady of Shalott, peering into a mirror, with your back turned on all the bustle and glamour of reality. And if a

---

1 鲁迅也说过:"儿童,着重的是吃,玩,认字,听些极普通、极紧要的常识。"
2 即托马斯·巴宾顿·麦考利(Thomas Babington Macaulay, 1800—1859),英国历史家,早年上学时期就以博闻强记、成绩优异出名。

可以说出一大篇高明的意见；只是在相反方面也有些话值得一说——而我此刻要说的正是这个。陈述某一种理由并不一定表明对于其他一切理由统统充耳不闻，正如一个人写了一本黑山游记，并不足以说明他从来也没有去过里士满。

人在幼小的时候理应当尽量什么也不干才好[1]——这一点看来是肯定无疑的了。因为，一方面，不定在什么地方，某位麦考利勋爵[2]似的人物，才智超人，在学校中对于优秀成绩的荣誉避之唯恐不及；另一方面，大多数小孩为了得到奖牌却付出过大的代价，以致后来变得头脑空空，刚刚踏上生活道路，智力就已衰竭了[3]。在一个人整个少年时代，不管是自学或是接受别人的教育，情况莫不如此。约翰逊在牛津，[4]有一位愚不可及的老先生对他讲过这么一派蠢话："年轻人，你现在要发奋读书，积累知识；因为，等你上了岁数，你就要发现钻研书本会变成一种令人烦恼的苦工。"这位老先生似乎并不晓得：人一到了不戴眼镜就瞅不清东西、不拄拐棍儿就不能走路的时候，不光读书，很多事都要变成烦恼，有不少事情甚至根本办不到了。书籍自然是好东西，但书籍仅仅是生活的极为苍白的代用品。一个人如果把喧闹、神奇的现实生活撇在脑后，而像美人莎洛特[5]似的，只是坐在那里对着镜子顾影自怜，那是非常可惜

---

[3] 马克·吐温的《汤姆·索亚历险记》中有一个小学生为了得奖，死背了三千条《圣经》经文，把脑子用坏，成为白痴，即是此类。
[4] 约翰逊于1728—1729年间在牛津大学读书，因家贫未毕业而去。
[5] 英国诗人丁尼生诗中的一个女主人公。

man reads very hard, as the old anecdote reminds us, he will have little time for thought.

If you look back on your own education, I am sure it will not be the full, vivid, instructive hours of truancy that you regret; you would rather cancel some lacklustre periods between sleep and waking in the class. For my own part, I have attended a good many lectures in my time. I still remember that the spinning of a top is a case of Kinetic Stability. I still remember that Emphyteusis is not a disease, nor Stillicide a crime. But though I would not willingly part with such scraps of science, I do not set the same store by them as by certain other odds and ends that I came by in the open street while I was playing truant. This is not the moment to dilate on that mighty place of education, which was the favourite school of Dickens and of Balzac, and turns out yearly many inglorious masters in the Science of the Aspects of Life. Suffice it to say this: if a lad does not learn in the streets, it is because he has no faculty of learning. Nor is the truant always in the streets, for if he prefers, he may go out by the gardened suburbs into the country. He may pitch on some tuft of lilacs over a burn, and smoke innumerable pipes to the tune of the water on the stones. A bird will sing in the thicket. And there he may fall into a vein of kindly thought, and see things in a new perspective. Why, if this be not education, what is? We may conceive Mr. Worldly Wiseman accosting such a one, and the conversation that should thereupon ensue: —

---

1 也就是高尔基所上过的"社会大学"。

的事。同样，一个人如果过分用功读书，那会像老故事里讲的，他就很少有时间思考。

当你回顾自己的求学时代，我相信，你一定不会为了你在逃学中度过的那些内容丰富、兴味盎然、富有教益的时光而感到悔恨；恐怕你愿意在记忆中一笔勾销的倒是在课堂上半睡半醒中度过的某些黯然无光的时刻。就我个人来说，生平所听过的讲课可谓多矣。我听人讲过陀螺的旋转乃动力稳定性一例。又听人讲过永久佃耕权并非病名，檐水滴落权也不是什么罪名。但是，诸如此类片片断断的科学常识，我虽然不想丢掉，可也不像对于我逃学中在宽广的大街上所得到的那些零星见闻那样看重。此刻不是详谈这种了不起的教育场所的时候，不过它确是狄更斯和巴尔扎克所最喜爱的学校，[1]而且年年都造就出来许许多多通晓人间世相的无名大师。对此，一句话说完：要是哪个孩子在十字街头什么也学不到，那只能说明他缺乏学习能力。而且，逃学的小孩也不一定非在街上，如果他高兴，也可以穿过有花草园林的近郊到乡下去。他可以到小河边去采摘一簇丁香花，也可以一边听着河水从石上流过的淙淙之声，一边大吸其烟斗。这时，一只小鸟在树丛中歌唱，他陷入一种温馨的情绪之中，用一种新的眼光来看待万物。如果这不算是教育，那么，究竟什么才算？我们可以设想，世故先生[2]碰上这么一个小伙子，于是他们二人之间进行了如此这般的一场对话：——

---

[2] 英国宗教小说家班扬的《天路历程》(*The Pilgrim's Progress*)中的一个角色。在下文对话中，作者让世故先生说话用古字眼儿，以模拟一种道学先生的口吻。

"How now, young fellow, what dost thou here?"

"Truly, sir, I take mine ease."

"Is not this the hour of the class? and should'st thou not be plying thy Book with diligence, to the end thou mayest obtain knowledge?"

"Nay, but thus also I follow after Learning, by your leave."

"Learning, quotha! After what fashion, I pray thee? Is it mathematics?"

"No, to be sure."

"Is it metaphysics?"

"Nor that."

"Is it some language?"

"Nay, it is no language."

"Is it a trade?"

"Nor a trade neither."

"Why, then, what is't?"

"Indeed, sir, as time may soon come for me to go upon Pilgrimage, I am desirous to note what is commonly done by persons in my case, and where are the ugliest Sloughs and Thickets on the Road; as also, what manner of staff is of the best service. Moreover, I lie here, by this water, to learn by root-of-heart a lesson which my master teaches me to call Peace, or Contentment."

Hereupon Mr. Worldly Wiseman was much commoved with passion, and shaking his cane with a very threatful countenance, broke forth upon this wise: "Learning, quotha!" said he; "I would have all such rogues scourged by the Hangman!"

"吁，少年，在此何为者？"

"不瞒您说，先生，我在这儿痛痛快快地玩儿。"

"此刻适为上课时间，汝胡不在校发奋苦读，以期学问有所深造乎？"

"对不起，我在这儿也是求学问呀！"

"异哉，汝所谓学问者！请教，尔在此求何种学问？其为数学乎？"

"当然不是。"

"莫非形而上学乎？"

"也不是。"

"或为某种语言乎？"

"不，也不是语言。"

"学买卖乎？"

"也不是买卖。"

"然则，汝究系何为者？"

"说实在话，先生，我很快就要登上人生的旅程，非常想观察一下别人处在我这种情况下究竟都在干些什么；我也想了解一下在人生道路上究竟什么地方有险恶的泥潭和丛莽，也想知道什么样的拐棍儿对上路最有用。还有，我躺在这里的河边，是为了从心灵深处学习人生的一课——这一课书，老师告诉我，就叫作宁静自安。"

听到此处，世故先生满脸怒容，气呼呼地挥动手杖，爆发出一阵吼叫："怪哉，如此学问！"他说："似汝等流氓无赖，唯有统统交付绞刑吏之手，痛加惩处，方称我心也！"

And so he would go his way, ruffling out his cravat with a crackle of starch, like a turkey when it spread its feathers.

Now this, of Mr. Wiseman's, is the common opinion. A fact is not called a fact, but a piece of gossip, if it does not fall into one of your scholastic categories. An inquiry must be in some acknowledged direction, with a name to go by; or else you are not inquiring at all, only lounging; and the workhouse is too good for you. It is supposed that all knowledge is at the bottom of a well, or the far end of a telescope. Sainte-Beuve, as he grew older, came to regard all experience as a single great book, in which to study for a few years ere we go hence; and it seemed all one to him whether you should read in Chapter xx., which is the differential calculus, or in Chapter xxxix., which is hearing the band play in the gardens. As a matter of fact, an intelligent person, looking out of his eyes and hearkening in his ears, with a smile on his face all the time, will get more true education than many another in a life of heroic vigils. There is certainly some chill and arid knowledge to be found upon the summits of formal and laborious science; but it is all round about you, and for the trouble of looking, that you will acquire the warm and palpitating facts of life. While others are filling their memory with a lumber of words, one-half of which they will forget before the week be out, your truant may learn some really useful art: to play the fiddle, to know a good cigar, or to speak with ease and opportunity to all varieties of men. Many who have "plied their book diligently, " and

---

1 英国的贫民收容所。关于济贫院的黑暗状况,最出名的描写见于狄更斯的《雾都孤儿》。

说完，他才上路，气得浑身发抖，连领带上的干浆糊都喀啪啪地响，像一只火鸡抖动羽毛大展翅。

世故先生讲的这一派话乃通常的看法。一种现象，倘若不能纳入经院课程的某一范畴之中，就不能叫作现象，只能算是瞎说。无论探讨什么，必须遵循某种名正言顺的公式；否则，你就不算是探讨，而是胡混——把你送进济贫院[1]去都算太便宜了你。据说，一切知识都藏在一口井的底下，或躲在一架望远镜的那一头上。其实，圣伯夫[2]上了年纪以后，把全部生活经验统统看作一部大书，花几年工夫念完了这一段，然后再去念另外一段。因此，在他看来，人从这部书的哪一段读起，究竟是第二十章——微分学，或是第三十九章，到花园去听乐队演奏，都没有什么关系。实际上，一个脸上总是含着微笑的聪明人，用眼睛看看，拿耳朵听听，要比许多苦苦熬夜的人更能受到真正的教育。在那常规的、艰苦的科学顶峰之上，当然可以找到一些冷冰冰、无趣味的知识；但在你身边，你只要睁开眼睛就能到处看到那些暖乎乎、使你心头扑扑跳动的生活现象。当其他学生正往脑子里塞那些乱七八糟的单词，其中总有一半他们不出一周就要忘得干干净净，逃学鬼却在校外学习着某些真正有用的本领：拉提琴呀，品尝一支上等雪茄烟呀，从容自然又恰当得体地对各色各样的人侃侃而谈呀，等等。然而，很多"发奋苦读"、通晓某一门众所

---

[2] 圣伯夫（Charles A. Sainte-Beuve, 1804—1869），法国文学评论家。

know all about some one branch or another of accepted lore, come out of the study with an ancient and owl-like demeanour, and prove dry, stockish, and dyspeptic in all the better and brighter parts of life. Many make a large fortune, who remain underbred and pathetically stupid to the last. And meanwhile there goes the idler, who began life along with them—by your leave, a different picture. He has had time to take care of his health and his spirits; he has been a great deal in the open air, which is the most salutary of all things for both body and mind; and if he has never read the great Book in very recondite places, he has dipped into it and skimmed it over to excellent purpose. Might not the student afford some Hebrew roots, and the business man some of his half-crowns, for a share of the idler's knowledge of life at large, and Art of Living? Nay, and the idler has another and more important quality than these. I mean his wisdom. He who has much looked on at the childish satisfaction of other people in their hobbies, will regard his own with only a very ironical indulgence. He will not be heard among the dogmatists. He will have a great and cool allowance for all sorts of people and opinions. If he finds no out-of-the-way truths, he will identify himself with no very burning falsehood. His way takes him along a by-road, not much frequented, but very even and pleasant, which is called Commonplace Lane, and leads to the Belvedere of Common-sense. Thence he shall command an agreeable, if no very noble prospect; and while others behold the East and West, the Devil and the Sunrise, he will be contentedly aware of a sort of morning hour upon all sublunary things, with an army of shadows running speedily and in many different directions into

公认的学问的人，一走出书斋就跟猫头鹰似的，脸上带出一副古板的呆相——这种人进入那些高高兴兴、活活泼泼的生活场合当中，总显得干巴巴、木呆呆，或者像是害着消化不良症。还有很多人发了大财，但是缺乏教养，一辈子愚蠢得可怜。而那位闲人先生呢，虽然跟这些人一同开始生活，可是——对不起，他过的日子却是别有天地。他尽有时间去保养自己的身心健康；他常在户外活动——这对于身体和精神都是极为有益的事；此外，对于人生这部大书，他虽然一碰到深奥难解之处就揭过去不念，但他稍稍翻阅、匆匆浏览的那一点点，他却真的抓住了要领。那么，我们的大学生不该匀出一点儿为记住几个希伯来词根所花的工夫，我们的商业主不该省下一点儿为赚几枚半克朗银币而伤的脑筋，也来学一学闲人对于生活的全面认识，分享一下他的生活艺术吗？不仅此也，闲人比他们还具有另外一种更为紧要的品性，那就是他的智慧。一个人如果常常观察别人对于个人兴趣爱好所流露出的孩子气般的满足，那他也会以一种幽默的宽容态度来对待自己的兴趣爱好。这样的人不会变成一个教条主义者。他对于各种人、各种意见都会采取一种雍容大度的体谅态度。尽管他发现不出什么石破天惊的真理，他也不会去附和什么荒谬绝伦的错误。他的一生走的是一条虽非熙来攘往但却平坦愉快的偏僻小路——它叫作平凡无奇之小巷，通向普通常识的望楼。从那里，他虽看不到什么宏伟的壮观，却能俯瞰一片赏心的小景。当别人都在观看东方与西方、恶魔之王与黎明之神，他却怡然自得地注意：当清晨降临于大

the great daylight of Eternity. The shadows and the generations, the shrill doctors and the plangent wars, go by into ultimate silence and emptiness; but underneath all this, a man may see, out of the Belvedere windows, much green and peaceful landscape; many fire-lit parlours; good people laughing, drinking, and making love as they did before the Flood or the French Revolution; and the old shepherd telling his tale under the hawthorn.

Extreme *busyness*, whether at school or college, kirk or market, is a symptom of deficient vitality; and a faculty for idleness implies a catholic appetite and a strong sense of personal identity. There is a sort of dead-alive, hackneyed people about, who are scarcely conscious of living except in the exercise of some conventional occupation. Bring these fellows into the country or set them aboard ship, and you will see how they pine for their desk or their study. They have no curiosity; they cannot give themselves over to random provocations; they do not take pleasure in the exercise of their faculties for its own sake; and unless Necessity lays about them with a stick, they will even stand still. It is no good speaking to such folk: they *cannot* be idle, their nature is not generous enough; and they pass those hours in a *sort of* coma, which are not dedicated to furious moiling in the gold-mill. When they do not require to go to office, when they are not hungry and have no mind to drink, the whole breathing world is a blank to them. If they have to wait an hour or so for a train, they fall into a stupid trance with their eyes open. To see them, you would suppose there was nothing to look at and no one to speak with; you would imagine they were paralysed or alienated; and yet very possible they are hard workers in their own

地万物，大群阴暗的幽灵都向着四面八方仓皇逃入永恒的白昼之中。那些阴暗的幽灵、已逝的世代、尖声叫喊的博士、轰轰烈烈的战争，都匆匆过去，进入了永久的沉寂和空虚；然而，我们从望楼的窗口中，透过这一切还看到了一片青葱的和平景象，看到灯火辉煌的客厅，看到善良的人们在欢笑，在饮酒，在求爱，不管处在大洪水到来之前或是法国革命前夕；我们也看到了牧羊老人在山楂树下讲说着他自己的故事。

不论在学校、学院、教堂、市场，过度的忙碌都是精力不足的表现；只有闲散才意味着爱好广泛和具有强烈的个人独立感。在我们周围，有一种奄奄无生气的庸人，他们只会履行某种习惯性的事务，除此以外，简直就不知道怎么才叫活着。如果我们把这些人弄到乡下或者放在船上，看吧，他们就要苦苦思念自己的办公桌或书房。他们没有好奇心；他们不可能因为什么偶然的刺激而全身心地钻进去；他们也不知道独立发挥自己的才能究竟会有什么乐趣；如果不是需要拿棍子抽打他们，他们甚至站住不动。跟这种人没有什么话好说的——他们没法儿闲着，他们的性格不够豁达；他们的日月全在黄金磨坊里的疯狂旋转中打发掉了，剩下几个钟头只好在昏迷状态中度过。当他们不必去办公室、肚子不饿、不想喝一杯的时候，那整个的人生世界对于他们来说就等于一片空白。如果他们必须等个把钟头火车，他们就只有睁着眼睛呆呆地发愣。跟这种人面面相对，你会觉得没啥可看也无话可谈；你会觉得他们是不是害了瘫痪病、异化了？然而，在他们那一行里，他们很可能是

way, and have good eyesight for a flaw in a deed or a turn of the market. They have been to school and college, but all the time they had their eye on the medal; they have gone about in the world and mixed with clever people, but all the time they were thinking of their own affairs. As if a man's soul were not too small to begin with, they have dwarfed and narrowed theirs by a life of all work and no play; until here they are at forty, with a listless attention, a mind vacant of all material of amusement, and not one thought to rub against another, while they wait for the train. Before he was breeched, he might have clambered on the boxes; when he was twenty, he would have stared at the girls; but now the pipe is smoked out, the snuff-box empty, and my gentleman sits bolt upright upon a bench, with lamentable eyes. This does not appeal to me as being Success in Life.

But it is not only the person himself who suffers from his busy habits, but his wife and children, his friends and relations, and down to the very people he sits with in a railway-carriage or an omnibus. Perpetual devotion to what a man calls his business, is only to be sustained by perpetual neglect of many other things. And it is not by any means certain that a man's business is the most important thing he has to do. To an impartial estimate it will seem clear that many of the wisest, most virtuous, and most beneficent parts that are to be played upon the Theatre of Life are filled by gratuitous performers, and pass, among the world at large, as phases of idleness. For in that Theatre, not only the walking gentlemen, singing chambermaids, and diligent fiddlers in the orchestra, but those who look on and clap their hands from the benches, do really play a part and fulfil important offices

辛辛苦苦的办事人，某项契约有了什么毛病、市场行情有了什么变化，他们能够明察秋毫。他们自然也上过中学、大学，但他们念书只是为了奖牌；他们在社会上走动，自然也接触了不少聪明人，但他们一心一意只想着自己的事务。本来嘛，一个人的心灵就够狭小了，他们过日子还要光干活、不玩儿，把自己的心灵弄得更加小气、更为狭隘。现在，他们年已四十，无精打采地坐在那儿等火车，脑子里没有一点儿别的思想，心里也没有一件可以高兴的事儿。在他穿着开裆裤的时候，大概也曾经在箱子上爬来爬去；他二十岁那年，大概也曾经目不转睛地看过人家大姑娘；但是，如今呵，这位绅士烟斗抽干了，鼻烟盒里空空如也，他只好目光凄然、直挺挺地坐在一条板凳上。——这个样子，在我看来，也算不得什么人生的成功。

然而，为了他那不知闲暇的生活习惯，吃苦头的不光是他自己，跟着他一起倒霉的还有他的老婆孩子、亲戚朋友，连在火车厢、公共马车里和他坐在一起的乘客也都包括在内。所谓始终不渝地忠于个人的事务，即意味着对于其他许多事情的始终不渝的疏忽。而且，一个人的事务也很难说一定就是他自己最要紧的事。公正无私地判断起来，可以清楚看出：在人生的大舞台上，许多最聪明、最崇高、最有益于世的角色，是由那些无报偿的扮演者来充当的，不过又往往被一般社会纳入不务正业的范围。因为，在人生舞台上，不仅是那些在台上踱来踱去的绅士、歌声婉转的侍女、乐队席中辛苦奏乐的提琴手，也包括那些坐在凳子上鼓掌的观众，大家全

towards the general result. You are no doubt very dependent on the care of your lawyer and stockbroker, of the guards and signalmen who convey you rapidly from place to place, and the policemen who walk the streets for your protection; but is there not a thought of gratitude in your heart for certain other benefactors who set you smiling when they fall in your way, or season your dinner with good company? Colonel Newcome helped to lose his friend's money; Fred Bayham had an ugly trick of borrowing shirts; and yet they were better people to fall among than Mr. Barnes. And though Falstaff was neither sober nor very honest, I think I could name one or two longfaced Barabbases whom the world could better have done without. Hazlitt mentions that he was more sensible of obligation to Northcote, who had never done him anything he could call a service, than to his whole circle of ostentatious friends; for he thought a good companion emphatically the greatest benefactor. I know there are people in the world who cannot feel grateful unless the favour has been done them at the cost of pain and difficulty. But this is a churlish disposition. A man may send you six sheets of letter-paper covered with the most entertaining gossip, or you may pass half an hour pleasantly, perhaps profitably, over an article of his; do you think the service would be greater if he had made the manuscript in his heart's blood, like a compact with the devil? Do you really fancy you should be more beholden to your correspondent, if he had been damning you all the while for your importunity? Pleasures are more beneficial than

---

1 这三个人都是著名英国小说家萨克雷的小说《纽科姆一家》(W. M. Thackeray: *The Newcomes*) 中的人物，前两者有缺点而憨厚，第三个则是个心地奸诈的坏蛋。

都充当着一定角色，完成着重要的任务，这才达到了共同的效果。毫无疑问，诸位的安危所系，自然离不开那些大律师、经纪人，离不开那些忙不迭地把你们从这一站送到那一站的护路队和信号兵，离不开那些在街上巡逻、保尊护驾的警察；但是，对于另外一些人，或则在人生道路上邂逅相逢、使你开颜一笑，或则席间暂遇、欢宴为之生色——对于这些有恩于你的人，难道在你心里就没有一丝一毫的感激之念吗？纽科姆上校让他的朋友破了财，弗来德·贝耶姆也爱用不光彩的手段骗别人的衬衫；然而，跟他们打交道总比跟巴恩斯先生打交道要好。[1]福斯塔夫既是酒鬼、又不怎么老实，但我可以指出一两个表面上一本正经的盗贼，世界上如果没有他们倒可以太平得多呢。黑兹利特说过，他觉得对于他那一伙赫赫有名的朋友，倒没有像对诺思科特[2]那样旧情难忘；虽然后者并没有给他帮过什么大忙，但是他认为一个好伙伴就是最大的恩人。我知道，世上尽有这样的人，如果别人对他的恩惠没有付出痛苦和艰难的代价，他们就觉得不值得感激。这是一种坏脾气。譬如说，有人寄给你一封信，密密麻麻六大张，写的都是非常有趣的闲话；或者，你花上半个小时，高高兴兴读了他的一篇文章，受益匪浅；难道这稿子非得叫他用自己的心头鲜血来写，就像跟魔鬼订合同似的，你才觉得他帮了大忙吗？再不然，当你有求于人，对方只有在信里把你臭骂一顿，你才对他感激不尽吗？愉愉快快的给予比义务性

---

[2] 19世纪英国与黑兹里特同时而不大出名的一个作家。

duties because, like the quality of mercy, they are not strained, and they are twice blest. There must always be two to a kiss, and there may be a score in a jest; but wherever there is an element of sacrifice, the favour is conferred with pain, and, among generous people, received with confusion. There is no duty we so much underrate as the duty of being happy. By being happy we sow anonymous benefits upon the world, which remain unknown even to ourselves, or when they are disclosed, surprise nobody so much as the benefactor. The other day, a ragged, barefoot boy ran down the street after a marble, with so jolly an air that he set everyone he passed into a good humour; one of these persons, who had been delivered from more than usually black thoughts, stopped the little fellow and gave him some money with this remark: "You see what sometimes comes of looking pleased." If he had looked pleased before, he had now to look both pleased and mystified. For my part, I justify this encouragement of smiling rather than tearful children; I do not wish to pay for tears anywhere but upon the stage; but I am prepared to deal largely in the opposite commodity. A happy man or woman is a better thing to find than a five-pound note. He or she is a radiating focus of goodwill; and their entrance into a room is as though another candle had been lighted. We need not care whether they could prove the forty-seventh proposition; they do a better thing than that, they practically demonstrate the great Theorem of the Liveableness of Life. Consequently, if a person cannot be happy without remaining idle, idle he should remain. It is a revolutionary precept; but thanks to hunger and

的施舍对人更为有益，因为它就像仁慈的品性一样，用不着勉强，因此也就使受者加倍地高兴。接吻，是两人之间的事；说笑话，二十个人也可以听；然而，一旦有所牺牲，施恩者既然觉得痛苦，受惠者（只要他们是心地高尚的人）自不免心中有愧。说到义务，我们常常把做人要高高兴兴的义务估计得太低了。实际上，当我们高高兴兴的时候，我们就在无形之中给社会带来了好处，只是我们自己毫不觉察罢了；一旦这种好处显露出来，最感到惊奇的倒是那位施恩者。几天前，一个衣服破烂、光着脚丫的小男孩在街上追赶一个小圆弹儿[1]，他那欢天喜地的样子把街上的每一个人都逗乐了。有一个人心里正在犯愁，见了他不禁破颜一笑。他拦住这个小家伙，给他一点儿钱，说："瞧，高兴了还有这种好处！"如果说这个小孩儿刚才是满脸高兴的话，现在脸上的表情可是又高兴又迷惑不解了。就我个人来说，我认为这样奖励笑嘻嘻的孩子比奖励泪汪汪的孩子要好。不论在哪儿，让我为了别人的眼泪（除非是在舞台上流的眼泪）而拿出钱来，我才不干；但是，为了笑声我却不惜付出大价钱。碰见一个快乐的男人或女人，比捡到一张五镑钞票还要好。这样的人像是某种善良愿望的辐射中心，他或她一进入你的屋子，就好似房间里又点亮了一支蜡烛。他们究竟能不能论证第四十七道命题，我们且不必管——他们给人带来的好处不止于此，因为他们所证明的是那尘世可以居住的伟大真理。因此，如果一个人觉得只有懒散着才快乐，那就让他懒散着吧。这是一条革命箴言；

---

[1] 一种用手弹着玩的儿童玩具。

the workhouse, one not easily to be abused; and within practical limits, it is one of the most incontestable truths in the whole Body of Morality. Look at one of your industrious fellows for a moment, I beseech you. He sows hurry and reaps indigestion; he puts a vast deal of activity out to interest, and receives a large measure of nervous derangement in return. Either he absents himself entirely from all fellowship, and lives a recluse in a garret, with carpet slippers and a leaden inkpot; or he comes among people swiftly and bitterly, in a contraction of his whole nervous system, to discharge some temper before he returns to work. I do not care how much or how well he works, this fellow is an evil feature in other people's lives. They would be happier if he were dead. They could easier do without his services in the Circumlocution Office, than they can tolerate his fractious spirits. He poisons life at the well-head. It is better to be beggared out of hand by a scapegrace nephew, than daily hag-ridden by a peevish uncle.

And what, in God's name, is all this pother about? For what cause do they embitter their own and other people's lives? That a man should publish three or thirty articles a year, that he should finish or not finish his great allegorical picture, are questions of little interest to the world. The ranks of life are full; and although a thousand fall, there are always some to go into the breach. When they told Joan of Arc she should be at home minding women's work, she answered there were plenty to spin and wash. And so, even with your own rare gifts! When nature is

不过，多亏世上还有饥饿和济贫所，人们也很难把它任意实行；放在适当范围以内，它在人类的全部道德体系中倒也不失为一条不容置疑的真理。请你看一看那黾勉从公的人吧：他播下了慌慌张张，收获了消化不良；他为了求利到处奔忙，得到的却是精神失常。他要么远离人群，脚穿毡拖鞋，蛰居于阁楼之中，日与黑铅墨水壶为伴，做一个与世隔绝之人；要么他就带着满脸苦相，浑身神经紧紧收缩，匆匆来到众人当中，大发一顿脾气，再回去办他的公事。这位先生究竟干了多少工作，工作得究竟如何，姑且不论；首先，他在别人的生活当中就扮演了一个面目可憎的角色。只有等他死了，别人才能快活一点儿。大家受不了他那暴躁的脾气，也用不着他在等因奉此的衙门里的那一套公事。一句话，他把生活的河流从源头上给污染了。我宁可让一个败家子的侄子把我勒索得精光，也不愿被一个脾气乖戾的伯伯天天缠得我神魂不安。

而且，上帝明鉴，这样子鸡犬不宁究竟图个什么？他们自己不好好过日子，又把别人挤对得难受，到底所为何来？某某人一年发表三篇或者三十篇文章，某某人的巨作寓意画完成了或者完不成，对于世界来说都是无关宏旨的事。人生的行列总是满满的；哪怕有一千个人死掉，也总会有人去填补他们的空缺。有人告诉贞德[1]说她应该待在家里做女人家该做的事；她回答说，纺线、洗衣服的人已经够多了。所以，就算你有罕见的天才，

---

[1] 又译"冉·达克"（1412—1431），法国民族女英雄。

"so careless of the single life," why should we coddle ourselves into the fancy that our own is of exceptional importance? Suppose Shakespeare had been knocked on the head some dark night in *Sir* Thomas Lucy's preserves, the world would have wagged on better or worse, the pitcher gone to the well, the scythe to the corn, and the student to his book; and no one been any the wiser of the loss. There are not many works extant, if you look the alternative all over, which are worth the price of a pound of tobacco to a man of limited means. This is a sobering reflection for the proudest of our earthly vanities. Even a tobacconist may, upon consideration, find no great cause for personal vainglory in the phrase; for although tobacco is an admirable sedative, the qualities necessary for retailing it are neither rare nor precious in themselves. Alas and alas! You may take it how you will, but the services of no single individual are indispensable. Atlas was just a gentleman with a protracted nightmare! And yet you see merchants who go and labour themselves into a great fortune, and thence into the bankruptcy court; scribblers who keep scribbling at little articles until their temper is a cross to all who come about them, as though Pharaoh should set the Israelites to make a pin instead of a pyramid; and fine young men who work themselves into a decline, and are driven off in a hearse with white plumes upon it. Would

---

1 据传说，莎士比亚少年时代曾到乡绅托马斯·卢西爵士的禁猎地去偷鹿，并曾受到惩罚，因此史蒂文森有此假想。

又怎么着？造物主既然"对于个体的生命漠不关心"，我们又何必那么溺爱自己，认为自己的生命特别重要呢？假如说，某个漆黑的夜晚，在托马斯·卢西爵士[1]的禁猎区里，莎士比亚被打碎了脑袋，不管是好是歹，地球照样还要转动，水罐子照样还要打水，镰刀照样还要割庄稼，学生照样还要念书，谁也不会明白自己到底受了什么损失。如果把事情全面掂量一下，就会觉得：在一个手头不怎么宽裕的人看来，世上流传的作品当中，值得他拿出一磅烟草来换的还真没有几本。想到这一点，我们在尘世上最洋洋得意的好名之心也会冷静下来了。不过，烟店老板听了这话也大可不必飘飘然忘乎所以；因为，只要他动脑筋想想，就明白，尽管烟草是一种很好的镇静剂，可是烟草零售并不需要多么稀罕、多么了不得的本领。这真是呜呼又哀哉！你爱怎么想就怎么想，可是，不管哪一个人的事业都不是离了他就不行的。即使那个捎天巨人阿特拉斯[2]也不过是一位长期受苦难折磨的可敬君子罢了。尽管如此，商业家还是不惜奔忙、劳碌，要先发一笔大财，再走进破产法院；小文人还要舞文弄墨，写出几篇小文章，脾气愈来愈坏，周围的人们躲他像躲灾星，好似法老王[3]逼着以色列人不修金字塔，改做扣针；漂漂亮亮的小伙子干活不停，直到体力衰竭，然后让一辆装饰着白羽毛的灵车送走了事。你想，难道

---

2 希腊神话中背负天体的巨人。
3 古埃及的国王，据《旧约·出埃及记》，埃及法老曾强迫以色列人做种种苦工、折磨他们。

you not suppose these persons had been whispered, by the Master of the Ceremonies, the promise of some momentous destiny, and that this lukewarm bullet on which they play their farces was the bull's-eye and centre-point of all the universe? And yet it is not so. The ends for which they gave away their priceless youth, for all they know, may be chimerical or hurtful; the glory and riches they expect may never come, or may find them indifferent; and they and the world they inhabit are so inconsiderable that the mind freezes at the thought.

典礼官[1]就没有向这些人悄悄暗示,许诺给他们某种了不起的命运,并且告诉他们:他们在此扮演人生喜剧的微温的弹丸之地[2]就是整个宇宙的中心吗?然而,事实并非如此。他们为之献出无比宝贵的青春的目标,很可能只是一场幻梦,甚或是有害无益之事;他们所期待的荣耀和财富可能永不来临,即使到来也无足轻重;他们连同他们所栖息的世界是如此渺小,叫人想起简直不寒而栗。

---

1 指尘世一切活动的"司仪",如"命运之神"之类。
2 比喻地球。

弗吉尼亚·吴尔夫

1882—1941

弗吉尼亚·吴尔夫(Virginia Woolf, 1882—1941)是20世纪著名的英国女作家,主要成就在小说方面——她是"意识流"文学的开创者之一,用这种创作方法写了许多小说,不注重情节,而着重于用抒情式的手法进行细致的心理描写,以便写出人物内心世界的活动。同时,她也是一位散文家,善于用轻快活泼的文笔写出她对于自己所喜爱的作家和作品的印象。她这方面的文章主要收入题为《普通读者》初集、二集的两本评论集中。在这两本书的扉页上,引着18世纪英国作家约翰逊博士的一段话:"能与普通读者的意见不谋而合,在我是高兴的事;因为,在决定诗歌荣誉的权利时,尽管高雅的敏感和学术的教条也起着作用,但一般来说应该根据那未受文学偏见污损的普通读者的常识。"吴尔夫在提到她的《普通读者》第二集时,说它是"一本并非专门性的评论著作,只是从一个作家的角度,而非从一个学者或批评家的角度,来谈一谈自己偶然读到的某些人物传记和作品。作为一个小说家,我自然常常会对某一本书发生兴趣,但我也常常为了自娱而随意读一读、写一写,并不想建立什么理论体系。"换句话说,她这些评论,是一个具有高度文化修养和丰富创作经验的作家,在创作事业之余,用随笔的形式、轻松的笔调,抒写自己对于其他作家、作品的印象的文章。

现在,从《普通读者》第二集里选译了两篇文章。

第一篇写的是英国女权运动的先驱者玛丽·沃斯通克拉夫特(1759—1797)。玛丽是18世纪法国革命时期一个思想激进的女作家和政论家,著有《女权论》等书。她高尚、纯洁、精明

Virginia Woolf

能干、热情如火,但由于在爱情婚姻问题上理想过高,而所遇非人,终遭蹉跌,演出悲剧;后虽遇救,且逢知己,结为良伴,但体质已亏,在分娩中死去——这后一次婚姻的结晶便是玛丽·戈德温,即以后的雪莱夫人。玛丽·沃斯通克拉夫特的一生可以说是做了她自己的理想的实验品,证明了:在一个污浊的社会环境中,只凭幻想、热情办事,是要付出巨大代价的。像这样的历史悲剧,"只可有一,不可有二"。

如果说玛丽·沃斯通克拉夫特为了自己的理想,拿一生的幸福做实验,有时到了"以身饲虎"的地步,简直有点女堂·吉诃德的味道(这里把堂·吉诃德当作一个有高尚理想而不切实际的典型),那么,多萝西·华兹华斯(1771—1855)就是截然不同的另一种典型了。多萝西是著名诗人威廉·华兹华斯的妹妹,也是他在诗歌创作中的亲密助手。她一生中除了料理家务、支持哥哥专心从事诗歌写作,就是细心观察自然、人生,在日记中忠实地记下自己的观察所得,也记下华兹华斯在诗歌创作中的艰辛历程。她这部日记,本来只为记录个人对自然与人生的印象,只供她兄妹二人传看,并不准备发表,但后来却成为诗歌史上一座朴实无华的纪念碑,成为文学史和诗歌研究者的宝贵原始资料。多萝西不求文名,却不自觉地成为英国文学史上著名的日记作家了。吴尔夫的文章对多萝西的性格和她这部日记的艺术特色都有描述,可供参看。

弗吉尼亚·吴尔夫不仅是20世纪英国"意识流"小说流派的一位代表作家,也是20世纪一位英国随笔大家。这一点,从文学历史的长河中来看,是愈来愈清楚了。

Mary Wollstonecraft

Great wars are strangely intermittent in their effects. The French Revolution took some people and tore them asunder; others it passed over without disturbing a hair of their heads. Jane Austen, it is said, never mentioned it; Charles Lamb ignored it; Beau Brummell never gave the matter a thought. But to Wordsworth and to Godwin it was the dawn; unmistakably they saw

France standing on the top of golden hours,
And human nature seeming born again.

Thus it would be easy for a picturesque historian to lay side by side the most glaring contrasts—here in Chesterfield Street was Beau Brummell letting his chin fall carefully upon his cravat and discussing

---

1 此语不确。兰姆在青年时代曾和当时其他激进英国青年一样热烈拥护法国革命，并因此受到保守人士的攻击。他跟本文所提到的戈德温、霍尔克罗夫特以及亨特、黑兹利特保持着终生的友谊。(Winifred F. Courtney: *Young Charles Lamb 1775-1802*)

玛丽·沃斯通克拉夫特

说来也怪，重大事变的影响往往是因人而异的。法国革命把有些人紧紧抓住不放，一撕两半儿；对另一些人，它却轻轻放过，不动他们一根毫毛。简·奥斯丁，据说对法国革命就没有提过一个字；查尔斯·兰姆对它不予理睬；[1] 博·布鲁梅尔[2]对这件事连想也不想。但是，对于华兹华斯和戈德温[3]来说，它却是时代的黎明，他们清清楚楚地看见

> 法兰西站在黄金时代的顶端，
> 人性似乎正在经历着新生。

因此，若有哪一位善于描绘情景的历史家要想进行一番鲜明的对比，很容易找到事例：一方面，在切斯特菲尔德大街，博·布鲁梅尔小心翼翼地把自己的下巴贴

---

2 博·布鲁梅尔（Beau Brummell即George Bryan Brummell，1778—1840），英国上流社会的名流，以讲究美衣美食著称。

3 戈德温（William Godwin，1756—1836），英国作家和社会思想家，他的《政治正义论》一书曾对18至19世纪之交的英国以至欧洲思想界产生过重要影响。

in a tone studiously free from vulgar emphasis the proper cut of the lapel of a coat; and here in Somers Town was a party of ill-dressed, excited young men, one with a head too big for his body and a nose too long for his face, holding forth day by day over the tea-cups upon human perfectibility, ideal unity, and the rights of man. There was also a woman present with very bright eyes and a very eager tongue, and the young men, who had middle-class names, like Barlow and Holcroft and Godwin, called her simply "Wollstonecraft", as if it did not matter whether she were married or unmarried, as if she were a young man like themselves.

Such glaring discords among intelligent people—for Charles Lamb and Godwin, Jane Austen and Mary Wollstonecraft were all highly intelligent—suggest how much influence circumstances have upon opinions. If Godwin had been brought up in the precincts of the Temple and had drunk deep of antiquity and old letters at Christ's Hospital, he might never have cared a straw for the future of man and his rights in general. If Jane Austen had lain as a child on the landing to prevent her father from thrashing her mother, her soul might have burnt with such a passion against tyranny that all her novels might have been consumed in one cry for justice.

Such had been Mary Wollstonecraft's first experience of the joys of married life. And then her sister Everina had been married miserably

---

1 霍尔克罗夫特（Thomas Holcroft，1745—1809），出身下层的英国演员和剧作家，思想激进，和戈德温是同道。

着领结，又煞费苦心地尽量摆脱说话中粗俗的强调语势，正在那里谈论着上衣翻领的体面样式；而同时，在萨默斯镇，却有一伙衣履不整、慷慨激昂的青年(其中有一个大脑瓜、长鼻子的小伙子)，天天在那里一边喝茶一边高谈阔论人类的可完善性、理想的和谐以及人的权利。在场的还有一位明目闪闪、快嘴快舌的女子——那几个名字叫作巴尔罗、霍尔克罗夫特[1]和戈德温的中产阶级青年，都不拘礼节地叫她"沃斯通克拉夫特"，并不管她结婚没结婚，好像她跟他们一样也是小伙子。

同是才智之士，见解却如此悬殊(查尔斯·兰姆、简·奥斯丁、玛丽·沃斯通克拉夫特都是才分很高的人)，足见环境对人思想的影响是如何之大。如果戈德温从小生长在伦敦法学院一带，又在基督慈幼学校[2]上学，朝夕沉浸于古风旧习、古代典籍之中，那么，对于人类的未来以及人的权利，他大概根本不会发生兴趣。如果简·奥斯丁还是个小女孩的时候，曾经躺在楼梯拐弯的地方挡住她父亲不让打她妈妈，[3]那么，在她灵魂深处很可能会燃起一股反抗暴政的怒火，而她的全部小说也许就会化为一声正义的呐喊了。

这正是玛丽·沃斯通克拉夫特最早经历的天伦之乐。接着，她妹妹爱芙利娜[4]悲惨地出嫁，在马车里把结婚戒

---

2 指伦敦基督慈幼学校，兰姆曾在此上学。(这句话说的实际上是兰姆小时候的事。)
3 这句话说的实际上是玛丽·沃斯通克拉夫特小时候的事。
4 玛丽的二妹。

and had bitten her wedding ring to pieces in the coach. Her brother had been a burden on her; her father's farm had failed, and in order to start that disreputable man with the red face and the violent temper and the dirty hair in life again she had gone into bondage among the aristocracy as a governess—in short, she had never known what happiness was, and, in its default, had fabricated a creed fitted to meet the sordid misery of real human life. The staple of her doctrine was that nothing mattered save independence. "Every obligation we receive from our fellow-creatures is a new shackle, takes from our native freedom, and debases the mind." Independence was the first necessity for a woman; not grace or charm, but energy and courage and the power to put her will into effect were her necessary qualities. It was her highest boast to be able to say, "I never yet resolved to do anything of consequence that I did not adhere readily to it." Certainly Mary could say this with truth. When she was a little more than thirty she could look back upon a series of actions which she had carried out in the teeth of opposition. She had taken a house by prodigious efforts for her friend Fanny, only to find that Fanny's mind was changed and she did not want a house after all. She had started a school. She had persuaded Fanny into marrying Mr. Skeys. She had thrown up her school and gone to Lisbon alone to nurse Fanny when she died. On the voyage back she had forced the captain of the ship to rescue a wrecked French vessel by threatening to expose him if he refused. And when, overcome by a passion for Fuseli, she declared her wish to live with him and was refused flatly by his wife, she had put her principle of decisive action instantly into effect, and had gone to Paris determined to make her living by her pen.

指咬成了碎片。她的兄弟是她的累赘。她父亲的农场破产，为了让这个赤红脸、脏头发、暴性子、名声坏的汉子能够重新找到一条生活出路，玛丽只好去为贵族做奴仆，当家庭教师。[1]一句话，她从来不知道什么是幸福；正因为缺少幸福，她就虚构出一套信条以对付那人类现实生活中的污浊与不幸。她那套信条的要领就是：独立高于一切。"我们从其他人那里所接受的任何恩惠对于自己都是一种新的羁绊，它会减损我们天赋的自由，败坏我们的心灵。"一个女人，第一需要是独立；对于女人来说，必不可少的素质并不是美貌或风韵，而是能力、勇气以及把意志化为行动的魄力。她最感到自豪的，是她能够说出这句话："任何重大行动，我一旦下了决心，就义无反顾，坚守不渝。"玛丽这句话说得丝毫不假。她刚过了三十岁，回顾往事，就有一大串行动都是不顾别人反对而坚持进行的。她费了很大劲儿为好朋友范妮找房子，房子弄到手，才知道范妮改变了主意，又不想要房子了。她创办了一所学校。她说服范妮跟一位斯奇先生结婚。后来，范妮在里斯本快死了，她把学校搁下，一个人跑去服侍她。在归航途中，遇见一只法国船失事，她强迫船长去搭救，威胁说，如果他不肯，就揭发他。后来，她陷入了对菲尤泽利[2]的爱情而无法自拔，表示想和他生活在一起，被后者的妻子断然拒绝。然后，为了实行自己行动要果断的原则，她立即去巴黎，靠笔杆子自谋生活。

---

[1] 玛丽曾为一个贵族当家庭教师，干了一年，被贵族夫人所辞退，理由是小孩子们爱家庭教师胜过爱自己的母亲。
[2] 英国画家，生于瑞士。玛丽与菲尤泽利夫妇是好朋友。

The Revolution thus was not merely an event that had happened outside her; it was an active agent in her own blood. She had been in revolt all her life—against tyranny, against law, against convention. The reformer's love of humanity, which has so much of hatred in it as well as love, fermented within her. The outbreak of revolution in France expressed some of her deepest theories and convictions, and she dashed off in the heat of that extraordinary moment those two eloquent and daring books—the *Reply to Burke* and the *Vindication of the Rights of Woman*, which are so true that they seem now to contain nothing new in them—their originality has become our commonplace. But when she was in Paris lodging by herself in a great house, and saw with her own eyes the King whom she despised driving past surrounded by National Guards and holding himself with greater dignity than she expected, then, "I can scarcely tell you why," the tears came to her eyes. "I am going to bed," the letter ended, "and, for the first time in my life, I cannot put out the candle." Things were not so simple after all. She could not understand even her own feelings. She saw the most cherished of her convictions put into practice—and her eyes filled with tears. She had won fame and independence and the right to live her own life—and she wanted something different. "I do not want to be loved like a goddess," she wrote, "but I wish to be necessary to you." For Imlay, the fascinating American to whom her letter was addressed, had been very

---

1 柏克（Edmund Burke，1729—1797），英国政论家和演说家，曾著《反思法国大革命》，反对法国革命，受到进步人士的批驳。
2 指路易十六。

因此，法国革命，对她来说，不仅仅是在身外发生的一场重大事件，而是使她热血沸腾的一种原动力。她一生都在反抗——反抗着暴政，反抗着法律，反抗着传统。改革家所怀抱的既包含着爱也包含着不少恨的那种对人类的爱，激荡着她的全部身心。法国革命的爆发，体现了她衷心服膺的理论和信念；在那巨变的高潮之中，她急急写出了两部语言雄辩、内容大胆的书——《答柏克[1]》和《女权论》。这两部书里所说出的真理，在今天看来已经不新鲜了——它们当初所包含的石破天惊之论已经转化为我们今天的老生常谈。她在巴黎，独自住在一所大房子里。当她亲眼看见她平常蔑视的法国国王[2]被国民自卫军监押着，坐在马车里从大街经过的时候，跟她想象的相反，他那神情居然还保持着几分尊严；于是，"我简直说不清为什么，"泪水竟涌进了她的眼睛里。"我要上床睡觉了，"这封信结束时写道："可是，在我生平第一次，我不能把蜡烛熄掉。"世事毕竟不是那样简单，连她自己的感情她也无法理解。她看到自己生平最珍爱的信仰实现了——然而她的眼睛里却充满了泪水。这时，她已经赢得了声誉、独立和安排个人生活的权利——但她还需要另外一样东西。"我并不需要像女神那样为人所爱，"她写道："但我希望我在你的眼里是不可缺少的。"她这封信写给伊姆利[3]——这个有着迷人风

---

3 即美国商人吉尔伯特·伊姆利（Captain Gilbert Imlay, 1754—1828）。玛丽与他同居两年，生了一个女孩，还帮他经营商业。玛丽恪守自己关于男女爱情的理论，未举行正式婚礼，伊姆利在正式文件中称她是"Mary Imlay, my best friend and wife"，但他有了新欢，就把玛丽遗弃。

good to her. Indeed, she had fallen passionately in love with him. But it was one of her theories that love should be free—"that mutual affection was marriage and that the marriage tie should not bind after the death of love, if love should die." And yet at the same time that she wanted freedom she wanted certainty. "I like the word affection," she wrote, "because it signifies something habitual."

The conflict of all these contradictions shows itself in her face, at once so resolute and so dreamy, so sensual and so intelligent, and beautiful into the bargain with its great coils of hair and the large bright eyes that Southey thought the most expressive he had ever seen. The life of such a woman was bound to be tempestuous. Every day she made theories by which life should be lived; and every day she came smack against the rock of other people's prejudices. Every day too—for she was no pedant, no cold-blooded theorist—something was born in her that thrust aside her theories and forced her to model them afresh. She acted upon her theory that she had no legal claim upon Imlay; she refused to marry him; but when he left her alone week after week with the child she had borne him her agony was unendurable.

Thus distracted, thus puzzling even to herself, the plausible and treacherous Imlay cannot be altogether blamed for failing to follow the rapidity of her changes and the alternate reason and unreason of her

度的美国人对她很好。事实上，她已经热烈地爱上了他。但是，她的理论当中有一条：爱，应该是自由的——"双方有情即是结婚，而爱情一旦不存，在爱情死亡之后婚姻的束缚亦不复存在。"话虽如此，在她需要自由的同时，她也需要明确性。她写道："我喜欢感情这个字眼儿，因为它意味着某种习以为常的东西。"

所有这一切矛盾冲突，在她的脸上就显露出来了：她脸上的表情既是坚定果断的，又是充满幻想的；既是多情善感的，又是聪颖过人的；此外，她那纷披的鬈发、明媚的大眼又非常美丽动人——据骚塞[1]说，她那一双大眼乃他所见过的最脉脉含情的眼睛。这样一个女人的一生注定是不会平静的。每天，她都在制订生活的原则；每天，她都要一头撞在别人的偏见所构成的岩石上。另外，她并不是冬烘先生，也不是冷冰冰的理论家；所以，每天总有一些新的想法在她头脑中产生，把她原来的理论条条推到一边，迫使她把它们重新加以熔铸。根据她自己的原则，她对于伊姆利并没有法律上的权利，因此，她拒绝跟他结婚。然而，当他撇下她和她为他所生下的孩子，接连几周没有音信的时候，她的痛苦却简直无法忍受了。

因此，她心烦意乱，处在一种连她自己也迷惑不解的状态之中。不过，像她心灵里不断发生的那些理性与非理性的相互交错和急剧变化，那个嘴巴很甜、内心诡诈的伊姆利摸不清头脑，也实在不能完全怪他。即使她

---

[1] 骚塞（Robert Southey, 1774—1843），英国诗人。

moods. Even friends whose liking was impartial were disturbed by her discrepancies. Mary had a passionate, an exuberant, love of Nature, and yet one night when the colours in the sky were so exquisite that Madeleine Schweizer could not help saying to her, "Come, Mary—come, nature lover—and enjoy this wonderful spectacle—this constant transition from colour to colour," Mary never took her eyes off the Baron de Wolzogen. "I must confess," wrote Madame Schweizer, "that this erotic absorption made such a disagreeable impression on me, that all my pleasure vanished." But if the sentimental Swiss was disconcerted by Mary's sensuality, Imlay, the shrewd man of business, was exasperated by her intelligence. Whenever he saw her he yielded to her charm, but then her quickness, her penetration, her uncompromising idealism harassed him. She saw through his excuses; she met all his reasons; she was even capable of managing his business. There was no peace with her—he must be off again. And then her letters followed him, torturing him with their sincerity and their insight. They were so outspoken; they pleaded so passionately to be told the truth; they showed such a contempt for soap and alum and wealth and comfort; they repeated, as he suspected, so truthfully that he had only to say the word, "and you shall never hear of me more," that he could not endure it. Tickling minnows he had hooked a dolphin, and the creature rushed him through the waters till he was dizzy and only wanted to escape. After all, though he had played at theory-making too, he was a business

---

1 玛丽的一位女友。

那些无偏无私的朋友们也被她那种矛盾多变的脾气弄得不知所措。玛丽本来非常热爱大自然景色；然而，一天夜晚，天空出现了说不出多么美丽的彩霞，马德琳·施魏策尔[1]忍不住向她说："来呀，玛丽，你这位热爱大自然的人，快来欣赏这一派奇景——看一看这多种色彩的不停变幻吧！"一瞧，玛丽的眼睛却直勾勾地盯住沃尔措根男爵。"我必须承认，"施魏策尔夫人写道，"这样迷恋美色，使我产生了很不愉快的印象，我心里的一团高兴立刻化为乌有。"如果这位多愁善感的瑞士妇女因为玛丽的色欲表示而感到慌乱不安的话，那么，那个狡猾的商人伊姆利却是因为她智力过人而感到恼火。每次见面，他都为她的风韵而心折；可是，她的机敏、她的洞察力、她那不肯妥协的理想主义又使他苦恼。他的所有借口，她一看即穿；他的一切理由，她全能驳倒；就连他的生意，她也能替他代办。跟她在一起简直没法儿安静——他只好走开。但是，她的信也接踵而来，以她那真情实意和敏锐眼光折磨着他。这些信开门见山，迫切地求他说出实情，而对于肥皂、明矾[2]、财富、舒适统统表示极大的鄙视；这些信再三真诚地表示（他也这样担心）：只要他说出那句话，"你就再也听不到我的消息了。"——对这一切，他实在无法忍受。他本来想抓几条小鲤鱼玩玩，却钓上来一只大海豚——这玩意儿不由分说，把他带到滚滚波涛之中，弄得他晕头转向，只求早点摆脱出来。尽管他有时候也玩弄一些编造理论的

---

2 伊姆利经营的商品。

man, he depended upon soap and alum; "the secondary pleasures of life," he had to admit, "are very necessary to my comfort." And among them was one that for ever evaded Mary's jealous scrutiny. Was it business, was it politics, was it a woman that perpetually took him away from her? He shillied and shallied; he was very charming when they met; then he disappeared again. Exasperated at last, and half insane with suspicion, she forced the truth from the cook. A little actress in a strolling company was his mistress, she learnt. True to her own creed of decisive action, Mary at once soaked her skirts so that she might sink unfailingly, and threw herself from Putney Bridge. But she was rescued; after unspeakable agony she recovered, and then her "unconquerable greatness of mind," her girlish creed of independence, asserted itself again, and she determined to make another bid for happiness and to earn her living without taking a penny from Imlay for herself or their child.

It was in this crisis that she again saw Godwin, the little man with the big head, whom she had met when the French Revolution was making the young men in Somers Town think that a new world was being born. She met him—but that is a euphemism, for in fact Mary Wollstonecraft actually visited him in his own house. Was it the effect of the French Revolution? Was it the blood she had seen spilt on the pavement and the cries of the furious crowd that had rung in her ears that made it seem a matter of no importance whether she put on her cloak and went to visit Godwin in Somers Town, or waited in Judd Street West for Godwin to come to her? And what strange upheaval of human life was it that inspired that curious man, who was so queer a mixture of meanness and

游戏，但他终究是个商人，他是靠贩卖肥皂、明矾为生的；而且，他自己也承认："人生中一些低俗的消遣，对我的舒适来说是必不可少的。"在这些消遣当中，有一件事，无论玛丽怎样千方百计追查，也查不出来：他老是不在玛丽身边，究竟是为了生意？为了政治？还是为了另一个女人？他躲躲闪闪，见了面又甜言蜜语，可是一晃就又没影儿了。最后，她气极了，猜来猜去简直要把她急疯，她从厨娘的嘴里逼出了实话。这才知道：有一个巡回剧团里的娇小的女演员是他的情妇。玛丽按照自己的果断行动的原则办事，把自己裙子泡湿以保证能在水里下沉，于是就从帕特尼桥上跳下河去。但是，她被人救了上来。经过一段难以言说的痛苦，她又活下来了。然后，她那"不可征服的伟大心灵"，她那少女一般纯真的独立的信念，重新占了上风。她决心再一次叩击幸福之门，自谋生计，不要伊姆利给她和孩子一个铜板。

在这紧要关头，她又见到了戈德温——也就是她过去在萨默斯镇认识的那个大脑瓜、小个子的青年。那时候，法国革命使得他们这些年轻人认识到：一个新的世界正在诞生。她遇见了他——但这是委婉的说法；因为，实际上玛丽是自己到他家去访问的。这算不算是法国革命的一种影响呢？是不是因为她亲眼看见过鲜血溅洒在人行道上，耳朵里听到过愤怒人群的呐喊，所以，她才觉得无论自己披上斗篷到萨默斯镇去找戈德温，或者就在贾德西街等着戈德温来找自己，都是无所谓的事了呢？在戈德温这个怪人身上，鄙俗小气与豁达大度、冷

magnanimity, of coldness and deep feeling—for the memoir of his wife could not have been written without unusual depth of heart—to hold the view that she did right—that he respected Mary for trampling upon the idiotic convention by which women's lives were tied down? He held the most extraordinary views on many subjects, and upon the relations of the sexes in particular. He thought that reason should influence even the love between men and women. He thought that there was something spiritual in their relationship. He had written that "marriage is a law, and the worst of all laws ... marriage is an affair of property, and the worst of all properties." He held the belief that if two people of the opposite sex like each other, they should live together without any ceremony, or, for living together is apt to blunt love, twenty doors off, say, in the same street. And he went further; he said that if another man liked your wife "this will create no difficulty. We may all enjoy her conversation, and we shall all be wise enough to consider the sensual intercourse a very trivial object." True, when he wrote those words he had never been in love; now for the first time he was to experience that sensation. It came very quietly and naturally, growing "with equal advances in the mind of each" from those talks in Somers Town, from those discussions upon everything under the sun which they held so improperly alone in his rooms. "It was friendship melting into love..."

漠无情与深情蜜意奇特地混合在一起[1]（像他为妻子所写的那部回忆录，若没有不同寻常的深厚感情，是写不出来的）——不知人类生活中哪一桩惊人的巨变启示了他，使他认识到玛丽做得很对——他尊敬玛丽，正因为她把束缚妇女一生的愚蠢传统踩在脚下。他对于很多问题的看法都很特别，尤其特别的是他对于两性关系问题的看法。他认为理性应该左右着男女之间的爱情。他还认为在男女关系上存在着某种纯精神的东西。他写道："婚姻是一种法律，而且，在一切法律中它是最坏的法律……婚姻又是一种财产关系，而且，在一切财产中它是最坏的财产。"他主张：如果一男一女相互喜爱，他们不必经过任何仪式就可以同居；如果同居容易使爱情减色，也可以住在同一条街上，譬如说，隔着二十道门。不仅如此，他还说：如果另外一个男人喜欢你的妻子，"这也不会产生什么难题。我们都可以和她交往，而且，我们既然都是有智慧的人，那么自会把肉欲关系看作不值一提的小事。"显然，他写这些话的时候，还根本没有恋爱的经验；现在，他对于爱情才有了亲身体会。在萨默斯镇，戈德温的房间里，他们两人单独在一起，不拘礼法地谈论着在阳光下发生的一切事情——这样，爱情悄悄地、无拘无束地到来了，"以同样的步调在双方心中增长。"他写道："友谊，自自然然融化为爱情……。按

---

[1] 戈德温原来是非英国国教派的牧师，后信仰无神论，成为一个有空想社会主义色彩的作家、理论家，为了谋生还做过书商。像他这样一个走过曲折生活道路的人，性格自然不会那样单纯。安德烈·莫洛亚的《雪莱传》对于戈德温的性格有不少描写（可能带有夸张），可参看。

he wrote. "When, in the course of things, the disclosure came, there was nothing in a manner for either party to disclose to the other." Certainly they were in agreement upon the most essential points; they were both of opinion, for instance, that marriage was unnecessary. They would continue to live apart. Only when Nature again intervened, and Mary found herself with child, was it worth while to lose valued friends, she asked, for the sake of a theory? She thought not, and they were married. And then that other theory—that it is best for husband and wife to live apart—was not that also incompatible with other feelings that were coming to birth in her? "A husband is a convenient part of the furniture of the house," she wrote. Indeed, she discovered that she was passionately domestic. Why not, then, revise that theory too, and share the same roof? Godwin should have a room some doors off to work in; and they should dine out separately if they liked—their work, their friends, should be separate. Thus they settled it, and the plan worked admirably. The arrangement combined "the novelty and lively sensation of a visit with the more delicious and heartfelt pleasures of domestic life". Mary admitted that she was happy; Godwin confessed that, after all one's philosophy, it was "extremely gratifying" to find that "there is someone who takes an interest in one's happiness". All sorts of powers and emotions were liberated in Mary by her new satisfaction. Trifles gave her an exquisite pleasure—the sight of Godwin and Imlay's child playing together; the thought of their own child who was to be born; a day's jaunt into the country. One day, meeting Imlay in the New Road, she greeted him without bitterness. But, as Godwin wrote, "Ours is not an idle happiness, a paradise of selfish and transitory pleasures." No, it

照事情的发展过程，关系明确之时，双方业已没有什么东西需要表白。"的确，他们两人在根本问题上的观点都是融合无间的，例如，他们都认为结婚没有必要。所以，他们打算继续分开居住。不过，大自然再一次进行了干预，玛丽发现自己怀了孕。她这才提出问题：难道值得为了一条原则而抛弃尊贵的朋友吗？回答当然是不值得。于是，他们就结了婚。另外，还有一条原则——丈夫和妻子最好分开居住——是不是也跟她新近产生的其他感情难以并存呢？她写道："丈夫是屋子里一件方便的家具。"确实，她发现自己现在对家务非常热心。因此，何不把这条原则也修改下，两个人都在同一屋顶之下过日子呢？戈德温可以隔几道门在另一间房子里做事；如果高兴，他们可以各自去外边吃饭——他们两个人的工作和朋友应该分开。他们的计划进行得很美满，生活就这样安定下来了。这种安排"把知友来访带来的那种新鲜活泼的意味跟家庭生活中真情实意的美妙乐趣"都结合在一起了。玛丽说自己是幸福的；戈德温也承认：多年来只跟哲学打交道，如今找到了"一个对自己的幸福密切关心的人"，那是"十分令人满意的"。过上新的生活心满意足，玛丽的力量和热情全部解放出来了。一点点琐碎小事也使她极端高兴，例如：看见戈德温跟伊姆利的小孩在一起玩儿，想起他们就要出生的婴儿，偶尔到乡下远足一天。一天，在新路碰上了伊姆利，玛丽毫无怨恨地向他问好，但是，戈德温写道："我们的幸福并非百无聊赖地打发日子，也不是自私的短暂欢乐的天

too was an experiment, as Mary's life had been an experiment from the start, an attempt to make human conventions conform more closely to human needs. And their marriage was only a beginning; all sorts of things were to follow after. Mary was going to have a child. She was going to write a book to be called *The Wrongs of Women*. She was going to reform education. She was going to come down to dinner the day after her child was born. She was going to employ a midwife and not a doctor at her confinement—but that experiment was her last. She died in child-birth. She whose sense of her own existence was so intense, who had cried out even in her misery, "I cannot bear to think of being no more—or losing myself—nay, it appears to me impossible that I should cease to exist," died at the age of thirty-six. But she has her revenge. Many millions have died and been forgotten in the hundred and thirty years that have passed since she was buried; and yet as we read her letters and listen to her arguments and consider her experiments, above all that most fruitful experiment, her relation with Godwin, and realise the high-handed and hot-blooded manner in which she cut her way to the quick of life, one form of immortality is hers undoubtedly: she is alive and active, she argues and experiments, we hear her voice and trace her influence even now among the living.

堂。"的确,这又是一番试验,正像玛丽的一生从开始起就是一种试验,一种使得人类的传统习俗如何能够更加密切地适应人类需要的尝试。他们两人结婚,只是试验的开头,各种各样的事情还要随之而来。玛丽的小孩子就要生下来了。她还要写一部书,叫作《妇女之苦》。她还要改革教育。她打算等孩子一生下来,第二天就下床来吃饭。她打算在分娩的时候,不请医生而雇一个接生婆——然而,这却是她最后一次试验了。她在分娩中死去了。这么一位女人,她生存的意志是那样强烈,在她极端痛苦之中,她仍然高叫:"我一想起自己就要死去——就要失去自己的生命——简直无法忍受。不,在我看来,我竟然不再生存——这简直是不可能的事。"但她终于在三十六岁上去世了。然而,她还是向命运进行了报复。在她入土之后的一百三十年来,千千万万死去的人都被忘记了;可是,当我们读着她的信札,听着她的论辩,再想一想她所进行过的种种试验,特别是那次最有成效的试验,亦即她和戈德温的结合,认清了她是怎样以大刀阔斧、热血沸腾的方式在人生要害处开辟着自己的道路,我们就可以看出,她毫无疑问地已经得到了永生——她现在仍然生气勃勃地活动着,争辩着,尝试着。我们仍然听得见她的呼声,甚至在活着的人们当中还能找到她的踪迹。

Dorothy Wordsworth

Two highly incongruous travellers, Mary Wollstonecraft and Dorothy Wordsworth, followed close upon each other's footsteps. Mary was in Altona on the Elbe in 1795 with her baby; three years later Dorothy came there with her brother and Coleridge. Both kept a record of their travels; both saw the same places, but the eyes with which they saw them were very different. Whatever Mary saw served to start her mind upon some theory, upon the effect of government, upon the state of the people, upon the mystery of her own soul. The beat of the oars on the waves made her ask, "Life, what are you? Where goes this breath? This *I* so much alive? In what element will it mix, giving and receiving fresh energy?" And sometimes she forgot to look at the sunset and looked instead at the Baron Wolzogen. Dorothy, on the other hand, noted what was before her accurately, literally, and with prosaic precision. "The walk very pleasing between Hamburgh and Altona. A large piece of ground planted with trees, and intersected by gravel walks. ... The ground on the opposite side of the Elbe appears marshy." Dorothy never railed against "the cloven hoof of despotism". Dorothy never asked

多萝西·华兹华斯

两个迥然不同的人，玛丽·沃斯通克拉夫特和多萝西·华兹华斯，曾经一前一后出外旅行。1795年，玛丽带着她的婴儿在易北河上的阿尔托纳住过一时；三年以后，多萝西跟着她哥哥和柯尔律治也到这里来了。她们两个人都写了旅行记——两个人游历的地方完全一样，但她们看待这些地方的眼光却大不相同。玛丽所看到的一切，促使她思考某种理论，思考政府的效能、人民的状况以及她自己心灵的奥秘。船桨拍打着水波的声音使她发出了这样的疑问："生命，你究竟是什么？这一口气究竟要飘流到何方？我还是像这样活着的我吗？在它发出并吸收了新的能量之后，它究竟要融化到什么样的元素中去呢？"有时候，她只顾盯着沃尔措根男爵，而忘了观看夕阳残照。而多萝西却将她眼前所见之物，用准确细密的文字实实在在、原原本本地记录下来。"从阿尔托纳散步到汉堡是非常愉快的。在一大片栽种着树木的土地上，有一条条沙砾小路穿过。……易北河对岸的地面上看来却是沼泽纵横。"多萝西从来不去骂那"专制主义的魔

"men's questions" about exports and imports; Dorothy never confused her own soul with the sky. This "*I* so much alive", was ruthlessly subordinated to the trees and the grass. For if she let "I" and its rights and its wrongs and its passions and its suffering get between her and the object, she would be calling the moon "the Queen of the Night"; she would be talking of dawn's "orient beams"; she would be soaring into reveries and rhapsodies and forgetting to find the exact phrase for the ripple of moonlight upon the lake. It was like "herrings in the water"—she could not have said that if she had been thinking about herself. So while Mary dashed her head against wall after wall, and cried out, "Surely something resides in this heart that is not perishable—and life is more than a dream", Dorothy went on methodically at Alfoxden noting the approach of spring. "The sloe in blossom, the hawthorn green, the larches in the park changed from black to green, in two or three days." And next day, 14th April 1798, "the evening very stormy, so we staid indoors. *Mary Wollstonecraft's Life*, &c., came." And the day after they walked in the squire's grounds and noticed that "Nature was very successfully striving to make beautiful what art had deformed—ruins, hermitages, &c., &c." There is no reference to Mary Wollstonecraft; it seems as if her life and all its storms had been swept away in one of those compendious et ceteras, and yet the next sentence reads like an unconscious comment. "Happily we cannot shape the huge hills, or carve out the valleys according to our fancy." No, we cannot reform, we must not rebel; we can only accept and try to understand the message of

鬼"。她从来不提那些关于出口、入口一类的"男人们的问题";她也不会把自己的灵魂和天空搅混在一起。"这样活着的我",对她来说,是无条件地从属于那些花草树木的。因为,如果她让"我"和它的是是非非、哀乐苦痛介入到她和客观事物之间,那么,她就得把月亮叫作"黑夜的女王",她就得大谈什么黎明时"灿烂夺目的光芒",她就要翱翔于梦幻和狂想的缥缈之境,而无心去为那湖面上月光粼粼的景色找出确切的词句加以描绘。还有,"水底的鲱鱼"——如果她尽顾想自己的心事,当然也就无暇去写了。因此,当玛丽一次又一次碰壁,高叫着:"在这颗心里一定存在着某种永生不灭的东西——人生绝不是幻梦一场",多萝西却在阿尔富克斯登[1]慢条斯理地记录着春天到来的脚步:"野李树开花了,山楂丛发青了,公园里的落叶松也由黑变绿——这都是在两三天之内发生的事。"第二天,即1798年4月14日,写道:"黄昏,风狂雨暴,我们足不出户。收到《玛丽·沃斯通克拉夫特传》等书。"次日,他们在乡绅的空地里散步,看到"不少为人力损毁得不成样子的东西,正由大自然着意装点、使之美化——荒废的房址,隐者的旧居,等等,等等"。对于玛丽·沃斯通克拉夫特则一字未提——似乎她那充满暴风雨的一生,用一个简单的"等等"就打发掉了;然而,下边的一句话好像是某种不自觉之中流露出来的评论:"幸好,我们无权根据个人意志去塑造大山,开辟峡谷。"是的,我们无权去改动什么,更不去抗拒;我们只能接受

---

[1] 在英格兰南部萨默塞特郡,华兹华斯兄妹于1797—1798年间在此居住。

Nature. And so the notes go on.

Spring passed; summer came; summer turned to autumn; it was winter, and then again the sloes were in blossom and the hawthorns green and spring had come. But it was spring in the North now, and Dorothy was living alone with her brother in a small cottage at Grasmere in the midst of the hills. Now after the hardships and separations of youth they were together under their own roof; now they could address themselves undisturbed to the absorbing occupation of living in the heart of Nature and trying, day by day, to read her meaning. They had money enough at last to let them live together without the need of earning a penny. No family duties or professional tasks distracted them. Dorothy could ramble all day on the hills and sit up talking to Coleridge all night without being scolded by her aunt for unwomanly behaviour. The hours were theirs from sunrise to sunset, and could be altered to suit the season. If it was fine, there was no need to come in; if it was wet, there was no need to get up. One could go to bed at any hour. One could let the dinner cool if the cuckoo were shouting on the hill and William had not found the exact epithet he wanted. Sunday was a day like any other. Custom, convention, everything was subordinated to the absorbing, exacting, exhausting task of living in the heart of Nature and writing poetry. For exhausting it was. William would make his head ache in the effort to find the right word. He would go on hammering at a poem until Dorothy was afraid to suggest an alteration. A chance phrase of hers would run in his head and make it impossible for him to get back

并尽量理解大自然的信息。——日记就这么样地写下去。

春去，夏来，夏又到秋；冉冉便是冬天，于是野李树又开了花，山楂树又发了青，再一次春回大地了。现在是北英格兰的春天，多萝西和她哥哥住在格拉思弥尔[1]高山丛中一个小村子里，经历了艰苦备尝、骨肉分离的少年时代，他们终于在自己的家屋中相聚；现在，他们生活在大自然的怀抱里，可以不受干扰地从事自己一心向往的事业，天天努力领会大自然的启示。他们手头宽裕，足够维持生活，无须为衣食奔走。既无家务之累，也无职业任务分他们的心。多萝西可以整个白天在山上跑着玩儿，晚上和柯尔律治谈上一个通宵，没有舅妈骂她不像个女孩儿家的样子。日出到日落，时间都属于他们自己，作息方式可以根据季节变化来加以调整。天气好，不必待在屋里；下雨天，躺在床上不起。什么时候睡觉都行。如果有一只杜鹃在山头兀自啼叫，而威廉一直想不出什么确切的词句来描写它，那就让做好的饭放凉也没关系。星期天跟其他日子没有什么区别。习惯，传统，一切，都得从属于那必须全神贯注、付出极大努力、令人疲惫不堪的唯一任务——在大自然的怀抱里生活、写诗。那真是把人磨得筋疲力尽。为了寻找一个准确的字眼儿，威廉用尽心血，累得头疼。每首诗，他总是推敲了再推敲，所以多萝西不敢提什么改动意见。她偶尔说了一句半句话，被他听见，记在脑子里，

---

[1] 地名，在英格兰北部著名的"湖区"（Lake District）。自1799年起华兹华斯兄妹以及后来的华兹华斯的妻子住在这里一所叫作"鸽舍"（Dove Cottage）的农屋里。

into the proper mood. He would come down to breakfast and sit "with his shirt neck unbuttoned, and his waistcoat open", writing a poem on a Butterfly which some story of hers had suggested, and he would eat nothing, and then he would begin altering the poem and again would be exhausted.

It is strange how vividly all this is brought before us considering that the diary is made up of brief notes such as any quiet woman might make of her garden's changes and her brother's moods and the progress of the seasons. It was warm and mild, she notes, after a day of rain. She met a cow in a field. "The cow looked at me, and I looked at the cow, and whenever I stirred the cow gave over eating." She met an old man who walked with two sticks—for days on end she met nothing more out of the way than a cow eating and an old man walking. And her motives for writing are common enough—"because I will not quarrel with myself, and because I shall give William pleasure by it when he comes home again." It is only gradually that the difference between this rough notebook and others discloses itself; only by degrees that the brief notes unfurl in the mind and open a whole landscape before us, that the plain statement proves to be aimed so directly at the object that if we look exactly along the line that it points we shall see precisely what she saw. "The moonlight lay upon the hills like snow." "The air was become still, the lake of a bright slate colour, the hills darkening. The bays shot into the low fading shores. Sheep resting. All things quiet." "There was no one waterfall above another—it was the sound of waters in the air—the

他的心情就再也无法平静下来。有时候，他下楼来吃早饭，却坐在餐桌旁，"衬衣的领口不扣，背心也敞开"，写着一首从她谈话中得到构思的咏蝴蝶诗，写着写着把吃东西都忘了，而且对那首诗改了又改，直到又是筋疲力尽为止。

这部完全由只言片语所构成的日记，竟能使这一些如此活灵活现地重现在我们眼前，想来真有点奇怪，因为任何一个性格沉静的妇女都能像这样地把她花园里的变化、她哥哥的种种心情和季节的转换记载下来。一整天的雨后（她记述道），天气温暖而和煦。她在田野里碰见一头母牛。"那头母牛望着我，我也望着那头母牛；我只要稍微动弹一下，那头母牛就停止吃草。"她还遇见过一个拄两根棍子走路的老人——一连多少天，除了吃草的母牛、走路的老人，她再也看不到什么不寻常的事情。而她记这些日记的目的也很平常——"因为，一来，我不想一个人在那里自寻烦恼；二来，等威廉回家，可以让他看了高兴一下。"只是，渐渐地这部简括的札记与其他札记的不同之处就显露出来了：随着这些短短的日记在我们心目中一点一点地展开，我们眼前便呈现出一片广阔的景象，这才看出那质朴无华的记述紧扣所描写的事物，只要我们的眼光朝着它所指出的方向看去。定可如实地看到她所见到的事物。"月光像雪一样落在山上。""空气一片寂静，湖水现出亮亮的蓝灰色，群山一派苍茫。湾流冲向那低低的、幽暗的湖滨。羊群在休息。一切都是静悄悄的。""那上游和下游的瀑布，好像并不是一个一个的瀑布，而像是从天而降的涛声——天上的

voice of the air." Even in such brief notes one feels the suggestive power which is the gift of the poet rather than of the naturalist, the power which, taking only the simplest facts, so orders them that the whole scene comes before us, heightened and composed, the lake in its quiet, the hills in their splendour. Yet she was no descriptive writer in the usual sense. Her first concern was to be truthful—grace and symmetry must be made subordinate to truth. But then truth is sought because to falsify the look of the stir of the breeze on the lake is to tamper with the spirit which inspires appearances. It is that spirit which goads her and urges her and keeps her faculties for ever on the stretch. A sight or a sound would not let her be till she had traced her perception along its course and fixed it in words, though they might be bald, or in an image, though it might be angular. Nature was a stern taskmistress. The exact prosaic detail must be rendered as well as the vast and visionary outline. Even when the distant hills trembled before her in the glory of a dream she must note with literal accuracy "the glittering silver line on the ridge of the backs of the sheep", or remark how "the crows at a little distance from us became white as silver as they flew in the sunshine, and when they went still further, they looked like shapes of water passing over the green fields". Always trained and in use, her powers of observation became in time so expert and so acute that a day's walk stored her mind's eye with a vast assembly of curious objects to be sorted at leisure. How strange the sheep looked mixed with the soldiers at Dumbarton Castle! For some reason the sheep looked their real size, but the soldiers looked like puppets. And then the movements of the sheep were so

声音。"即使在这样短短的日记中,我们也可以感觉到那种并非属于博物学者,而是属于诗人天赋的暗示能力,也就是说,抓住非常普通的事实,略加点染,那整个景象,宁静的湖水,壮丽的群山,就以浓郁的色调、天然的姿态出现在我们眼前。然而,她却又不是一般意义上的描写文作者。她首先关心的是力求真实——优美和对称都得附丽于真实才行。而真实之所以需要加以探索,又是因为如果在描写中把微风拂动湖水的景象稍加歪曲,也就有损那支配着表面风貌的精神。正是这种精神刺激着她,推动着她,使得她的才能得到充分发挥。每一种景象,每一种声音,只要她有感于心,她总要把这一感觉的来龙去脉进行一番探索,并且用文字把它记录下来,不管这文字多么质朴无华;或者把它凝练为某种形象,不管这形象多么生硬拙笨。大自然是一个严峻的女监工,她要求:无论那浩浩茫茫、幻影一般的外形轮廓,还是那毫发毕现的平凡细节,都得描摹出来。甚至当梦境般壮丽的远山在她面前巍巍颤动,她仍然要一丝不苟、原原本本地记下"羊群脊背上那闪闪烁烁的银白色的轮廓线",并且写道:"向远处望去,在阳光下飞翔的乌鸦变成了银白色;当它们向更远处飞时,就像水波荡漾似的在绿色的田野上滚动。"由于经常练习、运用,她的观察力磨炼得非常纯熟、敏锐;在外边步行一天,就能给她那心灵的眼睛贮存下好大一批奇闻异事,足够她在暇日从容加以拣选。譬如说,在邓巴顿城堡外,羊群和士兵混搅一起,又是多么奇怪的现象啊!不知什么原因,那些羊群看去和实物一样大小,而那些士兵却像是些木偶;那些羊群的动作姿

natural and fearless, and the motion of the dwarf soldiers was so restless and apparently without meaning. It was extremely queer. Or lying in bed she would look up at the ceilling and think how the varnished beams were "as glossy as black rocks on a sunny day cased in ice". Yes, they "crossed each other in almost as intricate and fantastic a manner as I have seen the underboughs of a large beechtree withered by the depth of the shade above. ... It was like what I should suppose an underground cave or temple to be, with a dripping or moist roof, and the moonlight entering in upon it by some means or other, and yet the colours were more like melted gems. I lay looking up till the light of the fire faded away. ... I did not sleep much."

Indeed, she scarcely seemed to shut her eyes. They looked and they looked, urged on not only by an indefatigable curiosity but also by reverence, as if some secret of the utmost importance lay hidden beneath the surface. Her pen sometimes stammers with the intensity of the emotion that she controlled as De Quincey said that her tongue stammered with the conflict between her ardour and her shyness when she spoke. But controlled she was. Emotional and impulsive by nature, her eyes "wild and starting", tormented by feelings which almost mastered her, still she must control, still she must repress, or she would fail in her task—she would cease to see. But if one subdued oneself, and resigned one's private agitations, then, as if in reward, Nature would bestow an exquisite satisfaction. "Rydale was very beautiful, with spear-shaped streaks of polished steel. ... It calls home the heart to quietness.

态自自然然、无所畏惧，而那些侏儒似的士兵的行动却是躁乱不安、看起来毫无意义。——这真是奇怪极了。有时候，她躺在床上，仰望天花板，觉得那些上了油漆的屋梁"发出光泽，好像是在阳光下一条条冰封着的乌黑岩石"。是的，它们"相互交叉，使我想起自己见过的一株浓荫覆顶、风雨剥蚀的大山毛榉树——它那枝柯交错、纷歧披离之状仿佛与这些屋梁近似……天花板好似我假想中的一个地下洞窟或宫殿，窟顶潮湿滴水，月光曲曲折折泻入，色调犹如颜色浑然冲淡的宝石。我躺着仰望，直到炉火熄灭。……一夜很少成眠。"

确实，她似乎总是把眼睛睁得大大的，不停地观察着，不光是为了那不知疲倦的好奇心，也是由于崇敬的心情，觉得有某种至关重要的秘密隐藏在事物的表面底下。有时候，由于她尽量控制自己的热烈感情，她的笔下不免吞吞吐吐。正像德·昆西说的，她说话时因为热情与羞怯相冲突而有点儿口吃。但她还是控制住了自己。她的脾气本来是容易感情冲动的，为那几乎支配了她的情感所折磨，她的眼睛常常带着"狂热而吃惊的神情"；但她必须控制自己，压抑自己，不然的话，她就无法完成自己的任务——她就只好停止自己的观察活动。然而，对于一个能克制自己，能捐弃自己的隐秘激情的人，好像作为报偿一样，大自然就要给予一种异乎寻常的满足。她写道："雷德尔[1]的景色非常美丽，天空上泛出好像一片片叶子似的发亮的钢灰色条纹。……这使得我的心归于宁

---

[1] 英格兰西北部湖区的地名。

I had been very melancholy," she wrote. For did not Coleridge come walking over the hills and tap at the cottage door late at night—did she not carry a letter from Coleridge hidden safe in her bosom?

Thus giving to Nature, thus receiving from Nature, it seemed, as the arduous and ascetic days went by, that Nature and Dorothy had grown together in perfect sympathy—a sympathy not cold or vegetable or inhuman because at the core of it burnt that other love for "my beloved", her brother, who was indeed its heart and inspiration. William and Nature and Dorothy herself, were they not one being? Did they not compose a trinity, self-contained and self-sufficient and independent whether indoors or out? They sit indoors. It was

about ten o'clock and a quiet night. The fire flickers and the watch ticks. I hear nothing but the breathing of my Beloved as he now and then pushes his book forward, and turns over a leaf.

And now it is an April day, and they take the old cloak and lie in John's grove out of doors together.

William heard me breathing, and rustling now and then, but we both lay still and unseen by one another. He thought that it would be sweet thus to lie in the grave, to hear the peaceful sounds of the earth, and just to know that our dear friends were near. The lake was still; there was a boat out.

静。我本来是非常忧郁的。"因为，柯尔律治不是曾经翻山越岭，深夜来到他们居住的农舍敲门——而她不是也曾经把柯尔律治的一封信深深藏在怀里带回来吗？

　　这样，一方面向大自然做出奉献，一方面又从大自然得到报偿。随着这辛勤、刻苦的岁月的流逝，在大自然和多萝西之间似乎发展出某种水乳交融般的共鸣——这共鸣并不是冷冰冰、木呆呆、无人情味的，因为在它的核心之中还燃烧着对于"我亲爱的人"，亦即对于她的哥哥的热爱，而他实际上是这一共鸣的中心和鼓舞者。威廉，大自然，多萝西，岂就不是同一个存在吗？无论在室内、户外，他们岂不总是构成一个万物皆备、无求于人、独立不羁的三位一体吗？他们在室内静坐，这时——

　　大约十点钟，在一个静悄悄的夜晚。炉火摇曳，钟声嘀嗒。除了我亲爱的人呼吸之外，我什么声音也听不见——他不时推推书本，翻过一张书页。

　　4月里的一天，他们带上破斗篷，到屋子外边的约翰丛林里躺下。

　　威廉时而听见我的呼吸声和衣服沙沙声，但是我们两个人都静静地躺着，谁也看不见谁。他认为如果像这样躺在坟墓里，谛听大地宁静的声音，而且知道自己亲爱的朋友就在身边，倒是很美妙的事。湖水平静；有一只小船在湖面上。

It was a strange love, profound, almost dumb, as if brother and sister had grown together and shared not the speech but the mood, so that they hardly knew which felt, which spoke, which saw the daffodils or the sleeping city; only Dorothy stored the mood in prose, and later William came and bathed in it and made it into poetry. But one could not act without the other. They must feel, they must think, they must be together. So now, when they had lain out on the hill-side they would rise and go home and make tea, and Dorothy would write to Coleridge, and they would sow the scarlet beans together, and William would work at his "Leech Gatherer", and Dorothy would copy the lines for him. Rapt but controlled, free yet strictly ordered, the homely narrative moves naturally from ecstasy on the hills to baking bread and ironing linen and fetching William his supper in the cottage.

The cottage, though its garden ran up into the fells, was on the highroad. Through her parlour window Dorothy looked out and saw whoever might be passing—a tall beggar woman perhaps with her baby on her back; an old soldier; a coroneted landau with touring ladies peering inquisitively inside. The rich and the great she would let pass—they interested her no more than cathedrals or picture galleries or great cities; but she could never see a beggar at the door without asking him in and questioning him closely. Where had he been? What had he seen? How many children had he? She searched into the lives of the poor as if they held in them the same secret as the hills. A tramp eating cold bacon over the kitchen fire might have been a starry night, so closely she

这是一种奇异、奥妙而且几乎是无声的爱，好像这一对兄妹生长在一起，不仅语言，连心情也是完全相同的。因此他们简直不知道两个人之中究竟是谁在感受，谁在说话，谁在欣赏水仙花，谁在观看入睡的城市——不同之处仅仅在于：多萝西先把这种思绪写成散文、储存下来，然后威廉也来沉浸于其中，并把它写成诗歌。但两个人缺一不可。他们必须共同感受，共同思想，共同生存。这时正是如此：他们先在户外山坡上躺了一阵儿，起来回家弄茶；然后，多萝西给柯尔律治写信；接着，他们一块儿播种红花菜豆；然后，威廉写他的《采集水蛭的人》，多萝西为他抄写诗稿。既是心荡神移，又能有所控制；既是无拘无束，又能井然有序——这部日记娓娓叙来，既描写令人迷醉的山上风光，也述说着烤面包、熨衬衣以及在农舍里给威廉端晚饭这些家常琐事。

这所农舍，虽然后园延伸到荒野之中，门前却临着大路。从她的起居室窗口向外望去，多萝西可以看到路上走过的每一个人：一个高高大大的女乞丐，在她脊梁上也许还背着她的婴儿；一个老兵；一辆华贵的四轮马车，坐在里边游山玩水的贵妇人们好奇地向外窥看。那些有钱的贵人们，她都放过不管——她对于他们的兴趣，也不过像对于大教堂、画馆和大城市的一样。但是，如果她在门口遇见一个乞丐，她就一定要把他叫进屋里来，详详细细地打听一番：他从什么地方来？见过些什么？他有几个孩子？她对这些穷人们的生活寻根问底，仿佛其中也像群山似的隐藏着什么秘密。一个流浪汉在她的厨房里一边烤火、一边吃着冷咸肉，这对于她来说就如那星光灿

247

watched him; so clearly she noted how his old coat was patched "with three bellshaped patches of darker blue behind, where the buttons had been", how his beard of a fortnight's growth was like "grey plush". And then as they rambled on with their tales of seafaring and the press-gang and the Marquis of Granby, she never failed to capture the one phrase that sounds on in the mind after the story is forgotten, "What, you are stepping westward?" "To be sure there is great promise for virgins in Heaven." "She could trip lightly by the graves of those who died when they were young." The poor had their poetry as the hills had theirs. But it was out of doors, on the road or on the moor, not in the cottage parlour, that her imagination had freest play. Her happiest moments were passed tramping beside a jibbing horse on a wet Scottish road without certainty of bed or supper. All she knew was that there was some sight ahead, some grove of trees to be noted, some waterfall to be enquired into. On they tramped hour after hour in silence for the most part, though Coleridge, who was of the party, would suddenly begin to debate aloud the true meaning of the words majestic, sublime, and grand. They had to trudge on foot because the horse had thrown the cart over a bank and the harness was only mended with string and pocket-handkerchiefs. They were hungry, too, because Wordsworth had dropped the chicken and the bread into the lake, and they had nothing else for dinner. They were uncertain of the way, and did not know where

烂的夜空一样神奇；她仔仔细细打量着他，甚至于看清楚在他那破烂的外衣上"衬补着三块深蓝色、喇叭花形的补丁——那里原来该是三个扣子"，他那半个月没有刮的胡子就像是"灰色的长毛绒"。当这些人信口谈着什么航海呀，拉兵呀，格兰比侯爵[1]呀等等的故事的时候，她总会捕捉住他们话里的一言半语——它，在那些故事早被忘记的时候，还能久久地保留在她的心灵之中："怎么，你要往西方走吗？""当然，童贞的少女到了天堂就大有出息啦！""在那些夭折的年轻人坟墓旁边，她才能轻轻松松地走路呀。"穷人们，就像群山一样，也有自己的诗意。但是，只有走出农舍，到户外，到路上，到旷野里，她的想象力才得到最自由的发挥。当他们傍着一匹慢慢腾腾的马，在潮湿的苏格兰道路上徒步前进，既不知道能不能找到住的地方，也不知道能不能吃上晚饭的时候，她觉得那才是她最幸福的时刻。那时候，她只知道在前方有某个名胜，有一片丛林值得一记，有一个瀑布应该探访。他们一个小时接一个小时地向前走着，大部分时间里谁也不说话，只有柯尔律治（这次出游他参加了）不定什么时候突然大声讨论着"威严的""崇高的"和"雄伟的"这三个字眼儿的真正含义。他们不得不一步一步艰难地行走，因为那匹马在一个堤岸上把车弄翻了，断了的缰绳、肚带刚刚用小绳子、小手绢接了起来。此外，他们还饿着肚子，因为华兹华斯把鸡肉和面包都掉到湖里去了，此外又没有什么东西可以当饭吃。他们路也不熟，不知道该到哪里去找

---

[1] 18世纪的一个英国将军，曾任英军统帅。

they would find lodging: all they knew was that there was a waterfall ahead. At last Coleridge could stand it no longer. He had rheumatism in the joints; the Irish jaunting car provided no shelter from the weather; his companions were silent and absorbed. He left them. But William and Dorothy tramped on. They looked like tramps themselves. Dorothy's cheeks were brown as a gipsy's, her clothes were shabby, her gait was rapid and ungainly. But still she was indefatigable; her eye never failed her; she noticed everything. At last they reached the waterfall. And then all Dorothy's powers fell upon it. She searched out its character, she noted its resemblances, she defined its differences, with all the ardour of a discoverer, with all the exactness of a naturalist, with all the rapture of a lover. She possessed it at last—she had laid it up in her mind for ever. It had become one of those "inner visions" which she could call to mind at any time in their distinctness and in their particularity. It would come back to her long years afterwards when she was old and her mind had failed her; it would come back stilled and heightened and mixed with all the happiest memories of her past—with the thought of Racedown and Alfoxden and Coleridge reading "Christabel", and her beloved, her brother William. It would bring with it what no human being could give, what no human relation could offer—consolation and quiet. If, then, the passionate cry of Mary Wollstonecraft had reached her ears—"Surely something resides in this heart that is not perishable—and life is more than a dream"—she would have had no doubt whatever as to her answer. She would have said quite simply, "We looked about us, and felt that we were happy."

---

1 地名，在英格兰南部。1795年华兹华斯得到一笔遗赠，经济开始宽裕，曾在此一农舍居住。

住的地方——只知道前边有一个瀑布。最后,柯尔律治受不了啦。他有风湿性关节炎;那辆爱尔兰式的双轮马车根本不能遮风蔽雨;他那两个旅伴尽是在那里想自己的心事、不说话。他离开他们,自己走了。但是威廉和多萝西只管往前走。这时候,他们两个人的模样就跟流浪汉差不多了。多萝西面颊棕红,像个吉卜赛人;她衣服破碎,步子急促,走路的样子歪歪扭扭。但她不知疲倦,目光炯炯,注意观察一切。他们终于来到瀑布之下。于是,多萝西的全部身心都集中到瀑布上面了。她以发现者的热情、博物学家的细心、情人的狂喜探索它的特征,记下它的外貌,阐明它的与众不同之处。她终于占有了它——把它永远储存在自己的心灵之中了。从此,它便形成一个"内心的幻影",她随时都可以清清楚楚、仔仔细细回想起来。即使多年以后,她老了,记忆力不好了,它还会袭上心头;它袭上她的心头,静止了,纯化了,并且与她生平中所有最幸福的回忆——与她关于瑞思多恩[1]、关于阿尔富克斯登、关于柯尔律治朗诵《克丽丝特布尔》[2]、关于她那亲爱的哥哥威廉的回忆,交错在一起了。它给她带来的,是无人可以给予也是一般人与人的关系所无法提供的东西——即抚慰与安宁。因此,如果玛丽·沃斯通克拉夫特那激昂的呼声曾经传到她的耳边:"在这颗心里一定存在着某种永生不灭的东西——人生绝不是幻梦一场",那么,她自己的答案也是明确无疑的。她大概会简简单单地答道:"我们只要观察周围的一切,就会觉得自己是幸福的。"

---

2 柯尔律治的一首诗。

封面图片: rawpixel.com / Freepik